TAKING STOCK

LICENSED, CATERING & RETAIL TRADES

The Incorporated Society of Licensed Trade Stocktakers

Taking Stock is published by
The Incorporated Society of Licensed Trade Stocktakers

Compiled by   Bruce S. Thompson F.I.L.S.

Assisted by   Stephen Berry F.I.L.S., M.S.A.E.
                   Norman Clements F.I.L.S., M.H.C.I.M.A.
                   Trevor Knight F.I.L.S.
                   Michael Murdoch A.I.L.S., F.T.V.I.
                   John Tandy F.I.L.S., F.A.V.L.P.

Contributions from the following were much appreciated:

G. Andrews F.I.L.S.   W. Hindle B.Sc., A.I.L.S.
C. Berridge A.I.L.S.   E. Howard F.I.L.S.
A. Brown A.I.L.S.   P. Littler A.I.L.S., A.I.C.S.
D. Burgoyne A.I.L.S.   J. McDougall A.I.L.S.,
P. Card F.I.L.S., F.S.V.A.,   L.H.C.I.M.A., M.B.I.I.
   M.C.F.A.   R. Newman F.I.L.S.
B. Daykin F.I.L.S.,   P. Partington A.I.L.S.,
   F.T.V.I.   L.H.C.I.M.A.
G. Giles A.I.L.S.

and others

We should like to thank both Gavin Bowers, of Francesco's Restaurant, Edinburgh, and Vincent Rex F.R.I.C.S. for supplying useful material; and the National Licensed Victuallers' Association for allowing the use of extracts from the publication 'An ABC of Licensing Law'.

The Incorporated Society of Licensed Trade Stocktakers is deeply grateful to Jane Gough, who spent many hours typing manuscripts; to Elisabeth Hutchings, who edited the book and tolerated many last-minute changes; and to John McWilliam, the artist, and Andrew Dorward, the printer, who both gave invaluable help during the two years' preparation of this publication.

ii

INCORPORATED SOCIETY OF LICENSED TRADE
STOCKTAKERS LTD

Dear Reader,

It is with great pleasure and confidence that I commend to you this book on stock control and stocktaking.

Since our Society was established in 1953, I and my co-founders have seen it grow from a struggling infant to a mature adult, creating examinations and training courses etc., but above all setting strict standards of ethics, behaviour and competence which are now fully recognised throughout the British Isles.

This success has been achieved only through much hard work by many members; but space allows the mention of only a few.

The late George Webber, our first Chairman, was a wise and kindly person and a friend to all. He was succeeded by Norman Clements, the present Chairman, a man of great patience, with the widest knowledge of our profession, who has been the backbone of the Society since its inception. After sound and solid service from the founding Secretary, Paul Murphy, and the late Geoff Cross, John Watts developed the Society into a modern and commercially well-run body. An enthusiastic and energetic spell as Secretary by Ron Edwards was followed by that of Steve Berry, who has enhanced the image of the Society for members, and ensured full recognition by the trade.

Given the expert knowledge and wide experience of our members throughout the British Isles, I see nothing but success for the future of the Society; and I am delighted that so many people, both in and outside the stocktaking profession, will have the opportunity to benefit by reading this publication.

Yours sincerely,

President

CONTENTS

Introduction   vii

Section I – The Management of Licensed Premises

1. BOOKKEEPING, CASH REGISTERS, AND CONTROL
    PROCEDURES   3
    Bookkeeping   3
    Cash Registers   14
    Control Procedures   21

2. PROFIT AND LOSS ACCOUNTS, BALANCE SHEETS,
    AND VALUE ADDED TAX   31
    Profit and Loss Accounts and Balance Sheets   31
    Management – Profit and Loss Accounts – Discrepancies   36
    Value Added Tax   43

3. LICENSEES AND THE LAW   50
    Miscellaneous Matters   50
    Amusement Machines in Licensed Premises   71
    Bar Hygiene   76
    The Management of Licensed Premises: Summary of
    Guidelines for Licensees   79

Section II – Stocktaking

4. LIQUOR STOCKTAKING: THE YIELD, THE
    PHYSICAL COUNT   83
    Stocktaking   83
    The Yield   87
    The Physical Count   96

5. LIQUOR STOCKTAKING: THE STOCK REPORT   103
    Completing the Stock Sheets   103
    Progressing and Understanding the Report   113
    Additional Procedures   118
    Valuations and Trading Accounts   121

6. ALLOWANCES AND ADJUSTMENTS   126
    Allowances   126
    Miscellaneous Adjustments   132
    Year-end Adjustments   139

7. BROKERS, STOCKTAKERS AND CHANGEOVERS;
    GENERAL STOCKTAKING   142
    Brokers, Stocktakers and Changeovers   142
    The Stocktaker and Changeovers   146
    Wine and Changeovers   150
    General Stocktaking   152
    Changeovers: Final Certificate of Valuation and Statement
    of Settlement   155

8. FOOD AND ANCILLARY STOCKTAKING   159
    Food Stocktaking   159
    Shops and Retail Outlets: Valuation of Stock   170
    Shops and V.A.T.   175
    Stocktaking: Summary of Guidelines for Stocktakers   178

Section III – The Product Range

9. BEER AND BREWING; SPIRITS, FORTIFIED WINES
    AND LIQUEURS   181
    Beer and Brewing   181
    Beer and the Pub   186
    Spirits   189
    Fortified Wines   195
    Liqueurs   198

10. WINES   207
    Vintage Port   207
    Wines – Types and Production   210
    Wine-producing Countries and Areas   219
    The Wine List   225

11. FOOD AND TOBACCO   233
    Food   233
    Tobacco   262

Section IV – Appendices

APPENDIX 1
COMPUTERS AND CALCULATORS; HYDROMETERS   269
    Computers   269
    Calculators   270
    Hydrometers   273

APPENDIX 2
TABLES AND CHARTS   277

APPENDIX 3
GLOSSARY   297

APPENDIX 4
THE INCORPORATED SOCIETY OF LICENSED TRADE
STOCKTAKERS   302

APPENDIX 5
SAMPLE THEORY EXAMINATION PAPER   306
    Incorporated Society of Licensed Trade Stocktakers
    Theory Examination   306
    Answers to Sample Theory Examination Paper Questions   309

INDEX   319

INTRODUCTION

The Licensed Trade

As the third largest employer in the United Kingdom, the hotel and catering trade is vitally important, not only because it gives jobs to so many people, but also because those people supply a means of entertainment to millions of others. The liquor trade generates huge amounts of money throughout the country, and whisky in particular is a major item of export. Taxation, duty and rates account for a considerable proportion of the Chancellor's income; so the industry is one to be taken seriously.

Almost up to the point of delivery, liquor is under the strict control of Customs and Excise. In spite of this, several substantial frauds have been uncovered, and long prison sentences given. Once out of bond (the area where liquor is held until duty is paid), stock becomes mobile and is likely to be delivered to pubs, hotels, shops, night clubs, discos or 'cash and carry' outlets.

Because the industry is principally cash-orientated, the stock now becomes 'hot' and is subject to rigid control procedures. Members of the Incorporated Society of Licensed Trade Stocktakers are specially trained to monitor the movement of all beer, wine and spirits, to ensure that at each stage a proper return is made on the investment, and that its final destination is properly recorded.

Temptations are rife – fraud, theft, illegal distilling and diluting are just a few. Illicit stills have existed for over one hundred years; and it is hardly surprising that today the number of convictions involving alcohol is considerable, many for frauds brought to light as a direct result of a Stocktaker's diligence. It is a sad reflection on the human race that so many people are prone to dishonesty, which appears at every stage of the industry, from the supplier and his staff, through the delivery man, the publican and the person behind the bar, to the customer, who will often take as much as he can for as little as possible.

The Need for Stocktaking

With so much legislation in force, every publican needs to know what gross profit he is achieving. Conscientious ones will also want to monitor the operation and ensure that there are no 'leakages'. If satisfactory gross profit levels are not achieved, it is highly likely that enquiries by both Customs and Excise and the Inland Revenue will be initiated, which could result in substantial fines, penalties and repayments, or even, in serious cases, imprisonment.

Losses can occur through the use of wrong measures or incorrect glasses, or through failure to look after beer and dispense systems. They are not always the direct result of dishonesty.

Too many publicans and hoteliers wait until the end of a financial year to discover their true profit margins. This is inadvisable, and not to be recommended. A considerable amount of money could have been lost during the period, whereas regular stocktaking would have detected the problem at an early stage, enabling immediate action to be taken and the situation remedied.

Trading accounts (covering variable periods of time) will merely tell the client what gross profit he is achieving; extended results are much more complex, but extremely beneficial to any well-run operation. They indicate not only what gross profit has been made, but also what should have been made, and they also show a retail figure of any surplus or deficit. By using this system, the Stocktaker can monitor the profit margin of each individual item, highlight overstocking, and control the entire liquor operation both professionally and beneficially to the business.

No outlet is too small for stocktaking, but the period of time between stocks will be governed by both size and turnover. Where fully extended stocks are being carried out, the Stocktaker should attend at least once a month, and more frequently if results are bad. As already indicated, trading accounts can cover any period of time, but many clients like them done on a monthly, quarterly or half-yearly basis.

Responsibilities of Management

Stocktaking, whether carried out in shops, licensed premises, garages or garden centres, is all about the control of stock: in each situation, unless proper controls are applied, losses will occur. The basic principle can be exemplified, very simply, as follows. If a publican has fourteen bottles of whisky on 1st April and eight on 1st May, but in the meantime has purchased twelve, the Stocktaker will assume that he has sold eighteen bottles and will, therefore, expect the relevant income to amount to eighteen times the retail value of a bottle of whisky. If he makes this calculation for every single item, he will be able to reach a conclusion about what those premises should have taken in cash during a particular period. The actual cash figure will be compared with this hypothetical one, and the final result will be either a surplus or a deficit. Allowances must be properly recorded, because stock which is either lost or removed from the bar without being paid for may eventually turn a deficit into a surplus.

Temptations in the licensed trade are rife; so all managers, proprietors and licensees are strongly advised to be aware of the pitfalls of their employment, and to have regular stocktaking. The Stocktaker, too, must look out for dishonest practices, so that he can investigate deficits thoroughly and advise his client in a proper and efficient manner. Deficits are rarely caused by employees actually taking bottles away; the more common fraud is under-ringing. If a round comes to £2.90, the barman or barmaid may well ring up £0.90 and, at the end of the night, pocket the balance of £2.00. As a result, although the cash register reading will balance with the cash, the stock at the end of the period will show a deficit proportional to the cash removed. If stocktaking is not in operation, this sort of practice could continue for a very long time, if not indefinitely. It is not unheard of for a Stocktaker to go into premises where no-one has operated controls for quite some time, only to find, in his first month, substantial deficits of £500 to £1,000, which may well have been occurring for many years. Irrespective of his deficits, however, the client will still have to pay all his overheads; and he will find these the harder to cover, if he is losing income because of dishonest practices.

Qualities of a Stocktaker

Anybody considering stocktaking as a career must enjoy working with figures, and should have the ability to work unsupervised in what is a very challenging and exacting profession. The work done by a Stocktaker can very often determine both the future and the livelihood of bar staff, stewards, managers, cellarmen and many others. He must always be a true professional; he must look smart, and be physically fit. Kegs have to be moved, cases lifted and several other tasks performed which do require a certain amount of energy, and a client will quickly lose confidence if he sees that a Stocktaker is not able to perform the function properly. The Stocktaker must always set about the task in a sensible, mature and logical manner.

It is the Stocktaker's responsibility to make sure that all the information given to him is correct. He must ensure that dates of price increases are exact, and that off-sale figures look realistic. He will not necessarily accept the word of stewards or bar managers; he will want to check everything himself, in order to have confidence in his own figures. When his gross profit agrees with that produced by the accountant at the end of the year, it will give him job satisfaction, particularly if there were problems which he helped to solve and then to control by successive visits.

The Stocktaker should be able to co-operate with everybody, and he will often find that his work is that of a diplomat. Staff will be pressing, in their efforts to gather information from him. He should not appear offhand, but must at the same time recognise that to disclose any details would be a breach of confidence.

Client Relationships

Stocktakers are regarded by many clients as people to whom they can talk and, accordingly, put their troubles, problems or grievances without threat of gossip. Clients must be able to rely on their Stocktaker's retaining confidences. If he tells them about other clients' businesses, they will be apprehensive of his discussing theirs. Facts and figures are private to each establishment, and are given to a Stocktaker because he needs to know them, not so that they can be exposed to others.

A client will not have confidence in a Stocktaker until he has earned it. Because he is paying out money, and because his entire business depends on profitability, the client must know that results are correct. Accuracy is essential, short cuts should never be taken, and as many questions should be asked as necessary. A lack of interest will be noticed, as will unnecessary haste. The asking of questions not only indicates efficiency, but also serves to remind the client of any unusual transactions about which the Stocktaker should know, if accurate results are to be obtained. Such discussion will inspire confidence, and ultimately establish a good relationship between Stocktaker and client.

A clear, concise knowledge of products is important. There are so many varieties on the market that publicans need advice on purchasing, compiling wine lists, establishing selling prices etc. This sort of assistance builds up a good lasting relationship, and if the Stocktaker is able to help, he is well on his way to gaining acceptance.

The attitude of the Stocktaker must at all times be that of a professional person, and whilst the owner of the premises is his client, he must be scrupulously fair with the staff and management. His job is to liaise with everybody, without being too friendly, and at the same time to produce correct and proper results. The Stocktaker should always be unbiased, helpful, fair but firm. He will very often be blamed, where deficits occur, and will often find himself in the middle of arguments. His words may well be taken out of context, and he will find himself made the scapegoat; but by setting an example and being highly professional, a good Stocktaker will overcome all these problems.

The Client

The client is the one essential element in any stocktake, and the Stocktaker will always be dealing with a very wide cross-section of the community. Owners and managers are all different, and some need many more explanations than others concerning results, although these should always be clear, concise, accurate and easy to follow.

Every person running licensed premises would like nothing better than to have good results all the time, but unfortunately this seldom happens. Surpluses or deficits are not necessarily caused by dishonesty but are in many cases purely the result of bad or inaccurate paperwork. Some clients will not believe the results given to them when they are not what they expect, whereas others will accept them and try to solve their problems as soon as possible, thus displaying good management and saving themselves a lot of money. The Stocktaker should be able to get together with the client, run through the stock sheets, and indicate where he feels the problem may lie. It may be difficult in some instances to give precise answers, but with his own experience of the trade, and of the premises where he is acting, he should at least be able to give his client some pointers.

It is the Stocktaker's responsibility to advise clients as to pricing policy and to indicate any increases in cost which would substantially affect their eventual gross profits. It may well be that he will suggest new retail prices for a client, and help to keep him running to budget. In some cases, though, clients do not accept advice very readily, and think they 'know it all'. In such circumstances there is little that the Stocktaker can do; but by recording his thoughts in writing, he can at least ensure that the client has no grounds for saying that he has not been informed. Constructive advice, criticisms and comments should be given wherever possible.

The Scope of this Book

Though biased towards the stocktaking profession, this book is intended to benefit all those involved in the licensed or catering trades. Much of the material, which draws upon the in-depth knowledge and considerable range of experience gained by the authors, has never been published before. The work embodies standard policy which operates throughout the British Isles, though it is not necessarily adopted by all Stocktakers or companies.

SECTION I
THE MANAGEMENT OF LICENSED PREMISES

CHAPTER 1
BOOKKEEPING, CASH REGISTERS, AND CONTROL PROCEDURES

BOOKKEEPING

The keeping of accurate books is an integral part of any stocktaking system. It must be impressed upon clients that unless they are prepared to keep concise records, the effort expended by the Stocktaker and the money spent by themselves would both be to no avail. If accurate reports are to be prepared, the Stocktaker must know of all transactions within the operation. He needs to be aware of the purchases, returns, allowances and also details of income. Any promotional stock or discounts should also be notified to him, so that gross profits are maintained accurately. Where a trading account (see page 124) only is requested, less bookwork is necessary: all that is required is sight of statements, invoices or delivery notes, and details of income.

A good Stocktaker will always want to ensure that the information given to him is correct. For this reason he will not accept hearsay, but will want to examine all relevant bookwork, as follows:–

1. Goods Received Book – an analysis of all relevant purchases.
2. Delivery notes – usually unpriced, and generally left when the goods are delivered.
3. Invoices – priced versions of delivery notes.
4. Statements – analyses of all invoices for a particular month, with demands for payment.
5. Details of income for the period – a 'business done' figure is required, not a 'cash received' one (see page 10).
6. Petty Cash purchases.
7. Till readings or analysis.

Goods Received Book

To ensure accurate recording of purchases, clients should be encouraged to maintain a Goods Received Book, with all relevant delivery notes and invoices attached. (The Goods Received Book is generally entered from delivery notes; prices are entered once the invoices are to hand.) The Stocktaker would be responsible for checking all entries, transferring details on to his own stock sheets

3

(see page 105), and stamping all papers. Invoices received after the stock date would be presented on the next visit, and duly checked and stamped then. By the use of this system, any invoices not stamped would be detected by the Accounts Department and queried immediately.

The Goods Received Book as detailed on page 5 would show all purchases, including Petty Cash ones (see page 10), relative to the operation. Any returns should be entered and, in the case of draught beer, an estimate of the amount clearly noted. This figure can be used for the current stocktaking, and an adjustment made once the credit note comes through. Discounts (see page 134) normally appear in the 'invoice total' column, enabling the Stock-taker to make proper adjustments and to produce accurate gross profit figures.

The Stocktaker would be responsible for stamping off the Goods Received Book after each visit, and also for noting the number of the page on which the last item was entered. It is customary for such books to be kept in duplicate, and the top copy retained.

Returned Beer

If the Stocktaker is unable to ascertain how much draught beer was returned during a stock period, he should check with the staff; and if still uncertain, allow half a container, making any adjustment once the credit note becomes available. An entry should where possible be made in the Goods Received Book, with an estimate of the amount, at the time of return. (For further information on draught beer returns, see page 138.)

Promotional Stock

Promotional stock often creates problems, but unless instructions to the contrary have been issued by a responsible person, it should be treated as a purchase and accordingly entered through the Goods Received system. Whether, after this, it is written off or sold at full retail price would need to be determined, and appropriate adjust-ments made (see page 128).

Income

Income should always be extracted by the Stocktaker from unit records, and a mark put beneath the last entry. Staff tend to make errors, and often do not realise the seriousness of any discrepancies. From his own records, the Stocktaker will be able to determine the date of the commencement of the stock, and thereby ensure an accurate period. It is also advisable to check the last few days of the previous stock, to make sure that no adjustments were made after

DATE	SUPPLIER	QUANTITY	DESCRIPTION OF GOODS	PRICE	£	p.	INVOICE TOTAL £	p.
1/9	Society Brewery	3 × KILS	MILD BEER	57 – 60	172	80		
	01113	4 × KILS	BITTER BEER	63 – 00	252	00		
		6 × DOZ	GUINNESS	3 – 58	21	48		
		40 × DOZ	FRUIT JUICES	1 – 99	79	60		
		60 × DOZ	BABY MIXERS	1 – 50	90	00		
		24 × 1·5L	BELLS WHISKY	14 – 44	346	56		
		12 × 1·5L	SMIRNOFF	13 – 64	163	68		
		6 × BTS	BRISTOL CREAM	3 – 70	22	20		
		12 × 1·5L	DRY MARTINI	4 – 58	54	96		
		6 × BTS	BAILEYS IRISH	5 – 65	33	90		
		24 × LTRS	LIEBFRAUMILCH	3 – 12	74	88		
		106 DOZ	BOTTLES	·52	55	12		
		28	CASES	1 – 00	28	00		
	Credit	104 DOZ	BOTTLES	·52	(54	08)		
		27	CASES	1 – 00	(27	00)		
			TOTAL		1314	10		
			VAT		197	11	1511	21
2/9	Society Brewery	2 × KILS	MILD					
	02691	4 × KILS	BITTER					
		6 DOZ	STOUT					
		40 DOZ	FRUIT JUICES					
		60 DOZ	BABY MIXERS					
10/9	United Crisp Co.	18 BOXES	CRISPS	4·44	79	92		
	001511			VAT	11	98	91	90

Last stock up to close of business on *January 13th.*

	LOUNGE	PUB	FUNCTION	TOTAL
14/1/89	164.20	87.89	Closed	252.09
15/1/89	115.27	112.40	271.93	499.60
22/1/89	1206.20	720.19	186.92	2113.31
29/1/89	1381.33	693.04	470.10	2544.47
5/2/89	980.20	614.80	1200.04	2795.04
12/2/89	1014.00	780.04	315.00	2109.04
13/2/89	147.90	101.12	Closed	249.02
14/2/89	173.20	92.00	Closed	265.20
TOTAL	5182.30	3201.48	2443.99	10827.77

This stock as at close of business on *February 14th.*

the last visit which would now need taking into account. Details of income should be taken as found, and balanced off.

The client must confirm that all business has been raised. In some smaller units there may be outstanding accounts which have not been recorded. The Stocktaker would need to maintain a list of these, deducting them from the income as they are paid (provided that they have been raised as business or rung through the cash register at the date of payment), and adding any new accounts to the income at each visit. This would ensure that the actual income relative to any stock period was correct. The figure would probably not, however, reconcile with internal records, so the client should be made aware of the procedure adopted. Very often the Stocktaker will extract his information from a tabular ledger.

The Tabular Ledger

This is an analysis of a single day's transactions, and is often referred to as a Tab. Records of this sort are maintained only by larger establishments; they were originally compiled manually, but are now often produced on computers. The example on page 7 is considerably reduced in size: normally, every chargeable item, together with blank spaces, would be shown across the top. In the left-hand column there would be a space for each client, and also for each other source of income. In certain circumstances the sheet would be reversed, with the clients' names across the top and the facilities down the side.

The second example works on exactly the same principle, and would generally be compiled from information contained in the Tab. It is an analysis of those figures, and would normally be

	B/F	ROOM	B/FAST	LUNCH	DINNER	COCK'L BAR	LOUNGE BAR	DAILY TOTAL	CASH	LEDGER BAL	TRANS TO LGR	LEDGER A/C PD	C/F
Ledger Bal B/F										3206-24			
Smith	88.34	30.00	5.00		12.00	8.50		55.50					143.84
Jones		30.00	5.00	6.50			12.00	53.50			53.50		
Saunders	104.30	30.00	5.00			6.82		41.82	146.12				
Dinners					183.20	47.30		230.50	180.40		50.10		
Lunches				147.20				147.20	118.70		28.50		
Lounge Bar							317.20	317.20	317.20				
Cocktail Bar						143.30		143.30	143.30				
Young (Wdng Recn)		30.00		627.40		300.00	187.50	1144.90			1144.90		
Gold (Account Bar)									753.80			753.80	
TOTAL	192.64	120.00	15.00	781.10	195.20	505.92	516.70	2133.92	1659.52		1277.00	753.80	143.84
Less VAT		15.66	1.96	101.89	25.46	65.98	67.39	278.34					
NET DAILY BUSINESS		104.34	13.04	679.21	169.74	439.94	449.31	1855.58	1659.52		1277.00	753.80	143.84
LEDGER BALANCE C/F										3729.44			

WEEK ENDING

	MON	TUES	WED	THURS	FRI	SAT	SUN	TOTAL
BROUGHT FORWARD	192-64	143·84						
APARTMENTS								
ROOM	90-00							
ROOM HIRE	30-00							
TOTAL	120-00							
FOOD B'FAST	15-00							
BAR MEALS								
LUNCH	153-70							
DINNER	195-20							
HIGH TEA								
FUNCTIONS	627-40							
TOTAL	991-30							
LIQUOR LOUNGE (1)	576-70							
LOUNGE (2)	505-92							
FUNCTION (1)								
FUNCTION (2)								
WINES								
TOTAL	1022-62							
SUNDRIES								
DAILY TOTAL	2133-92							
TO LEDGER　　　　—	1277-00							
PETTY CASH　　　—	⌐							
ACCOUNTS PAID　+	753-80							
BANKED	1659-52							
CARRIED FORWARD	143-84							
V.A.T.	278-34							
NET BUSINESS	1855-58							

CASH
+
TRANS TO LEDGER

DAILY TOTAL　　　+
　　+　　　　　=　　PETTY CASH
BROUGHT FORWARD　+
CARRIED FORWARD
—
LEDGER ACCOUNTS PAID

	M	T	W	T	F	S	S	Total
ROOMS	3							
SLEEPERS	3							
LUNCHES	17							
DINNERS	16							
HIGH TEAS	⌐							

extended to supply weekly totals. The headings down the left-hand side would relate to the particular premises; and the total figures entered should all be the same as those on the Tab. Again, the Debtors Ledger (see page 12) must balance with these figures, so a weekly check should be carried out as follows:–

Opening ledger balance + transferred to ledger − ledger accounts paid = Closing ledger balance.

A column is shown for Petty Cash. This is not necessary if a proper system is used (see page 10), but it would be if cash were drawn on a daily basis to pay small creditors. The amount of money banked should agree with the total in the summary, as should the total of Petty Cash payments (if relevant).

The box in the bottom right-hand corner will show, when completed, the number of people partaking of each meal and sleeping on the premises.

Ledger Balance Brought Forward

This is the total balance of outstanding debtors as at close of business on the previous night. This figure and that on the tabular ledger should always agree. Discrepancies should be investigated immediately, as delays could increase the volume of work required to trace the error. Ledger control is a daily update of accounts put to ledger and those paid.

The explanatory notes which follow refer to the clients and other income sources listed in the example on page 7.

Smith: Mr Smith has an account outstanding to date of £88.34, which has been included in the previous day's total. He has charged several items to his room during the day, and is staying on at the hotel, so the total amount of £143.84 will be carried forward to the following day, but not included again in the 'business done' figure.

Jones: Mr Jones has stayed for one night. His company is paying the bill, so the account has been transferred to ledger, and thus removed from the daily 'business done' sheets. Once the account is entered in the Debtors Ledger, an invoice will be sent to his company.

Saunders: Mr Saunders had a 'brought forward' figure of £104.30 from the previous day's business. He has paid by cash and left the hotel, so his payment will form part of the day's banking figure, thus terminating any future bookwork concerning him.

Dinners, Lunches, Lounge Bar and Cocktail Bar: The daily business done in each department, split where applicable between liquor and food, must be entered, and credit accounts transferred to ledger as shown. Only cash received will be entered in the 'cash' column.

Young: Mr Young has had a wedding reception at the hotel. The business is raised under the appropriate headings, and all is trans-

ferred to ledger. From there, the total will be invoiced to him, and
when his cheque is received, it will be treated in the same way as Mr
Gold's.

Gold: Mr Gold has paid for a dinner dance held a month ago, so
his payment comes under 'cash' and 'ledger accounts paid'. The
business will not be raised again.

The advantage of the tabular ledger is that every transaction is
entered on a single sheet of paper. It is balanced daily, the ledger
balance is checked, and the cash income should agree with that
shown on the Tab. It is a total analysis of business done. (It is quite
usual for the daily balance to be calculated at about 10 o'clock in the
morning, to enable payments received for overnight accommodation etc. to appear as part of the previous day's business.)

The final figures would normally be transferred, with or without
V.A.T., into a principal ledger. The Stocktaker should always
establish whether these figures are gross or net. His own task is to
extract his figures from the weekly summary and (for any odd days)
from the daily Tab., listing them as shown on page 6.

The formula for checking the daily or weekly figures is as
follows:–

Daily total + brought forward = Cash + transferred to ledger +
carried forward − ledger accounts paid.

Deposits

Had a deposit been paid during the course of the day, the amount of
money would have been entered in the 'cash' column, the client's
name (with the word 'deposit' beside it) on the left-hand side, and
finally an entry in the 'ledger accounts paid' column. It would be
held as a credit entry or overpayment in the ledger, and then
eradicated by the business being raised on the day of the event. If
the deposit were insufficient to cover the function, the client would
become a debtor for the balance.

Petty Cash

Petty Cash refers to cash held on the premises for the purchase of
any small items for which it is not practical to pay by cheque or use
the normal purchase system. It would be customary in most premises for a float to be maintained for this purpose, always containing
cash and properly authorised vouchers amounting to the value of
the float. Payments from the float are frequently referred to as
payouts, and must be accounted for accurately on a weekly basis. In
larger establishments, an Imprest Book (or Petty Cash Analysis)
would be kept, controlling the movement of all such money. The
Stocktaker would need to check this, to ensure that no liquor or food

SUPPLIER	No.	BAR	FOOD	STATIONERY	REPAIRS	VAT	TOTAL
Float 5/9/88							150-00
J. Bright	1	7-20				1-08	8-28
D. Foggerty	2		2-20			—	2-20
J. Johnstone	3		3-00			—	3-00
Envelope Co.	4			4-50		-68	5-18
L. Marvel	5	5-10				-77	5-87
Morton - Joiners	6				17-50	2-63	20-13
Barclay - Glaziers	7				6-40	-96	7-36
Stamps	8			20-00			20-00
J. Nugent	9		14-20				14-20
		12-30	19-40	24-50	23-90	6-12	86-22
Weekly Total							86-22
Cheque 12/9/88							86-22
Float 12/9/88							150-00

had been purchased without being entered in the Goods Received Book: he would ascertain, from the Petty Cash vouchers, what had been purchased for the amounts of money recorded.

As can be seen from this very basic example, the value of vouchers is redeemed each week to bring the float up to its normal level. The Stocktaker can isolate any expenditure relevant to him, to keep his 'purchase' figure accurate. Petty Cash systems vary considerably from premises to premises, especially in the number of headings and frequency of reimbursement, but their principle remains basically the same.

Debtors Ledger

This is an index card or book detailing any debts due to the business. It generally has three columns, the first one indicating the amount due, the second one the amount paid, and the third one any outstanding balance. The following examples show a debt raised of £808.00, a part-payment of £500.00 on 1st September, and the balance paid later.

Had Mr Fisher elected to pay a deposit towards a future dinner party, it would have been treated as a payment and held as a credit in the ledger until such time as the function was raised and entered as a debit balance. Any difference would be due either to or from the client.

Cash Reconciliation

It sometimes happens that a client requests the Stocktaker to check the cash and prepare a reconciliation. This is more likely to happen in clubs and managed houses, and can form a vital part of stock control. To prepare it, the Stocktaker would have to check each of the following, and then present his reconciliation in the format shown below:–

> House float (if any)
> Cash takings
> Bankings
> Cash in hand
> Payments (supported by authorised vouchers)

House Float	£500.00	Till Floats	£300.00
Income	£6,300.00	Banking	£4,500.00
		Payments	£850.00
		Cash	£1,150.00
	£6,800.00		£6,800.00

This example shows an exact balance, which is rare. There would normally be small differences which would be shown on the report.

MR. A. FISHER – 12 Society Crescent
Mosspit – Stafford

#	Day	Mo	Yr	Description	DEBIT		CREDIT		BALANCE	
1	23	8	88	To Wedding Reception	722	46			722	46
2	27	8	88	To accommodation	85	54			808	00
3	1	9	88	By part. Payment			500	00	308	00
4	4	10	88	By final Payment			308	00	—	
5	2	1	89	By deposit (function 24 - 6 - 89)			300	00	(300	00)
6	24	6	89	To Dinner Party	347	50			47	50
7	30	6	89	By cheque			47	50	—	
8										
9										
10										
11										
12										
13										
14										
15										
16										
17										
18										
19										
20										
21										
22										
23										
24										
25										

CASH BALANCE

...... *Society Hotel* .... House　　Date ... 26 : 9 : 88 ...

Bankings checked: .... *John Smith* ......

	£	p				£	p
House Float	1000	00	Till Floats			200	00
Sunday 380 -04			Large Notes				
Monday 710 - 93			£20 Notes	260 -00			
Tuesday 605- 40			£10 Notes	980 - 00			
Wednesday 508 - 43			£5 Notes	400 - 00			
Thursday 810 - 22			£1 Notes/Coins	80 - 00			
Friday 1263- 41			50p pieces	65 -00			
Saturday 1608 -27	5886	70	20p pieces	26 -00			
			10p pieces	60 - 00			
			5p pieces	15 - 00			
FRUIT MACHINE	486	20	2p pieces	20 - 00			
JUKE BOX	210	38	1p pieces	8 - 28	1914	28
			Cheques				
			Wilson 26/9 10 -00				
	7583	28	Thompson 26/9 20 -00		30	00
Less P Cash	208	40					
Less Bankings	5210	20	Tokens			20	40
	2164·	68				2164	68

If for some reason the cash shortage was substantial, it would be the Stocktaker's responsibility to report this immediately. A typical sheet for itemising the balance is shown above.

CASH REGISTERS

Many years ago, the only method of taking cash behind a bar was by using the original 'wooden box' or single drawer, fitted to the underside of the counter. The only security was provided by a bell which sounded each time the drawer was opened. Later came the so-called 'press down' model, which provided a continuous reading. This machine was designed according to the old currency system: there were keys for pence up to eleven, shillings up to nineteen, and (usually) pounds up to two or three only. The bell remained, in this design; but in addition, when the flat lid was raised for a reading to be taken, a second counter registered the number of openings, thus creating some, though very minimal, degree of security within the operation. The successor to this was the electric or mechanical register, which provided an audit roll with X and Z key readings.

With the introduction of decimal currency, a new type of cash register was introduced, on which staff were able to punch in a key representing a particular product, rather than a monetary amount, and read the 'total cash due' amount shown in the window. Current models of cash registers are now computerised, and can be set up not only to record cash takings, but also to list individual commodity sales and provide print-outs of stock on hand, sales at cost, retail etc. So much information can be obtained from the machine that it requires a dedicated licensee to absorb the limitless print-outs – which are, in many cases, totally superfluous to a publican's requirements.

What some machines will do (provided the correct opening stock figures are entered and other information properly keyed in) is to indicate the volume of stock which should be on a client's premises at any given time. All purchases must be recorded in the machine, and sales are automatically deducted from the total stockpiling. No allowance is generally made for pipe cleaning, complimentary drinks, or other transactions where cash is not received over the counter. If deficits are occurring, a comparison between the individual sales figures on the stock report and those shown on the cash register may identify where the shortfall is, and whether cash or stock is involved.

Till rolls are available on almost all makes of machine; basically, these produce a summary of business done during any one period. It is customary and advisable to read and clear a till on a daily basis. Of the keys provided for these purposes the most important, as far as the Stocktaker is concerned, are as follows:–

X This key is generally used when the till is cleared at the end of each night, or after the lunchtime session. It merely gives a reading, and does not interfere with the cumulative figures. In older machines, the figure will still represent business 'done to date' on that machine, and the barman or manager will have to deduct the previous day's total from his current figure to obtain the net income figure for the period (see page 20).

Z   Generally, the Z key will clear the machine completely,
           leaving a zero total and no cumulative figures. This key
           should be retained by responsible people only, and never
           handed to bar staff. Clients should be encouraged to take
           a Z reading on the day of each stocktake. Though it is
           unlikely that the income figure will match exactly, any
           major discrepancies can be investigated at once, as can
           any breaks in continuity caused by zeroing of the till roll,
           or change of till part-way through the period.

GTZ   This key, often known as the 'grand total', was originally
or Z2   introduced for the exclusive use of the Stocktaker. It
           overrode all other keys, giving direct access to cash
           register readings during the stock period, irrespective of
           whether or not the machine had been reset. The advan-
           tage of this facility is that the Stocktaker has a figure with
           which to compare the income given to him. The system
           does not always work, however, particularly if there is a
           large volume of credit sales, e.g. drinks given out at
           wedding receptions, which are not recorded through the
           till. It nevertheless provides a guide for the Stocktaker,
           and can save him much wasted time.

Pre-set Cash Registers

These are classified in terms of their 'alpha/numeric' facilities:
'alpha' signifies that the machine will print a product name (usually
an eight-character description). There are three types of machines:–

1. Numeric tills, which record information by number only.
2. Cheaper alpha/numeric tills, which provide product descrip-
    tions on till print-outs only.
3. True alpha/numeric tills, which provide product descriptions on
    display as well as on all till print-outs.

Pre-set cash registers have 'department keys', which are one-touch
entry keys or buttons on main till lay-outs, usually numbered
between 30 and 100, depending on the type of till. These might be
labelled 'whisky', 'gin', 'vodka', 'beer pint' etc., and the bar staff will
press the key for the item sold rather than for a monetary amount.
The cash register automatically converts this into money and shows
on its display board a cash total for the particular sale.

The P.L.U. (Price Look Up) key is for items not on the main
lay-out, such as cocktails, special promotions etc. Entry is by code
number, followed by depression of the P.L.U. key. Each item can if
required be linked to a main section such as beer, spirits or liqueurs.
In normal circumstances, several hundred codes are available. The
P.L.U. numbers do not have to be consecutive. For example, in cases

where table wines are set up, it is common for the P.L.U. numbers to be the same as the numbers on the wine list, half-bottles being numbered 100 plus the wine list number.

On some of the more modern tills, the department keys are now used for tracking sales and the one-touch entry keys set up as P.L.U.s. If, therefore, the till had 100 one-touch entry keys, the first 100 numbers would be allocated to them, and the P.L.U.s entered as numbers would commence at code number 101.

Till Set-up

Pre-set tills do tend to delay service, and the design of the till lay-out must be carefully planned. Bottled beer, minerals, spirits etc. should be set up in their own areas on the keyboard, and preferably colour-coded. As already indicated, P.L.U. keys can be connected with any department, but in some cases it may be preferable for them to be linked to an unused department key, so that the total of the P.L.U. sales can be identified.

The use of miscellaneous keys is to be strongly discouraged in all circumstances.

The more up-to-date machines now have a facility called the 'shift key level', which allows two or more completely independent pricing levels to be set up. The changeover from one level of prices to another is usually made by inputting a code number or changing a switch. This particular type of machine is suitable for establishments which specialise in promotions, or operate 'happy hour' prices.

Advantages to Stocktaking

All the comments below refer to the information available from a periodic reading made during the stocktaking period. The manual for the particular cash register, or its supplier, will indicate how these print-outs can be obtained.

1. The reading provides an independent check on the income figures.
2. By checking his stock sales against cash register print-outs, the Stocktaker can obtain an independent check on his figures.
3. The reports show the number of units, and total amount of sales of each item, during a particular period. Thus, if the known price multiplied by the unit does not equal the amount shown, it is apparent that a price has been changed during the stocktaking period. Such readings also clearly indicate if any stock has been brought into the premises which has not been properly recorded.
4. If any price changes have occurred during the stock period, it is quite easy to calculate accurately the necessary adjustment to

enter as an allowance. For instance, if 100 items have been sold and the original bar price was 50p, then a till amount for these sales would be £50.00. If this is not the figure shown, the difference represents the positive or negative amount.

5.   Where postmix or premix containers are being used, the Stocktaker can extract the correct information and ensure that the right selling price is being charged. If records are kept over a period, the reading may help to indicate whether the equipment needs servicing.

6.   In premises where flow meters are in operation for dispensing draught beer, the readings can be checked to ascertain whether losses are occurring.

7.   In places where stock problems exist, reference to such readings may help to identify the cause of the deficiencies.

Disadvantages to Stocktaking

1.   It is a very time-consuming exercise to analyse the till readings against stock sales; and as already indicated, a considerable proportion of the information acquired would be superfluous.

2.   To produce a truly meaningful report of the till sales against stocktaking figures, the allowances must be calculated not only in the normal way, but also item by item, as dictated by the till set-up.

Advantages to the Client

1.   Provided the correct keys are pressed, pre-set tills do ensure that the correct prices are being charged.

2.   Price changes can be made at any time, without being delayed until the stocktake.

3.   Readings may be taken at any given time which indicate the total number of whiskies, vodkas, pints of beer, sherries etc. sold during the period. Clients can, at any particular time, carry out spot checks on any items which they suspect may have been lost or stolen. This information can be of great value, especially if deficits are being incurred, but is only useful in conjunction with proper stocktaking.

Disadvantage to the Client

Pre-set tills do tend to slow down bar service. It is often the case that only one person can use the register at a time; and if a barman is entering drinks served as part of a large round, he may monopolise the cash register for the entire period that he is serving the one customer. For this reason, it may be desirable, if changing to pre-set tills, to increase their number within the operation.

Till Summary Sheets

Till readings can indicate dishonest practices. In normal circumstances, a variation of up to £1 either way may be considered acceptable; but it may well indicate malpractice. The number of 'no sale' rings can also be useful in any investigation (see page 41). It is always advantageous to advise clients to use a till summary sheet, completed each night, and to make a separate note of overages and shortages as shown in the following example. The second example shows a form designed to maintain cumulative records of till differences. It assumes that a reading is taken twice a day (after close

TILL SUMMARY SHEET

TILL SUMMARY			
		Date	2 /9/ 88
Till Reading	843 — 98		
Cash in Drawer	824 — 21		
Cheques	—		
Large Notes	710 — 00		
£1 pieces/notes	91 — 00	Over-ring	£20 — 00
50p pieces	10 — 50		
20p pieces	6 — 80		
10p pieces	18 — 40		
5p pieces	21 — 35		
2p pieces	4 — 80		
1p pieces	2 — 96		
Other TOKENS	8 — 40		
Total	£ 874 — 21	Till Reading	843 — 98
Less Float	50 — 00	Adjustments	£ 20 — 00
Actual Drawings	£ 824 — 21		£823 — 98
		Over/Short	+ · 23p

Signature...... John Smith ....

BRANCH _Society Hotel_   PERIOD FROM _6/2/89_

BAR _Cocktail_   TO _____

DAY	ACCUMULATED READING	RECORDED SALES	ACTUAL CASH	DIFF + OR −	BAR HAND INTLS
14					
14					
13					
13					
12					
12					
11					
11					
10					
10					
9					
9					
8	210 286 − 91	139 − 58	139 − 60	+ ·02	RB.
8	210 147 − 33	77 − 93	77 − 40	− ·53	GH.
7	210 069 − 40	101 − 99	102 − 14	+ ·15	JL
7	209 967 − 41	78 − 68	78 − 30	− ·38	DM
6	209 888 − 73	127 − 53	130 − 02	+ 2·49	JL
6	209 761 − 20	198 · 03	191 − 10	− 6·93	DM
5	209 563 − 17	93 − 02	93 − 03	+ ·01	JL
5	209 470 − 15	138 − 34	138 − 69	+ ·35	DM
4	209 331 − 81	135 − 27	135 − 40	+ ·13	JL
4	209 196 − 54	77 − 82	77 − 80	− ·02	DM
3	209 118 − 72	212 − 22	220 − 22	+ 8·00	JL
3	208 906 − 50	195 − 53	195 · 61	+ ·08	DM
2	208 710 − 97	20 − 44	20 − 36	− ·08	JL
2	208 690 − 53	150 − 16	150 − 16	—	DM
1	208 540 − 37	129 − 97	130 − 08	+ ·11	JL
1	208 410 − 40	66 − 92	66 − 90	− ·02	DM

of business at lunchtime, and in the evening), and will be useful in showing up any trends in till discrepancies. It also assumes that the till is not being cleared and that the readings have been accumulated over a period of time, perhaps since the last stock. This means that the figure shown on the previous print-out must be deducted from the current one, thus giving the recorded sales for the period in question.

Credit Sales

Where a tabular ledger is in use, it is normal practice to ring up credit sales (those charged to a room, function or table) on a separate key. The reading is balanced off with the checks and appropriate entries made through the bookkeeping system. In smaller premises, where less meticulous records are maintained, this practice could create uncertainty about income figures, and perhaps duplication (the amount being rung in again when paid). Care must be taken to separate credit sales of food and of liquor, if correct stock results are to be produced.

Sample Till Print-outs

On the next three pages are shown till print-outs, with explanations and indications of what the Stocktaker should look for when analysing their contents.

CONTROL PROCEDURES

Cellar Control Systems

There is unlikely to be a cellar control system within premises unless more than one bar exists. In single-bar operations, the only advantage of such a system would be to monitor the control of stock within the premises.

In normal circumstances, where more than one bar exists, the purpose of cellar control is to provide individual results for each bar, enabling management to monitor the operation of every outlet. The basic system involves control of stock in and out of the cellar. Using a cellar ledger, the Stocktaker would establish which bar had received stock issued from the cellar, and charge it to that bar. In certain cases, it is not possible to operate a cellar control system, for example if draught beer is being dispensed to all the bars from one keg, or postmixes or premixes are being dispensed from one container. It is possible to have meters installed, to indicate the volume of beer going to each outlet, but these are not always precise, and the reading may require an adjustment. Accuracy can generally be ensured if readings are recorded before and after pipe cleaning,

PtCIDER		0.61%
01	172	*153.08
PtGUIN		1.74%
02	456	*437.76
PtLIGHT		5.57%
03	1778	*1404.62
PtHEAVY		11.55%
04	3466	*2911.44
PtLAGER		28.31%
05	8295	*7133.70
1/2 CIDER		0.26%
06	148	*66.60
1/2 GUIN		0.30%
07	155	*74.40
1/2 LIGHT		0.66%
08	415	*166.00
1/2 HEAVY		1.64%
09	981	*412.02
1/2 LAGER		2.11%
10	1235	*531.05
PtMcEwH		0.01%
11	3	*2.52
PtMcEwL		0.02%
12	5	*3.95
1/2McEwH		0.01%
16	5	*2.10
1/2McEwL		0.01%
17	5	*2.00
		52.78%
1G	17119	*13301.24
GIN		2.51%
13	957	*631.62
VODKA		10.02%
14	3824	*2523.84
WHISKY		12.33%
15	4709	*3107.94
DarkRUM		1.08%
18	413	*272.58
BRANDY		0.96%
19	288	*241.92
BACARDI		2.21%
20	786	*558.06
C/TREAU		1.01%
21	326	*254.28
CanCLUB		0.22%
22	72	*56.16
D/BUIE		0.08%
23	27	*21.06
MALTS		0.11%
24	39	*28.47
SpWHISK		0.82%
25	286	*205.92

B/RUM		0.00%
26	0	*0.00
DrySHER		0.06%
27	29	*14.21
SwSHER		0.68%
28	350	*171.50
MARTINI		1.11%
29	595	*279.65
ADVOCAT		0.05%
30	24	*11.76
CAMPARI		0.73%
31	267	*184.23
TiaMARI		0.28%
32	92	*71.76
MALIBU		0.28%
33	105	*69.30
PERNOD		0.39%
34	126	*98.28
GLAYVA		0.10%
35	33	*25.74
CID&BAB		0.19%
36	63	*48.51
CINZANO		0.10%
37	52	*24.44
RedWINE		0.00%
38	0	*0.00
Wh WINE		0.51%
39	196	*129.36
		35.84%
2G	13659	*9030.59
BtBEER		0.00%
41	1	*0.53
Bt EXPRT		0.12%
42	52	*29.64
BtPILS		2.06%
43	683	*519.08
BtSpBRW		0.60%
44	213	*151.23
SwSTOUT		0.77%
46	339	*193.23
BtCIDER		0.01%
47	6	*3.66
BtGUIN		0.01%
48	5	*2.95
N/CASTL		0.64%
49	193	*162.12
FOWLERS		0.01%
51	5	*2.85
BARBCAN		0.28%
52	117	*70.20
PaleALE		0.10%
53	31	*25.73

Till print-out, giving a line-by-line record of consumption.

This constitutes an ideal consumption analysis for cross-checking against the usage figures on the Stocktaker's 'Reported Sales' sheet.

```
WHISKY      47Q        MRTINI      29Q        R/STR       16Q
 1.09%    38.54         0.65%    23.20         0.68%    24.00
WHISKY      57Q        MARTIN      23Q        CIDER       56Q
 1.45%    51.30         0.58%    20.70         1.03%    36.51
MIXER      411Q        APPLET       3Q        CIDER       15Q
 2.33%    82.20         0.05%     1.95         0.27%     9.81
MIXER      353Q        APPLET       2Q        PILS        30Q
 2.00%    70.60         0.03%     1.40         0.81%    28.68
STELLA       3Q        BRANDY       4Q        PILS        18Q
 0.10%     3.60         0.11%     3.96         0.50%    17.88
STELLA       8Q        BRANDY      18Q        EKU          1Q
 0.29%    10.24         0.53%    18.90         0.06%     2.15
LIQUER      56Q                               C BERG       1Q
 1.66%    58.80                                0.02%     0.78
LIQUER      34Q               —Z2—             SBITE        3Q
 1.06%    37.40       PERIODICAL  TOTAL         0.09%     3.48
JDANIE      12Q        PT80/-     124Q        SBITE        2Q
 0.35%    12.60         3.70%   130.58         0.07%     2.60
JDANIE      28Q        PT80/-     119Q        GROLSH      14Q
 0.87%    30.80         3.57%   125.85         0.55%    19.52
PORT         2Q        SPEC        98Q        GROLSH      30Q
 0.05%     2.00         2.81%    99.15         1.28%    45.12
PORT         1Q        SPECAL      82Q        FURST        7Q
 0.03%     1.10         2.48%    87.60         0.26%     9.48
*VODKA     153Q        CIDER       32Q        FURST       29Q
 3.69%   130.05         1.00%    35.28         1.19%    42.23
*VODKA     161Q        CIDER       11Q        SANNIG       1Q
 4.11%   144.90         0.34%    12.15         0.02%     0.99
DASH       174Q        LAGER      369Q
 0.74%    26.10        11.03%   308.85
DASH        65Q        LAGER      252Q
 0.27%     9.75         7.92%   279.40
AZZURO       1Q        EXPORT       3Q
 0.03%     1.25         0.08%     3.15
GWINE        1Q        EXPORT       3Q
 0.02%     0.83         0.08%     3.15
MALIBU       6Q        MURPH       71Q
 0.17%     6.30         2.33%    82.13
MALIBU       8Q        MURPH       49Q
 0.24%     8.80         1.68%    59.50
PERNOD       5Q        1/2PT      100Q
 0.14%     5.00         1.71%    60.40
PERNOD       2Q        1/2PT       52Q
 0.05%     2.10         0.96%    34.01
RUM          9Q        BECKS       13Q
 0.21%     7.47         0.35%    12.41
RUM         12Q        BECKS       22Q
 0.30%    10.80         0.62%    21.95
COKE       118Q        CHLITZ       4Q
 1.84%    64.90         0.14%     5.00
COKE        51Q        SCHLIT      10Q
 0.86%    30.60         0.36%    12.92
BBCHAM       3Q        R/STR       11Q
 0.06%     2.40         0.43%    15.29
```

Till print-out, giving separate analyses of stock sold during, and outwith, the 'Happy Hour'.

For example, vodka sales (*) were as follows: during 'Happy Hour' – 153 @ 85p = £130.05; outwith 'Happy Hour' – 161 @ 90p = £144.90.

Till report, using P.L.U. numbers rather than individual item descriptions.

This identifies a particular product or category by a number which, on being entered in the till, is converted to a pre-set value. The Stocktaker must be informed of the product that relates to each number, so that he can prepare a comparison against the actual stock sales.

For example, item 1 (*) represents bitter beer, so the sales shown are 178 pints @ 82p per pint = £145.96.

◀

Till print-out, which provides a detailed line-by-line sales report and also totals sales by category (e.g. spirits (*), liqueurs (*) etc.), as on the Stock Report.

The system used here also has the facility to produce the total allowance for items sold more cheaply during the 'Happy Hour' (*), i.e. − £71.86.

```
. 10.          #..
0196.           z.
  .    .         *.
0178.           ..
* . 145,96      1..
0000.           ..
  .   0,00      2..
0000.           ..
  .   0,00      3..
0000.           ..
  .   0,00      4..
0381.           ..
  . 270,51      5..
0765.           ..
  . 698,12      6..
0091.           ..
  .  94,86      7..
0272.           ..
  . 242,65      8..
0000.           ..
  .   0,00      9..
0525.           ..
  . 378,00     11..
0051.           ..
  .  36,21     12..
0000.           ..
  .   0,00     13..
0000.           ..
  .   0,00     14..
1722.           ..
  . 840,38     15..
0196.           ..
  .  89,14     16..
0014.           ..
  .   7,39     17..
0081.           ..
  .  36,10     18..
0000.           ..
  .   0,00     19..
4276.           ..
.2839,32+T      ..
  .    .         *.
.2839,32 S      ..
.2839,32  T     ..
0344.           ..

  .    .         *.
```

▶

DPT

```
 SPIRITS        Q        2211
*   21.23%            1499.64
*LIQUEURS       Q          28
    0.37%               26.24
 MALTS          Q          20
    0.25%               17.45
 WINES          Q           5
    0.07%                4.75
 BRANDIES       Q          34
    0.43%               30.60
 VERMOUTHS      Q          75
    0.71%               50.35
 DRAUGHT BEER   Q        4668
   58.96               4163.90
 BOTLD BEER     Q         676
    7.40%              522.57
 OFF SALES      Q          55
    2.11%              148.95
 SOFT DRINKS    Q         769
    4.58%              323.68
 CIGARS         Q         504
    1.56%              110.20
 BAR LUNCHES    Q          28
    0.48%               34.20
 BAR SUPPERS    Q          10
    0.23%               16.05
 SUNDRY ITEMS   Q         544
    1.61%              113.54
                Q           1
    0.00%               0.00
 GRS TL         Q        9628
  100.00%            7062.12

-DPT            Q           0
                         0.00
```

TRANS

```
ST%2            Q           0
                         0.00

NET                      7062.12

TAKBL1                   7062.12
VAT                       921.15

* H/HOUR        Q         410
                        -71.86
 ITEM%2         Q           0
                         0.00
 REFUND         Q           0
                         0.00
```

so that proper allowances can be made. Brewers, however, are sometimes reluctant to fit meters.

Requisitions: It is normal policy for the person in charge of each bar to fill in a requisition form prior to departure each night. This sheet, as shown in the example, must be comprehensively and legibly completed, indicating size of bottle and brand of spirit. A line should be drawn beneath the last item, and nothing entered thereafter. The book, which is generally in duplicate, would go to the cellarman, who would issue the stock, sign the book, and return it, showing clearly any item not available. He would request a signature from the person in the bar receiving the goods. It is important for requisition books to be properly numbered and pages used sequentially, so that the cellarman or Stocktaker can quickly identify any missing sheets and act accordingly. If there are cellar discrepancies, it could be that a requisition has been omitted from the cellar ledger; and the Stocktaker, by checking numbers, will probably be able to obtain the missing information from the duplicate and balance the ledger.

Very often requisition books are of different colours, one for each bar. This assists the cellarman and also the Stocktaker, if he has to go through the requisitions to identify any cellar discrepancies. Normally the Stocktaker would take the top copies with him, in case of future queries.

Cellar Ledger: A typical ledger is shown in the following example. All incoming stock is entered and added on to the closing stock. Items going out of the cellar are recorded beneath the name of the actual bar to which they go. This figure is deducted from the closing figure, creating a new balance which should always correspond with the actual stock in the cellar. To facilitate proper control, it is advisable to have a separate page for each individual item and size of bottle.

The cellarman or other responsible person should be encouraged to check his cellar on a weekly basis, and ensure that his count corresponds with the figure shown on the ledger. If there are discrepancies he should be able, in dealing with so short a period of time, to account for them; but if unable to do so, he should not balance the ledger, but notify the differences to the Stocktaker, who will either be able to resolve the problem or record a cellar outage.

On the Stocktaker's visit, he must check the purchases off from the delivery notes or invoices, compare them with the entries in the Goods Received Book, and then record the total of stock going to each outlet, so that he can charge that quantity to its respective bar. He will then stamp or sign off the cellar ledger, leaving the correct opening figure and a new start for the forthcoming period. The normal procedure is for the Stocktaker to make entries on his sheets

THE MANAGEMENT OF LICENSED PREMISES

STOCK TRANSFER 342432

DEPARTMENT *Lounge* DATE 2/9/88

QTY.	ITEM	Received	Entered in Control Ledger
3	Grouse 1.5	✓	✓
1	Bells 40oz	✓	✓
2	Grouse ½ gall	✓	✓
1	Dimple Haig BTL	✓	✓
2	Bristol Cream BTL	✓	✓
1	Sweet Martini 1.5	✓	✓
2	McEwans Export doz.	✓	✓
2	Babycham doz	✓	✓
1	Carlsberg Lager 11 gall	✓	✓

SIGNED BARMAN *S.M...*

CELLARMAN *B.Ro...*

N.B. I) Use every line: Cross out those not used
      II) Insert carbon paper.

DATE	REFERENCES	PURCHASES	BAR 1 Public	BAR 2 Cocktail	BAR 3 Lounge	BAR 4 Function	BAR 5 Off Sales	BAR 6	Total	Closing Stock
31/5	B/Fwd.	36	10	6	3	8			(27)	9
31/5	21925	12								21
2/6	163		6						(6)	15
2/6	105			3					(3)	12
4/6	394					4			(4)	8
5/6	231				2				(2)	6
7/6	23674	12								18
11/6	108			4					(4)	14
13/6	235				4				(4)	10
14/6	110			3					(3)	7
14/6	25191	6								13
16/6	165			(2)		2				13
18/6	395		6						(6)	7
20/6		66	22	14	9	14		Stocktake J.P.B.	(59)	7
21/6	27233	18								25
21/6	238				3				(3)	22
23/6	166					4			(4)	18
25/6	396		5						(5)	13
26/6	167			3					(3)	10
26/6	008						1		(1)	9
27/6	239				3				(3)	6

CELLAR STOCK CARD — Society Whisky 1·5 Litre

from delivery notes or invoices, before balancing the ledger. Any discrepancies will be highlighted when the cellar balance is calculated.

As will be seen from the example, all purchases and credits are clearly entered, with the delivery or credit note number entered in the second column under 'references'. Also entered here are the requisition note numbers for any transfers to the bars. For an internal transfer such as the one on 16th June, Bar 2 has been credited and Bar 4 charged; but as this is a transfer purely between bars, the final balance is not affected. In the event of off-sales or other cellar transactions, the Stocktaker must determine the price the item was sold at and then make an appropriate allowance against the cellar. (The assumption here is that this income was credited to the cellar and not to one of the bars; if it had been credited to the latter, the item would be charged to that bar, and an allowance made there.)

The figures in the top row represent totals requisitioned to each bar since the last stock; these, added to any subsequent requisitions, are shown for 20th June, when the figures were totalled ready for the Stocktaker. Beneath this date the Stocktaker should draw a line and sign the ledger off, if necessary changing the balance so as to give the correct opening figure for the next stock.

Staff should be discouraged from making internal transfers; but it does happen. The procedure is to assign, either on a special transfer book or on a separate page of the requisition sheet, the purchase to the bar to which it was transferred, and a corresponding credit to the other. Part-bottles should be gauged as accurately as possible and entered, preferably in tenths (though in practice it is more likely to be in denominations of one quarter).

It is always advisable, both in multi- and in single-bar operations, for the Stocktaker to record delivery note numbers and dates of delivery separately for each company. This should be done on separate sheets of paper; it not only provides a check on future stocks, if there is doubt as to whether a certain invoice has been entered, but also allows the Stocktaker to see the purchase pattern. If, for instance, beer is delivered every Friday, he might notice one week's delivery missing, and be able, because he is still on his client's premises, to make immediate investigations.

In some cases a cellar ledger is not maintained; the Stocktaker will then have to work off requisitions and delivery notes. The only practical method here is to count the number of items transferred to each bar and enter those as purchases. This is laborious, and because the staff will not have checked their balances during the period in question, the results are rarely correct and major cellar discrepancies are likely to appear. It is always advisable to encourage clients, if they want separate results, to keep a cellar ledger, even though it entails extra work.

Bin cards operate in exactly the same way as cellar ledgers, but are normally loose-leaf; entries are made when stock is put into or taken out of the cellar. These cards are generally kept at the point of dispense. Their format is similar to the cellar ledger card shown on page 27.

In some cases, the cellar and one bar are combined and operated as a single unit. If the Stocktaker is requested to produce separate results for another bar on the premises, he would not be able to operate a cellar ledger system, but would have to use requisition notes to establish transfers, and credit those figures against purchases in the main bar. Provided accurate records are kept, realistic results should be attainable for each outlet.

Stock Rotation

'Stock rotation' refers simply to the use of older stock before the latest delivery. This helps to ensure that the customer gets a consistently fresh product and that stock does not become out of date. Supplies of bottled beer, cans and minerals should be stacked underneath or behind any remaining in the storeroom; and when staff are 'bottling up' a bar, they should put the new stock behind any still left on the shelf.

The modern practice of cramming bottle shelves twelve or more deep, and replacing every few sold, makes stock rotation very difficult, and this is why it is often neglected – to the detriment of stock quality. Neat rows three to six deep, with just over a day's maximum sales, look more attractive and are far easier to rotate.

If keg or draught beer is allowed to lie too long in the cellar and becomes out of date, it may be that the supplier will refuse credit on grounds of age. The write-off in this instance could be considerable.

With the exception of some ciders, all bottles and cans now have a 'best before' date. Dates for bottles appear on the edge or bottom of labels, or on the back, or on the top or edge of crown corks (caps). Dates for cans appear on the top or bottom panel, or on the plastic strip which binds a four-pack together. The period from production to 'best before' date varies from about one month to twenty-four months.

Keg and draught beers may have, in place of a 'best before' date, a production date, sometimes in the form of a very simple code. The 'best condition' life is usually judged to expire from three to eight weeks after production. Individual breweries should be contacted for specific details.

Stocktakers are mainly concerned with dating at change of ownership valuations (see page 146), when every effort should be made to ensure that the buyer does not pay for out-of-date stock. If stock rotation has not been adhered to, losses to the vendor can be considerable.

Stock Quantities

Overstocking: Overstocking can be a major problem. Many millions of pounds are tied up in superfluous stock throughout the country's licensed premises. There are many with five to ten cases of rum or ruby port in the storeroom – and a sale of two bottles per month. These costly purchases are usually made just prior to the Budget in an effort to save money, but since many premises run on an overdraft, it is likely that the money thus tied up would be better released and put to good use. The only way to benefit by buying excessive bulk is perhaps in the case of vintage port or fine wines; but this is only relevant to the 'up-market' section of the trade, and even there only to be undertaken with expert advice.

Overstocking is likely to produce untidy stock, which can both encourage pilfering and make the loss harder to detect. Rotation, too, becomes more difficult.

Par Stocks: Many establishments set a level of stock to be held in any one bar. This is referred to as 'par stock', and requisitions would be based on the numbers needed to bring this stock up to the designated level. If the par stock of vodka magnums was three, this figure would never be exceeded; but if two had been used in the bar, the barman would requisition two to bring his stock up to the correct level. Generally, stock in use is not included, and the system only applies to full bottles.

CHAPTER 2
PROFIT AND LOSS ACCOUNTS, BALANCE SHEETS, AND VALUE ADDED TAX

PROFIT AND LOSS ACCOUNTS AND BALANCE SHEETS

Accounts for hotels and public houses are similar to those for any other type of business, and are made up of two main documents, the profit and loss account and the balance sheet.

The following examples relate to a small hotel, and are typical accounts for this type of operation. In 1987 there was a small loss of £742, but with increased gross profits and stringent control of overheads, the figure for the following year has reversed this, and a profit of just over £10,000 has emerged. It should be noted that a fee of £625 for stocktaking appears in the later set of accounts: the employment of a Stocktaker may well help to explain why profits have increased so considerably.

The Profit and Loss Account

This document shows the performance of the business throughout the previous financial year, and provides a comparison with that of the preceding year. Profit margins, both net and gross, are shown, the former after overheads have been deducted, and the latter after the cost of sales only (the actual cost element of the products sold) has been taken into account. In the example shown on page 32, the turnover up to 26th June 1988 totalled £134,895, from which a gross profit of £90,462 (67%) was achieved. This particular set of accounts breaks down the turnover into three separate categories, each of which is producing a realistic profit. Liquor has produced a 40.9% gross profit (£10,787 divided by £26,358) and food and accommodation between them 73.2%. (It is preferable to separate food and accommodation, but in practice this can be difficult, because so many establishments operate inclusive terms, and in almost all cases the charges for bed and breakfast are combined in a single figure. To facilitate good management – and to assist the Stocktaker – it is advisable, where practicable, to allocate income from rooms, bars and catering separately, within the hotel records. If breakfast is included in the accommodation figure, the breakfast charge can be multiplied by the number of sleepers, and that figure

31

PROFIT AND LOSS ACCOUNT
YEAR ENDED 26 JUNE 1988

	Sales £	Cost of Sales £	Gross Profit £	1987 £
FOOD AND				
ACCOMMODATION	106,746	28,528	78,218	67,643
BAR	26,358	15,571	10,787	9,259
SUNDRY	1,791	334	1,457	580
	134,895	44,433	90,462	77,482
Gaming machine income		1,439		582
Less: expenses		636		465
			803	117
			91,265	77,599

OVERHEADS		
Wages and national insurance	30,341	22,697
Laundry and cleaning	5,336	5,882
Entertainment	1,922	3,989
Rates	4,417	3,321
Insurance	1,446	1,200
Postage, printing, stationery and advertising	993	2,123
Motor expenses	1,114	1,673
Staff uniforms	360	1,508
Repairs and renewals	5,853	4,859
Heat and light	8,270	10,280
Telephone	1,359	1,347
Rental and leasing charges	1,263	1,276
Accountancy	764	493
Bank interest and charges	981	489
Stocktaking fees	625	–
Loan interest	10,800	10,800
Sundry	69	141
Depreciation	5,275	6,263
	81,188	78,341
NET PROFIT/(LOSS) for year	£10,077	£(742)

added on to the catering income.) Sundry income has arisen from the sale of postcards, stationery, and other commodities not classed as food or drink; the gaming machine income amounted to £803 after deduction of rental. Before the deduction of overheads, therefore, this particular establishment had made profits of £91,265.

This figure is known as the gross profit, and it must be large enough to absorb all the overheads, of which the biggest is generally wages. In this instance wages account for £30,341, or 22.5% of turnover, which is probably about right for the size of establishment. The items listed on this particular profit and loss account are the standard ones, but any other heading can be introduced if the accountant sees fit. The figure arrived at after deducting these overheads is known as the net profit, and is the most important figure on the document. In this case the unit has made £10,077; but it should be noted that in the previous year there was a loss of £742, and one can see clearly from the accounts that the improvement in the current year's figures is due to an increase in gross profits.

All these figures are the personal concern of the owner or company who runs the establishment, and no Stocktaker to whom profit and loss accounts or balance sheets are shown should ever discuss them with anyone else. The bank interest charges and loan interest do not reflect on the operation of the business, but simply indicate the manner in which the proprietors have chosen to finance the hotel. The depreciation figure is a 'book' one, worked out on an annual average basis to represent the decreasing value of the assets of the business. In certain circumstances, and very rarely, this figure may increase; but this would only occur when appreciating assets are held on the premises, such as antiques or rare commodities. The depreciation figure, together with loan and interest charges and any other unusual overheads, is frequently added back to the net profit, so as to show a realistic trading result over a given period.

Any professional valuer assessing a business will study its profit and loss account in great depth. He will look at the trading account to see if gross profit levels are acceptable, and study each of the overheads to determine whether they compare realistically with those of similar businesses.

The Balance Sheet

Unlike the profit and loss account, the balance sheet shows the state of the business and its assets at any one time, usually the last day of the financial year. It shows the fixed assets, which generally represent the 'bricks and mortar' value of the building, together with fixtures, fittings and motor vehicles. In the example, 'goodwill' is

BALANCE SHEET
AS AT 26 JUNE 1988

	£	*1988* £	*1987* £
GOODWILL			
At cost		5,000	5,000
FIXED ASSETS			
Property and improvements			
As at 26 June 1987	67,272		
Improvements during year	1,858		
		69,130	67,272
Furniture, fixtures and fittings			
As at 26 June 1987	27,524		
Purchased during year	611		
	28,135		
Depreciation for year	4,220		
		23,915	27,524
Motor vehicle			
As at 26 June 1987	4,219		
Depreciation for year	1,055		
		3,164	4,219
		101,209	104,015
CURRENT ASSETS			
Stock	3,500		3,900
Debtors and prepayments	–		196
Value Added Tax	1,048		2,448
Cash on hand	250		250
	4,798		6,794
CURRENT LIABILITIES			
Creditors and accrued charges	26,933		26,992
Bank overdraft	2,837		7,583
	29,770		34,575
NET CURRENT LIABILITIES		(24,972)	(27,781)
TOTAL NET ASSETS		£76,237	£76,234

	1988	1987
£	£	£

Represented by:

JOINT CAPITAL ACCOUNT

As at 26 June 1987	6,961	14,944
Profit/(loss) for year	10,077	(742)
	17,038	14,202
Personal drawings	10,074	7,241
	6,964	6,961

LOAN ACCOUNTS

Development Loans Ltd	1,773	1,773
Society Finance Co.	67,500	67,500
	£76,237	£76,234

shown as an asset, but some accountants prefer not to include this in the final document.

Total fixed assets are shown as £101,209; but unless a recent valuation of the premises has been carried out, this figure is unlikely to be accurate, and that is why so many bank managers and financial institutions ask for an up-to-date valuation to be prepared before they grant loans. There are several factors which determine the value of a property, amongst which are the situation and condition of the building, the potential, past trading experience, and the rate of inflation.

Depreciation is generally calculated to write off the cost of any tangible fixed assets as fairly as possible over their effective normal lives. Accountants have differing views on this, but generally furnishings and fittings would be written off over a period of ten to fifteen years, whereas the period for vehicles and mechanical equipment would probably be five. Leasehold property would be written off over the period of the lease; freehold buildings (if the state of the business permitted) would be written off over as short a period as possible. In this way, a company can build up considerable assets and substantial borrowing power in later years.

The asset figures at the bottom of the balance sheet vary on a day-to-day basis, and can in theory be converted into cash at any given time. Set against them are any liabilities. If these are far in excess of current assets, the business is weak and would be termed 'not liquid'. If the current liabilities were higher than both the current assets and the fixed assets, the business would be in serious financial difficulty. The figure which represents the difference between the total current liabilities and the total current assets is termed the 'net current liability', whereas the 'total net assets' figure represents the fixed and current assets combined, less any liabilities.

The final part of the balance sheet indicates how the net assets were financed.

MANAGEMENT — PROFIT AND LOSS ACCOUNTS — DISCREPANCIES

The role of management is complex, and varies according to the size of the establishment and the extent of the responsibility entrusted to the particular manager. The list below covers the various aspects for which he might be expected to take responsibility:–

The food and beverage operation	Marketing
Stores and supplies	Costing and planning
Housekeeping and general cleanliness	Budgetary control
Maintenance	Bookkeeping and accounts
General standards	Production of results
Staff and personnel training	Liaising with Head Office

In bigger establishments, it is probable that the general manager will delegate responsibility for the liquor and food operation to one of his subordinates, who will be referred to as the food and beverage manager and who will provide a direct contact between the Stocktaker and the establishment. This assistant manager will be directly responsible for each of the following:–

1. Monitoring and control of deliveries and stores.
2. Control of wet and dry stocks.
3. The prevention of pilferage.
4. Staff liaison and discipline.
5. Delegating responsibilities, and ensuring that they are properly understood.
6. The maintenance of proper records.
7. The production of satisfactory gross profits.
8. Liaison with the Stocktaker.
9. Understanding the stock report, and knowing how to act on any information supplied.

Stocktaking is carried out not simply to indicate whether there is a surplus or a deficit, but also to promote proper management, supply information and statistics, ensure proper pricing, monitor costs, control allowances, and enable management to check that stock levels are being maintained at the correct level.

Profit and loss accounts can be very beneficial to the management team, and are frequently produced on a monthly basis. The following example shows considerable shortfalls in profitability, and is typical of some hotels and pubs today.

Annual Profit and Loss Account

Last Year £		This Year £
	Sales	
81,280	Rooms	106,970
174,900	Food	182,510
158,860	Liquor and tobacco	141,060
1,560	Sundries	1,690
£416,600	Total Sales	£432,230
	Cost of Sales	
115,840	Provisions	116,090
87,590	Liquor and tobacco	88,430
£203,430	Total Cost of Sales	£204,520
213,170	Gross Profit	227,710
	Expenses	
118,810	Salaries and wages	125,250
15,350	Lighting and heating	15,920
8,670	Rates	8,610
2,120	Insurance	2,160
2,980	Cleaning materials	3,030
12,260	Laundry and dry cleaning	12,950
2,250	Stationery, printing and postage	2,200
1,480	Telephone	1,310
5,000	Advertising	5,710
650	Commissions	450
970	Professional Charges	1,000
490	Entertainments	380
4,170	Petty Cash and Sundries	3,910
21,420	Repairs and Renewals	19,010
8,220	Depreciation	8,610
£204,840		£210,500
£ 8,330	NET PROFIT	£17,210

The gross profit on food, last year, was 33.7%; this year it is 36.4%. This is a slight improvement, but the turnover has remained almost static, and if inflation is taken into account, the figure has actually decreased. As far as the liquor and tobacco operation is concerned, the hotel's gross profit has been reduced from 44.8% to 37.3%. This is a highly unsatisfactory situation, and one which should set alarm bells ringing. Each individual establishment will set its own targets for profitability, but whatever figures were budgeted for in this particular establishment, it must be fairly apparent that they have not been met. It is an easy task for any Stocktaker to calculate the gross profit which should have been achieved; and in these particular circumstances, it would be essential for a Stocktaker to be asked to produce this figure, and to try to establish why the actual ones were so low. Had a gross profit of 50% been achieved in both liquor and food, the current profits would have increased by £42,735. This would have been a much more realistic profit in relation to the size of operation, and one which few businessmen would not welcome.

The example indicates how stocktaking can be used to increase profitability – and, indeed, how little the service costs, when one considers the potential increase in profitability ensured by proper controls.

The gross profit shown by a Stocktaker, or by the accountant, is the actual figure achieved. Their figures should agree, and if there are serious discrepancies, reasons should be sought without delay. The surplus or deficit figure (see page 117) is the key to the detection of discrepancies within the operation of the business, and helps to determine whether the budgeted profits will be achieved or not. It is, however, of no use to management if they are unaware of the reasons for high surpluses or deficits; on the following pages, possible reasons for fluctuations are detailed, together with suggestions for controlling them.

Possible Reasons for High Deficits
Wrong Measures or Selling Prices in Use: It may be that staff, through inadequate training, are using the wrong size of measure. For instance, they might be using a sherry measure for liqueurs, instead of a one-sixth gill, or a wine measure for Martini, when the hotel instruction is to use a one-third measure. Selling prices do vary, and can be confusing for staff inexperienced in the trade. It is imperative that a clear and concise list be displayed behind the bar, so that they know exactly what price to charge for each drink and also what measure to use.

Excessive Beer Wastage: Draught beer, particularly traditional ale, can be the source of a lot of wastage claims; and very often staff, through inexperience, do not treat it with the respect it deserves, and thus increase losses. Pipes must be cleaned regularly, and all beer used as quickly as possible after delivery, to prevent build-ups of yeast and the serving of out-of-date beer. In many establishments it is common practice for staff to pour pints down the sink, in some cases because of frothing. This is extremely wasteful; it is also usually unnecessary, and can indicate bad cellar work.

Stock out on Loan: If a neighbouring pub or hotel has run short on a particular item, the staff may borrow stock and return it after their next delivery. As such loans are often for two or three days only, proper transfer slips may not have been completed; accordingly, if a stock is done prior to the delivery, the Stocktaker may not know of the transaction, and may consequently assume that the stock has been sold.

Incorrect Income or Business not Raised: Errors can occur when income is extracted. As stated, it is the Stocktaker's responsibility to ensure that he has obtained the correct figures; but in certain circumstances, it may be very difficult for him to achieve this. If, therefore, when leaving the premises, he feels dissatisfied with the figures given to him, he should make it quite clear to his client that the result does depend upon the accuracy of the income figure. In many instances, where functions have been held at the premises, the business may not yet have been raised through the books; it is important for the Stocktaker to check, before he leaves, that none is still outstanding. (The assumption here is that the hotel uses the tabular system described on page 6. If, on the other hand, the cash will be recorded only when the client pays, the Stocktaker must add the amount to the present income figure, and make a note reminding himself to reduce by an equal amount the income figure for the later period, in which the payment is made.)

Inadequate Control of Allowances: To ensure accurate stock results, it is important for all allowances to be recorded properly. Unless money passes over the bar counter for each transaction, a note must be made in the allowance book or a charge made to the client. The Stocktaker must be notified of all allowances and must make the necessary adjustments (see page 126).

Short Deliveries or Errors by Suppliers: It is the duty of all staff employed at hotels and pubs to monitor deliveries, and ensure that they receive what they actually sign for. Short deliveries are common; but the Stocktaker will take as having been delivered what he finds entered on the invoice or delivery note.

Stock not Seen by the Stocktaker: When there are private bars, or wine displays, or when stock is not stored in the usual place, the manager may forget to tell the Stocktaker about the stock concerned, which may then fail to be taken into account.

Returned Beer not Recorded: Because it sometimes takes several weeks to procure credit notes, it is important for a record to be kept of any beer returned to a supplier. If no record is kept, the Stocktaker will probably not know of such a return, and will not make any allowance in his figures. The manager or cellarman should assess the volume of beer in each keg; the Stocktaker will use this figure, and make any adjustment once the credit is received.

Deliveries Relating to the Previous Period: If a delivery came to light which had been omitted during the previous stock, its inclusion in the current one would create a deficit.

Dishonesty: This is a very broad category. Some 'fiddles' are detailed on the following pages, but it would be virtually impossible to list every type which exists today.

Possible Reasons for High Surpluses

Purchases not Recorded: If – as is quite common – delivery notes are lost, the Stocktaker will receive no record of certain purchases. This is particularly likely to happen when goods are purchased through 'cash and carry', on a Petty Cash voucher. It is extremely important that the Stocktaker be notified of all purchases relative to the liquor operation.

Wrongly Allocated Income: Income can be wrongly allocated if, for instance, food money is recorded through the bar, or corkage or room hire charges are raised as bar income. Unless the Stocktaker is informed, or notices sudden surges in income, he is unlikely to realise what is happening.

Borrowed Stock: If stock is borrowed from other premises and not recorded, this creates a surplus on the result – with a corresponding deficit during the next stock period, after the item in question has been returned.

Income Raised from the Previous Period: If income for a function was raised during the stock period which in fact related to the previous stock, then a surplus should show. A corresponding deficit should be apparent, however, for the previous period.

Pilferage – Some Methods

1. *Not Charging for Drink:*   This often occurs when the friends or family of staff are within the premises as customers: they are supplied with drink for which no charge is made, or a discount is given. The result is a deficit.
2. *Under-ringing:*   This involves not ringing up the true amount of money on the cash register, and removing a corresponding amount before the end of the session.
3. *Collusion by Bar and Floor Staff:*   Where floor waitresses are involved, it is always a possibility that they and the bar staff are 'working together'. Customers will probably be served their drinks and charged the correct prices, but the staff, knowing that the customers cannot see the cash register, may appropriate some or all of the money.
4. *Supplying Short Measures to Clients:*   By inflating the surplus, this would permit staff to remove either stock or cash, which would not show up on any stocktake. It would contravene the Weights and Measures Act, and the hotel would be liable to prosecution.

5. *Diluted Spirits:* This again would create inflated surpluses, allowing staff to remove stock or cash. The only way in which a Stocktaker could accurately detect this fraud would be by using a hydrometer (see page 274).

6. *Direct Theft:* This would involve cash or stock, and the discrepancies would show up on the Stocktaker's report. Staff themselves may be drinking without paying, and this would have the same effect on results.

The list is endless; but there are control methods of which Stocktakers should be aware, and which they can recommend to clients. Several of these are listed below.

Security Procedures

1. *Comparison of Till Records against Stock Sales:* This is possible only where computerised tills (see page 16) are used. Any major discrepancy between the sale figure of each commodity produced by the Stocktaker and that shown on the cash register should cause immediate concern.

2. *Daily Overages and Shortages:* An analysis of till overages and shortages might indicate whether staff have been misappropriating cash. Small discrepancies will frequently occur and will usually be tolerated, but if differences between amounts of cash in the till and readings are considerable, either up or down, it may well suggest dishonest practices.

3. *Till Rolls and 'No Sales':* It is an acknowledged fact that, because of the number of people asking for change for cigarette and fruit machines, there will be several 'no sales' rung up on the cash register. However, excessive rings should immediately be investigated, because they might indicate that the barman was ringing up a 'no sale' instead of a cash amount, then pocketing the balance. Similarly, excessive sales of small amounts might suggest the ringing up of part-charges.

4. *Z Readings:* It is worth ensuring that a Z reading (see page 16) is done at each stocktake. This will not necessarily prove any fraud, especially where there are considerable credit sales, but it will help the Stocktaker to determine whether all cash has been put through the books. It is also a good idea to ensure that the till has not been zeroed and re-started during the stock period.

5. *Abnormal Sales of Particular Commodities:* It is always worth checking to see if any particular item is selling more than usual. If this is the case, then a worthwhile exercise is to operate an 'empty for full' system. This would entail having a par stock (see page 30) in each bar; and for each full bottle requested from the cellar, the bar staff would have to produce an empty one.

This (at least theoretically) would discourage the bringing in of stock, or the theft of full bottles.

6. *Brought-in Stock:* As mentioned under 'Abnormal Sales of Particular Commodities', it is important to check the sales of individual items; and if a decrease is found in the sale of any particular commodity, it is worth checking that stock is not being brought in and sold for personal gain.

7. *Off-sales:* If the number of off-sales has suddenly increased during the stock period, it may be that quarter- and half-bottles, officially sold at off-sale prices, are being sold at normal retail prices through the optic, and that staff are pocketing the difference. Verification of full bottle sales can often be found by checking the till roll.

8. *Bottle and Case Counts:* On an extended stock report, these would not necessarily affect the result; but any discrepancies might indicate malpractice.

A Stocktaker is not always able to highlight where discrepancies are occurring. He should, however, be able to indicate to clients how they might be occurring, and to suggest preventive measures. Keen supervision is always needed; and if suspicions have been raised concerning cash, it is always helpful to have a spare till drawer ready with its float, to replace the one in use during the business period. A till reading can be taken at any time, and the contents of the drawer counted at leisure. This procedure would detect under-ringing by staff intending to take cash out of the till drawer later.

Prior to notifying the client of any deficits, the Stocktaker would need to ensure that the income given to him was correct, that the allowance figures were complete, and that all purchases had been properly recorded, with details of any returned beer. Once he had satisfied himself that his information was correct, he would look at various possible reasons for high deficits, consider the situation, and decide if any preventive controls would be advantageous in the circumstances.

In some cases, it might be a good idea to suggest to the client that he employs someone (perhaps one of the Stocktaker's professional colleagues) to come in as a customer and watch the operation, to see if any dubious activities take place. The cash register should be monitored to ensure that it is not being exchanged for short periods of time.

Precautionary Measures for Stocktakers

The Stocktaker should check

1. That each bottle contains what the label says, and that the content is of the correct proof (see page 273).

Once this stock has been counted, it will be ready to be analysed against the Cellar Ledger (the Caledonian Hotel, Princes Street, Edinburgh).

A hydrometer is essential for checking the proof of spirits, as in this regular exercise (the Caledonian Hotel, Princes Street, Edinburgh).

2. That draught beer kegs and other containers are genuinely full, and that caps have not been replaced on empty ones.
3. That spirit bottles in the cellar are sealed.
4. That all full spirit cases are properly secured (check the bottom).
5. That stacked cases are all full and that the ones at the bottom are the same as those at the top.

VALUE ADDED TAX

Value Added Tax, commonly referred to as V.A.T., was introduced on 1st April 1973; it is administered by Customs and Excise. The original rate was 10%, later reduced to 8%; at the time of writing, the rate is 15%.

The original concept was that a tax would be applied on the purchase of all luxury items, and that essentials would be exempt and described as 'zero rated'. The scheme has changed, mainly to comply with Common Market regulations, but items such as food (purchased in shops), newspapers, books, children's clothes, nappies etc. are still not subject to tax. Food eaten in restaurants and 'carry out' food (only if hot), along with most other items, are 'standard rated', which means that, provided the vendor is registered for V.A.T., a surcharge will be added. The registered trader will have to charge his clients 15% on their purchases, and forward the total to the government; but he will be able to reclaim from the same source the 15% that he originally paid on the goods. The ultimate losers are those individuals not registered for V.A.T., who are unable to reclaim the surcharge.

Every individual or company with turnover (as from March 1989) of or above £23,600 must register for V.A.T.; this figure is known as the threshold, and tends to be increased each year at the Budget. Once registered, individuals or companies are bound by law to declare, every three months, their taxable earnings and payments, which are known as input and output taxes.

A typical V.A.T. Return (Form 100) is shown on page 45; as will be clearly seen, the amount payable or recoverable is the difference between the output figure and the input figure. Since not all items are subject to tax, a high degree of accurate bookkeeping is necessary, to maintain records properly and satisfy the Customs and Excise, who regularly inspect the books and accounts of registered individuals and companies. The publican, restaurateur or hotelier will pay V.A.T. on most of his purchases, the major exception being food, which is zero rated. The person completing the V.A.T. return will have to declare every input, even though no V.A.T. is payable,

and he will have to charge tax to all customers who purchase meals
or snacks within the premises. Thus 15% will be added to all bills,
and subsequently (at the end of each quarter) forwarded to the
Customs and Excise, with any V.A.T. paid on purchases deducted
from that amount.

In 1973, when V.A.T. was introduced, the prices of beer, wine
and spirits were not increased, and the duty payable by brewers and
distillers was reduced by the same amount as was added for V.A.T.
This meant there was no immediate surge in prices, and allowed
people time to register and become accustomed to the new regulations. Today the government is benefiting by the additional 5% on
the V.A.T. rate, and by V.A.T. income from individuals who, not
being registered, are unable to reclaim their tax.

As already stated, V.A.T. has two components, output tax, which
is that due on sales or business done, and input tax, which is that due
on purchases.

The V.A.T. Return

The main figures being asked for on a Return are:–

1. Output Tax.
2. Output Total (or sales excluding V.A.T.).
3. Input Tax.
4. Input Total (or purchases excluding V.A.T.).
5. V.A.T. payable.

To arrive at these figures, the trader must observe the following
procedure:–

1. To produce the output tax figure, he must record and add
    together all his income for the period. As far as the publican or
    hotelier is concerned, V.A.T. is payable on virtually all sources
    of income, and therefore if his total turnover for the period
    amounted to £29,504.50, his tax at 15% would be £3,848.41,
    which leaves a standard rate sales figure of £25,656.09.

    The V.A.T. figure is arrived at by taking 15/115ths (or
    3/23rds) of the turnover figure. A common way of arriving at
    the net figure is to divide the gross amount by 1.15. A straight
    deduction of 15% should never be made, because the original
    figure already includes the V.A.T. element; accordingly, any
    such calculation would be incorrect.

    To check these figures, all that is necessary is to add 15% of
    the net amount on to that amount: the total figure should agree
    with the gross turnover prior to deduction of V.A.T.

Value Added Tax Return

For the period

01 06 88 to 31 08 88

H M Customs and Excise

Due to reach the VAT Central Unit by 30 09 88
These dates must not be altered.

For Official Use

Registration No | Period

08 88

Before you fill in this form please read the notes on the other side. You must complete all boxes — writing "none" where necessary. If you need to show an exact amount of pounds, please write "00" in the pence column. Don't put a dash or leave the column blank. Please write clearly in ink. You must ensure that the completed form and any VAT payable are received no later than the due date by the Controller, VAT Central Unit, H M Customs and Excise, 21 Victoria Avenue, SOUTHEND-ON-SEA X

SS99 1AB

WARNING

If this return and any tax due are not received by the due date you will be liable to a surcharge.

An envelope is enclosed for your use.

For Official Use

£ | p

FOR OFFICIAL USE

		£	p
VAT DUE in this period on OUTPUTS (sales, etc), certain postal imports and services received from abroad	1	5310	43
Underdeclarations of VAT made on previous returns (but not those notified in writing by Customs and Excise)	2		
TOTAL VAT DUE (box 1 + box 2)	3	5310	43
VAT DEDUCTIBLE in this period on INPUTS (purchases, etc)	4	3011	73
Overdeclarations of VAT made on previous returns (but not those notified in writing by Customs and Excise)	5		
TOTAL VAT DEDUCTIBLE (box 4 + box 5)	6	3011	73
NET VAT PAYABLE OR REPAYABLE (Difference between boxes 3 and 6)	7	2298	70

Please tick only ONE of these boxes:

box 3 greater than box 6 — payment by credit transfer

box 6 greater than box 3 — repayment due

payment enclosed ✓

		£	p
Value of Outputs (excluding any VAT)	8	40714	00
Value of Inputs (excluding any VAT)	9	23090	00

How to pay the VAT due

Cross all cheques and postal orders "A/C Payee only" and make them payable to "H M Customs and Excise". Make credit transfers through account 3078027 at National Girobank or 10-70-50 52055000 for Bank Giros and keep your payment slip. You can order pre-printed booklets of credit transfer slips from your local VAT office. In your own interest do not send notes, coins, or uncrossed postal orders through the post.
Please write your VAT registration number on the back of all cheques and credit transfer slips.

Please tick box(es) if the statement(s) apply:

box 5 includes bad debt relief

box 8 includes exempt outputs

box 8 includes exports

Retail schemes If you have used any of the schemes in the period covered by this return please tick the box(es) to show all the schemes used.

| A | B | C | D | E | F | G | H | J |

Remember, you could be liable to a financial penalty if your return and all the VAT payable are not received by the due date.
DECLARATION by the signatory to be completed by or on behalf of the person named above.

I, JOHN SMITH .... declare that the
(full name of signatory in BLOCK LETTERS)
information given above is true and complete.

Signed John Smith .... Date 10/8/88 19......
*(Proprietor, partner, director, secretary, responsible officer, committee member of club or association, duly authorised person) *Delete as necessary

FOR OFFICIAL USE

VAT 100 F3790 (October 1987)

The following table shows the calculation of output tax (V.A.T. on sales) for a single V.A.T. quarter.

V.A.T. Quarter May 1st–July 31st 1988

		Bar	Food	Machines
		£	£	£
May	7	2,271.60	399.75	181.40
	14	2,409.70	426.70	
	21	2,471.40	471.40	190.60
	28	2,379.60	470.80	
June	4	2,571.70	496.00	200.40
	11	2,496.90	505.10	
	18	2,611.40	501.40	177.80
	25	2,577.70	499.90	
July	2	2,399.80	477.80	181.60
	9	2,610.70	502.00	
	16	2,577.20	510.90	197.70
	23	2,666.40	536.00	
	30	2,704.50	540.60	181.80
(1 day)	31	274.70	40.40	
		33,023.30	6,378.75	1,311.30

Total business for period (V.A.T inclusive)	£40,713.35
V.A.T. content	£5,310.43
Net business	£35,402.92

2. To produce the input tax figure, all purchases for the period must be recorded with a separate column showing the V.A.T. element. By law, all invoices coming from a company registered for V.A.T. must show their registration number (see page 48); and though this is not obligatory, the V.A.T. content will in most cases be shown as a separate figure, which the trader will thus not need to calculate.

    The analysis sheet which follows shows how input tax (V.A.T. on purchases) is extracted from invoice totals.

On the V.A.T. Return Form 100 (see page 45) the figure of £5,310.43, being the V.A.T. due on outputs or sales, would be entered in boxes 1 and 3. Once completed for the full period, the input V.A.T. (in this instance assumed to be £3,011.73) would be entered in boxes 4 and 6. The difference between the two would be either payable or refundable.

OCTOBER 1988

	CODE	CHEQUE No.	TOTAL	WAGES & DRAWINGS	PRINTING STATS	ADVERTISING	HP	MOTOR	TRADE	VAT	NET
Accounting Services Ltd.	256	789481	750-00						652-18	97-82	652-18
Customs & Excise	257	789482	540-30						540-30		540-30
Typing Services	258	789483	45-00		45-00						45-00
Burgoyne	259	789484	375-00	375-00							375-00
G.P.O. (car tax)	260	789485	100-00					100-00			100-00
Automobile Association	261	789486	52-50					45-65		6-85	45-65
Nelson + Co.	262	789487	98-90						86-00	12-90	86-00
B. Telecom	263	789488	33-46						29-10	4-36	29-10
Campbell	264	789489	136-66	136-66							136-66
Society Brewers	265	789490	204-70						178-00	26-70	178-00
Registrar of Companies	266	789491	40-00						40-00		40-00
Blight Press	267	789492	62-74			54-56				8-18	54-56
Hunter Garages	268	789493	350-00					304-34		45-66	304-34
Andrew Owens Ltd.	269	789494	54-26		47-18					7-08	47-18
Clark	270	789495	140-00	140-00							140-00
Typing Services	271	789496	19-71		19-71						19-71
Drawings	272	789497	450-00	450-00							450-00
Inland Revenue		s/o	200-00						200-00		200-00
Rent		s/o	174-50						174-50		174-50
City Finance		s/o	197-89				197-89				197-89
			4025-62	1101-66	111-89	54-56	197-89	449-99	1900-08	209-55	3816-07

Society Stocktakers Ltd   8/11/89
        Strange Street
        Stafford

    0785-42618

INVOICE

Black Bush Hotel – Stafford

To visiting the above premises, taking a physical count of stock, extending the figures and producing an extended stock report

FEE			VAT
Stocktake 1/11/89	£	110.00	16.50
Goods Received Book	£	8.00	1.20
Total	£	118.00	17.70
Total VAT	£	17.70	
INVOICE TOTAL	£	135.70	

THIS AMOUNT DUE WITHIN 28 DAYS

It is absolutely essential for V.A.T. calculations to be done correctly; and whenever V.A.T. is charged to a client, it must by law be declared to the Customs and Excise. On the other hand, it is in one's own interest to reclaim as much as possible, so recording of the V.A.T. element in all purchases, including Petty Cash ones, is highly beneficial to the individual concerned.

If a trader is not registered for V.A.T., he cannot reclaim V.A.T. on purchases – but neither does he have to add it to sales. No V.A.T. returns need be completed until his annual turnover exceeds the threshold figure or the quarterly limit.

A typical V.A.T. invoice is shown on page 48.

V.A.T. on Deficits

Customs and Excise can charge V.A.T. on stock deficits. The ruling is that once a transaction has occurred, and a drink has passed over the counter, V.A.T. is payable; but if theft or loss occurs prior to the point of sale, e.g. through short deliveries, payment cannot be enforced. In all instances, however, the onus rests on the licensee to prove that the loss occurred prior to a sale having been made.

Without the aid of regular stocktaking, deficits assessed by the Customs and Excise could be overestimated; and it is only on the basis of extended reports, where sales mix ratios, allowances etc. are clearly detailed, that any such assessments could be contested.

CHAPTER 3
LICENSEES AND THE LAW

MISCELLANEOUS MATTERS

The following extracts are taken from 'An ABC of Licensing Law' (sixty-third edition, October 1988), and are printed here with acknowledgement to the National Licensed Victuallers' Association.

Annual Licensing Meeting

The annual licensing meeting must be held in the first fortnight of February in every year and is fixed at a meeting of the justices held at least twenty-one days beforehand. The justices may adjourn the annual licensing meeting beyond the day appointed in order to consider any application already lodged but no new applications may be made at such adjourned sessions. All powers of the justices may be exercised at the annual licensing meeting. (See also 'Licensing Sessions'.)

Appeals

There is a right of appeal to the crown court against any decision of the licensing justices in the following circumstances:

(a) where the justices have granted or refused to grant a new justices' licence or an ordinary removal of a justices' licence

(b) where the justices have refused to grant the renewal, transfer or special removal of a licence

(c) where the justices have made an order for structural alterations or have refused consent for the making of alterations

(d) where any decision has been made by the justices as to the conditions of a justices' on-licence

(e) where there is a refusal to declare a Provisional Grant final or to affirm it or to give consent on the application of the Holder of a Provisional Licence to a modification of plans

(f) where the justices have granted a Restriction Order

(g) where there are decisions relating to the grant, revocation or imposition of Conditions relating to Special Hours Certificates

(h) where the justices have revoked a justices' licence.

In addition there is also a right of appeal against any conviction by a court of summary jurisdiction where the convicted person did not plead guilty or admit the truth of the information, or if he pleaded guilty, against his sentence.

Bar

Section 201 of the Licensing Act 1964 gives the following statutory definition: '"bar" includes any place exclusively or mainly used for the sale and consumption of intoxicating liquor'. (See also 'Children'.)

Betting, Gaming and Lotteries

The following summarises the position so far as licensed premises are concerned:

Amusements with Prizes Machines: Coin operated machines are legal, if and only if, the player obtains nothing except a chance to play again or the return of his coin.

Under Section 34 of the Gaming Act 1968, the licensing justices may grant a permit for certain types of coin operated gaming machines in the public rooms of licensed premises. The conditions of this section must be strictly observed. These include:

(a)   no player may pay more than 10p for each chance to win
(b)   a player may only receive in respect of any one playing of the game a money prize not exceeding £2 or a prize other than money not exceeding £4 or a token or tokens exchangeable for such a prize.

If a tenant licensee wishes to install such machines he should first obtain the consent of his brewer. The supplier of the machines cannot make a charge calculated as a proportion of the takings but may only receive a fixed rent for the hire of the machine.

The fee chargeable on the grant of a permit is £25 and in addition there is gaming machine licence duty payable.

Betting: It is an offence, for which there are severe penalties, to allow betting and the passing of betting slips on licensed premises – apart from a room in respect of which a betting office licence is held. Such a room must be enclosed and there must be direct access to it from the street without going through a part of the premises in which alcoholic liquor is sold or consumed.

Applications for betting office licences are made to a betting licensing committee whose members are appointed from the justices for the petty sessions area and notices of application must be served and advertised in accordance with the procedure laid down by the Act. Such applications in respect of licensed premises may not be greatly favoured by the justices and can be refused if the premises are not suitable or there are sufficient facilities in the area.

The Act provides that no offence is committed where all the

persons concerned in betting transactions either reside or work on the premises or hold a bookmaker's permit or act on behalf of the holder of a bookmaker's permit, but licensees must exercise extreme caution so far as such transactions are concerned.

Gaming: There are heavy penalties for breach of any of the provisions of the Gaming Act, 1968 and so where a licensee lets a room to a club, society or organisation, he must ensure that he has adequate control over what takes place in such a room in relation to gaming.

Lotteries: Certain lotteries, draws and sweepstakes are permissible on licensed premises and these may be summarised as follows:

Small Lotteries: Small lotteries incidental to entertainments. The kind of entertainment would be functions such as dinners, dances, sporting events or events of a similar character where a lottery is not the main reason why people attend. All proceeds from the lottery and the entertainment must be for purposes other than private gain. The promoter may receive expenses for printing the tickets, expenses for providing the entertainment and lottery and expenses up to £50 to provide prizes. No cash may be given as a prize and tickets can only be sold on the premises where the entertainment is taking place and only when it is in progress. This kind of lottery will be familiar to licensees where, for example, a tombola or a raffle takes place at a banquet.

Private Lotteries: These have to be promoted by and confined to members of a society or people who live or work in the same premises.

Societies' Lotteries: These are lotteries promoted by a society established and conducted for charitable purposes or participation in or support of athletic sport or games or cultural activities or other purposes not connected with private or commercial gain. Such societies must be registered with the appropriate local authority under the Lotteries and Amusements Act 1976.

Local Lotteries: These are lotteries run by a local authority under a scheme registered with the Gaming Board. There are special provisions under the Lotteries and Amusements Act 1976 as to tickets, expenses, prizes and other matters.

Charity race nights must fall within one of the above categories in order to be lawful.

Children

Licensees and their employees may not sell intoxicating liquor to a person under 18. It is however a defence for the person who made the sale to prove (a) that he exercised all due diligence to avoid the commission of such offence or (b) that he had no reason to suspect that the person was under 18.

It is also an offence for a licensee or his employee knowingly to allow any person to sell intoxicating liquor to a person under 18 or knowingly allow a person under 18 to consume intoxicating liquor in a bar.

Where a licensee is charged with an offence by reason of the act or default of another person it is a defence for him to prove that he exercised all due diligence to avoid the commission of the offence.

It is also an offence for anyone under 18 to buy or attempt to buy intoxicating liquor on licensed premises or to consume intoxicating liquor in a bar. No person may purchase or attempt to purchase any intoxicating liquor for consumption in a bar by a person under the age of 18. Sale to a person purchasing for such a purpose would amount to aiding and abetting if done with knowledge and would be punishable accordingly. The only exception is that beer, porter, cider or perry may be sold or supplied to and consumed by, a person over the age of 16, if for consumption with a meal in a part of the premises which is set apart for the service of meals and is not a bar within the scope of Section 169 of the Licensing Act, 1964. (See below.)

Licensees and their employees may not knowingly deliver and a licensee may not knowingly allow any person to deliver for consumption off the premises any intoxicating liquor to any person under the age of 18. The exception is where the delivery is made at the home or working place of the purchaser or where the person under 18 is a member of the licensee's family or his employee and is employed as a messenger to deliver intoxicating liquor.

A person convicted of an offence under the above provisions is liable to a fine of up to £400. The licensee on a second or subsequent conviction may forfeit his licence.

Tobacco or cigarette papers may not be sold to persons apparently under 16 years of age; provided that no offence will be committed in the case of the sale of tobacco not in the form of cigarettes, if the vendor does not know and has no reason to believe that the tobacco is for the use of the person to whom it is sold. These provisions do not apply where the person to whom the tobacco or cigarette papers are sold is at the time employed by a manufacturer or dealer in tobacco for the purposes of his business or is a boy messenger in uniform in the employment of a messenger company and employed as such at the time.

Section 168 of the Licensing Act, 1964, provides that children under 14 must not be allowed to be in any bar or other part of licensed premises exclusively or mainly used for the sale and consumption of intoxicating liquor. This, however, does not apply to a child of the licence-holder or a child who is resident but not employed in the licensed premises; nor to a child who passes through a bar to or from another part of the premises, not being a bar, where there is no other convenient way (but see below).

With regard to the employment of children in licensed premises, Section 170 of the Licensing Act, 1964, prohibits the employment of persons under 18 years of age in any bar of licensed premises at any time when the bar is open for the sale and consumption of intoxicating liquor; the Children and Young Persons Act, 1933, contains important provisions concerning which a local authority may make bye-laws; therefore in all cases enquiry should be made of the local authority.

Sections 168 to 170 of the Licensing Act, 1964, do not apply to a bar at any time when it is, as is usual in the premises in question, set apart for the service of table meals and not used for the sale or supply of intoxicating liquor otherwise than to persons having table meals there and for consumption by such persons as an ancillary to a meal.

Cider

A licence for the sale of wine only does not include cider. Strengthened cider and perry do, however, come within the scope of a wine licence.

Consumption of Liquor

As a general rule intoxicating liquor may be consumed on licensed premises only during permitted hours of sale. Exceptions to this rule are as follows:

Drinking-up time: A period of 20 minutes is allowed at the end of any period of permitted hours for the consumption of alcoholic liquors purchased during such hours. This period also applies to permitted hours as extended by a special order of exemption.

Meals: If the liquor has been supplied during permitted hours with a meal for consumption therewith, it may be consumed with that meal for half an hour after the conclusion of any period of permitted hours.

Residents: Residents in licensed premises may buy and consume intoxicating liquor at any time. Intoxicating liquor may also lawfully be supplied outside permitted hours to, and for consumption by, any private friends of a resident who are *bona fide* entertained by him at his own expense.

Licensees: A licensee, or any person carrying on or in charge of the business, may at his own expense entertain his private friends at any time whether or not he is himself residing on the premises.

Employees: Persons employed in licensed premises may be supplied with intoxicating liquor for consumption on the premises outside permitted hours provided that such liquor is supplied at the expense of their employer, or of the person carrying on or in charge of the business on the premises.

Unlicensed premises: Liquor may be consumed on unlicensed premises when it has been brought in by the customer. (See also 'Extended Hours'.)

Entertainment Licences

The law relating to music and dancing and other public entertainment varies dependant upon the location of the premises concerned. The position is as follows:–

Premises in a London borough or the City of London: No premises may be used for public dancing or music or any other public entertainment of the like kind unless a licence has been granted by the council (i.e. the council of the appropriate London borough or, if the premises are situated in the City of London, the Common Council). Licences are granted for periods up to one year and are subject to renewal and may be transferred. Fees are fixed by the Council.

Any person who intends to apply for a new entertainments licence should make a preliminary enquiry of the council which is empowered to make regulations prescribing generally the terms, conditions and restrictions subject to which licences are granted, renewed, or transferred. Notice of application must be given to the council, the commissioner of police, and the fire authority. Advertising and additional notices may be prescribed by the council. Where an application for the grant, renewal, transfer or variation of the terms of the licence has been refused there is a right of appeal to the magistrates' court and thereafter to the crown court.

Any person who is concerned in the provision of such entertainment or who allows premises to be used for such a purpose without a licence can be find up to £2,000 or sentenced to three months imprisonment or both.

Elsewhere: No public dancing or music or any other public entertainment of a like kind may be provided without an entertainments licence granted by the district council for the area. An applicant for the grant, renewal or transfer of an entertainments licence must give not less than 28 days' notice of his intention to make the application to the district council, chief officer of police and the fire authority. The district council can make regulations as to the details to be given and as to the giving of additional notices. It is necessary always to make enquiry of the council who will be able to provide a copy of the regulations made.

The council can grant the licence subject to conditions and restrictions and will take account of any observations made by the police or fire authorities.

Where a licence is in force and application for renewal has been made then the licence will continue in force beyond its expiry date until the application had been decided.

Where the grant, renewal or transfer of an entertainments licence is refused or terms, restrictions or conditions are imposed or the licence is revoked then the applicant has a right of appeal to the magistrates' court. The time prescribed for appealing is 21 days from his being notified of the authority's decision. There is also a right of appeal to the crown court against the decision of the magistrates' court.

Entertainment licences cover one or more of the following:– music, dancing, boxing, wrestling, or similar activities. There are special provisions relating to places of public religious worship, outdoor entertainments and pleasure fairs.

The licences are granted for a year or such shorter period as may be specified and are renewable. Licences may be granted also merely for one or more particular occasions. Fees for all forms of entertainments licences are fixed by each council and vary considerably.

If an entertainment for which a licence is required is held without a licence or in contravention of the terms of the licence an offence is committed for which the fine is up to £2,000.

Extended Hours

Supper Hour Certificate: Section 68 of the Licensing Act, 1964, applies to premises that the licensing justices are satisfied are structurally adapted and *bona fide* used or intended to be used for the purposes of habitually providing, for the accommodation of persons frequenting the premises, substantial refreshment to which the sale and supply of intoxicating liquor is ancillary. Where the licensee elects to take advantage of the provisions of the Section there is added to the permitted hours the hour following the general licensing hours. On Sundays, Christmas Day and Good Friday the period between the first and second parts of the general licensing hours is also added but on weekdays this period is covered by being part of the general licensing laws. Liquor may only be sold and supplied for consumption at a table meal supplied at the same time in a part of the premises usually set apart for the service of table meals. During these additional periods no person may consume liquor except as an ancillary to his meal.

Procedure for obtaining justices' certificate: If any licensee desires to take advantage of the special privileges accorded by the Act to establishments of this kind, he must give, at least one week before the meeting at which he intends to make application for the justices' certificate, notice in writing of his intention to:

    (a)   the clerk to the justices,

(b)   the chief officer of police for the district or in the Metropolitan Police District the Commissioner of Police for the Metropolis.

The application can be made at any licensing sessions.

The licensee must give 14 days' notice to the police before availing himself of the privilege of Section 68 and such notice can be incorporated in the notice of application if given 14 days before the licensing session at which the application is to be considered by the licensing justices.

The justices are to satisfy themselves 'in such manner as they think fit' that the requirements of Section 68 have been met. Presumably the applicant will be heard in support of his application, but apparently the justices may hear anyone they please in opposition as well.

If the justices grant their certificate and as soon as the 14 days' notice to the police has expired, the licensee has the benefit of the additional hour, subject to the above conditions. He must forthwith keep permanently affixed in a consipcuous place on the premises a notice stating the effect of the provisions of Section 68 of the Act. The provisions will then continue to apply to the premises until the licensee gives at least 14 days' notice in writing before the expiration of any licensing year (April 5th) to the police that he intends to cease to avail himself of the provisions, which will then cease to apply to his premises at the end of the licensing year in question.

Withdrawal of the justices' certificate: The justices can withdraw their certificate from an hotel or restaurant at any licensing session. They must give at least seven days' notice of their intention to do so to the licensee and thereafter the matter is to proceed on the same lines as if notice has been served of opposition to the renewal of the licence.

Special Hours Certificate: Licensing justices may grant with or without limitations a special hours certificate if they are satisfied:–

(a)   that an entertainments licence is in force for the premises and
(b)   that the whole or the relevant part of the premises is structurally adapted and *bona fide* used or intended to be used for persons resorting to the premises for the purpose of providing music and dancing and substantial refreshment to which the sale of intoxicating liquor is ancillary.

The justices may grant the certificate for part of the year only and for part of the premises only. It may also be limited to particular days of the week and on other days the permitted hours of the premises will not be affected by the provisions relating to special hours certificates. The justices have power to limit the certificate to particular times of the day and may provide different limitations for different days. The justices may exercise this power of limitation at the time of an application for a certificate or where an application is made to revoke an existing certificate. Furthermore, the police may at any time apply to the justices to exercise this power.

Before a licensee uses a special hours certificate he must give 14 days written notice to the police, but such notice can be incorporated in the original notice of application if given 14 days prior to the date on which the application is to be heard.

Where a special hours certificate is in force the permitted hours (subject to any limitations) extend until 2 o'clock the following morning. In those parts of the Metropolis designated by the Home Secretary the terminal hour is 3 a.m. It should, however, be borne in mind that if the music and dancing ends between midnight and 2 o'clock in the morning the permitted hours end when the music and dancing ends. These hours apply to all weekdays, including Saturdays and including also Christmas Day when not a Sunday.

The police may also apply to revoke the certificate if the premises have not been used in accordance with (b) above, if there have been breaches of the law relating to permitted hours or if it is expedient to revoke by reason of disorderly or indecent conduct in the premises. If the entertainments licence ceases to be in force the certificate is thereby revoked.

Extended Hours Order: Where premises which, in addition to supplying substantial meals, also provide live musical or other entertainment, the justices may, at any licensing session, make an extended hours order. The effect of such an order is to extend the permitted hours on weekdays until 1 a.m. while the entertainment and the meals continue.

The justices have a discretion as to whether or not to grant such an order and also they may limit the operation of the order to particular days or times of the year or to a time earlier than 1 a.m. In making any order the justices will have particular regard to the comfort and convenience of the occupiers of neighbouring premises. The justices have power to revoke the order when, on application by the police, they are satisfied that it is expedient to do so.

Extension of Permitted Hours

A petty sessional court may grant to any on-licence holder in respect of premises in the immediate neighbourhood of a market or the like, an order extending the permitted hours for the sale of liquor on those premises during such time as shall be specified in such order. A notice of the days and times referred to in the order **must** be kept affixed outside the premises. It should be noted that this order, known as a 'general order of exemption', does not cease to have effect when the person to whom is had been granted ceases to hold the licence but continues for the benefit of any person to whom the licence is transferred.

In the Metropolis and City of London the Commissioner of Police and elsewhere a petty sessional court may also grant an order known as a 'Special Order of Exemption' to an on-licensee under which the permitted hours are extended on his premises for a special occasion. The Hight Court has considered in detail the basis on which these extensions should be granted. There are three main rules:

(a) the occasion should be special from a national or local point of view

(b) the more frequent the occasion the less likely it can be regarded as special

(c) if the occasion is created by the licensee solely for the purpose of his business then it is not likely to be capable of being a special occasion.

Magistrates can use their own judgement based on their own local knowledge and what may be a special occasion in one area may not necessarily be so in another.

The holder of a general or special order of exemption must produce it for examination if requested to do so by a police officer or a justice of the peace.

Hours Permitted for the Sale of Intoxicating Liquor

As a general rule liquor may be **consumed** during the following hours of sale. (For exceptions see 'Consumption of Liquor' and 'Extension of Permitted Hours'.)

Weekdays: **Premises licensed for consumption on the premises** – The general licensing hours for on-licensed premises are 11 a.m. to 11 p.m.

The licensing justices in any licensing district, if they are satisfied that the requirements of the district make it desirable, have power to vary the weekday hours for their district by fixing an earlier opening hour not being earlier than 10 a.m. This variation may be made for different weekdays and for different periods of not less than eight consecutive weeks, but the hours for the whole of the year must be fixed at the annual licensing meeting.

The powers of the justices above referred to may be exercised by them at any general annual licensing meeting. They must give notice of their intention to consider any proposal to make or vary any such order in two local newspapers circulating in their district. They may also give notice in any other way they think fit. Interested parties will have the right to be heard. The justices must appoint the same hours for the whole of their district.

Sundays: The general licensing hours for on-licensed and off-licensed premises in England (except Monmouthshire) on Sundays, Christmas Day and Good Friday, are 12 noon to 3 p.m. and 7 p.m. to 10.30 p.m. In Wales and Monmouthshire these hours apply on Christmas Day and Good Friday and also on Sundays where the local government electors in any particular area have so determined by a poll held in accordance with the provisions of the Licensing Act, 1964. Otherwise in Wales and Monmouthshire there are no permitted hours on Sundays.

Off-licences: The permitted hours in respect of premises licensed for the sale of intoxicating liquor for consumption off the premises only, begin at 8 a.m. and end with the evening terminal hour. Where in on-licensed premises there is a part set aside solely for off-sales, such part may on application to the justices enjoy the permitted hours for off-licences. There must, however, be no internal communication available to customers with a part of the premises where sakes take place for consumption on the premises. The general licensing hours apply on Sundays, Christmas Day and Good Friday. (See 'Sundays' above.)

Registered Clubs: The permitted hours for registered clubs are on weekdays other than Christmas Day or Good Friday the general licensing hours. On Sundays, Christmas Day and Good Friday, the hours are fixed by the rules of the club provided that they do not exceed $5\frac{1}{2}$ hours and do not begin earlier than noon or end later than 10.30 p.m. There must be a break of at least 2 hours in the afternoon including the hours from 3.00 p.m. to 5.00 p.m., and there may not be more than $3\frac{1}{2}$ hours after 5.00 p.m.

Innkeeper

An innkeeper is one who keeps an establishment held out by the proprietor as offering food, drink and if so required, sleeping accommodation, without special contract to any traveller presenting himself who appears able and willing to pay a reasonable sum for the services and facilities provided and who is in a fit state to be received (Hotel Proprietors Act, 1956). He is compelled to receive all comers at any hour of the day or night until his house is full. Subject to the above he cannot pick and choose, but must receive any traveller desirous of being received. The innkeeper who objects without sufficient cause to receive a traveller is liable to an action for the private injury as well as to an indictment for the public wrong. He is bound to take care of his guest's goods and he has a lien on them for his reasonable charges. The lien, which does not extend to vehicles or their contents, is exercisable by a sale by auction after a lapse of six weeks and after a month's notice in one London and one local newspaper. An innkeeper warrants that his premises are, for the purpose of personal use by his guest, as safe as reasonable care and skill can make them, except as to defects which could not be discovered by reasonable care or skill on the part of anyone. An innkeeper, if he causes a copy of the notice set out in the schedule of the Hotel Proprietors' Act, 1956, printed in plain type to be exhibited in a conspicious place where it can be conveniently read by guests at the reception office or desk or if none, at the main entrance to the inn, limits his liability to any one guest to £50 for one article, or £100 in the aggregate, except:–

(a) in the case of loss or damage through the default, neglect or wilful act of the innkeeper or his staff, or
(b) when goods are expressly deposited with him or his employee for safe custody, or
(c) he refuses to receive the goods for deposit or through his default a guest who wished to do so, was unable to deposit the goods expressly for safe custody.

An innkeeper is not subject to the strict innkeepers' liability for the loss of, or damage to, his guests' vehicles or animals brought to his inn, but an innkeeper into whose custody vehicles are expressly delivered would be liable for their loss or damage unless the innkeeper has contracted out of such liability and presumably an innkeeper may avoid even his limited liability if he can show that the guest's goods were lost or damaged by the guest's own neglect. An innkeeper must keep a register of all aliens of 16 years and upwards staying at his premises, in the form prescribed by the Secretary of State. In the case of British subjects the register must show the name and address of the guest and date of his arrival at the inn.

Intoxicating Liquors

Intoxicating liquors include most spirits, wine, beer, cider, and any fermented distilled or spirituous liquor but does not include:–

(a) any liquor of a gravity not exceeding 1,016° and of a strength not exceeding 1.2%
(b) perfumes
(c) flavouring essences recognised by the Commissioners of Customs & Excise as not being intended for consumption as or with dutiable alcoholic liquor
(d) spirits, wine or made-wine so medicated as to be in the opinion of the Commissioners intended for use as a medicine and not as a drink.

Justices' Licence

A justices' on-licence means a licence authorising sale for consumption either on or off the premises for which the licence is granted and a justices' off-licence authorises sale for consumption off the premises only.

There are various kinds of justices' on-licences as follows:

(a)   intoxicating liquor of all descriptions
(b)   beer, cider and wine only
(c)   beer and cider only
(d)   cider only
(e)   wine only.

A justices' off-licence is either a licence for the sale of intoxicating liquor of all descriptions or for the sale of beer, cider and wine only.

An application for a justices' licence is made to the licensing justices at a licensing sessions. Applications may be made either for the grant of a new licence or for the ordinary or special removal of a justices' licence or the transfer of a justices' licence.

In the case of any of these applications notice in the prescribed form must be served not less than 21 days before the licensing sessions on the clerk to the licensing justices, the chief officer of police, and the local authority. In the case of an application for the transfer of a licence notice must similarly be given to the holder of the licence, and in the case of a removal notice must be given to the registered owner of the premises of which it is sought to remove the licence.

Except in the case of an application for the transfer of a licence the following further notifications have to be given:

Not more than 28 days before the licensing sessions a notice of the application must be displayed for a period of 7 days in a place where it can be conveniently read by the public on or near the premises proposed to be licensed.

Not more than 28 days nor less than 14 days before the licensing sessions notice of the application must be advertised in a newspaper circulating in the place where the premises to be licensed are situated.

Notice of the application must be given to the fire authority for the area.

Where the premises for which a licence is sought are about to be constructed or are in the course of construction application can be made for a provisional licence on the basis of plans which show the premises as they would be if completed. If a provisional licence is granted then on the necessary notice being given it must be brought into force by the justices if the premises have been completed in accordance with the approved plans and the holder of the provisional licence is not disqualified and is a fit and proper person to hold a justices' licence. Application for a final order may be made prior to completion if it is likely that the premises will be completed before the next licensing sessions. In such circumstances the justices may decide that the licence can be made final before that sessions by a single licensing justice. There are provisions under which a provisional licence application can be made purely on the basis of a site plan together with a description of what is proposed and with a detailed plan to be submitted at a later stage.

Landlord and Tenant

The Landlord and Tenant Act 1954 contains provisions which give a measure of security for tenants of off-licensed premises and certain types of on-licensed premises. Tenants of public houses and certain other premises where intoxicating liquor is sold for consumption on the premises are in general excluded unless a substantial proportion of the business consists of transactions other than the sale of intoxicating liquor.

All tenants have a right to claim compensation for improvements under the Landlord and Tenant Act 1927 if they are improvements which are not required by the Tenancy Agreement or by an other legal obligation. There is a very detailed procedure to be followed and tenants should seek detailed advice before undertaking such improvements.

Licensing Sessions

In addition to the annual licensing meeting, the justices must hold not less than four transfer sessions at as near regular intervals as practicable. The licensing sessions for each twelve months are fixed at the general annual licensing meeting or at the meeting at which the date of the general annual licensing meeting is itself fixed.

All powers of the justices may be exercised at any licensing session except for the following which are exercisable only at general annual licensing meetings:

(a)   the power to renew except where renewal is not applied for at the preceding general annual licensing meeting and reasonable cause shown for not applying at that time

(b)   the power to make regulations restricting the frequency with which applications for special removal or transfer may be made

(c)   the power to extinguish licences in suspense by reason of war circumstances, on the grounds of the conduct of the licence holder or his fitness to hold the licence

(d) the power to make orders varying the general licensing hours in the licensing district.

The justices may divide the business of any licensing sessions between different benches sitting at the same time. (See also 'Annual Licensing Meeting'.)

Measures

Under the provisions of the Weights and Measures Act, 1985, draught beer and cider may be sold by retail only in quantities of one-third, one-half or multiples of one-half pint and must be served in a capacity measure of the same quantity as the liquor. This restriction does not apply in the case of mixed drinks such as shandy, nor does it apply where beer or cider is measured by a duly stamped measuring instrument designed to dispense a pre-determined quantity and is dispensed in the sight of the customer.

Whisky, gin, rum and vodka may be sold by retail for on consumption only in quantities of one-fourth, one-fifth, or one-sixth of a gill or multiples of those quantities and a notice must be prominently displayed indicating in which of these quantities these drinks are supplied. Mixed drinks containing a mixture of three or more liquids are exempted from this requirement as also are mixed drinks where the quantity of spirits is expressly requested by the customer. Other intoxicating liquors sold in quantities of less than half-a-pint may be sold by the glass or nip or in any other way.

All intoxicating liquor in a closed container, except wine, has to be marked with the quantity by capacity measurement unless the quantity is less than 3 fluid ounces or more than 1 gallon.

Wine sold in carafes can only be sold in certain prescribed quantities, namely, ¼, ½, ¾ or 1 litre, 10 fl. oz, or 20 fl. oz. The licensee is required to display a statement setting out the quantities in which wine in carafes or other open vessels is sold. There is no obligation to specify the quantity of wine if sold by the glass.

Notices on Licensed Premises

Every licence holder must keep painted or fixed in a conspicuous place on his premises in such form and manner as the licensing justices direct (as to which enquiry should be made of their clerk) his name, followed by the word 'Licensed' and words sufficient to indicate what is sold and the class of licence held. If the dealing is in wine or beer only, or both, these words must appear and the fact indicated whether the licence be only a six-day or early closing one. It is an offence to have any words or letters on the premises importing that authority is held to sell any liquor which in fact is not authorised by the licence. Non-observance of any of the foregoing provisions involves a penalty not exceeding £50.

There are also other notices of great importance and variety of which the principal ones are as follows:

Licensing Act 1964: Where the licensee operates a special hours certificate, a supper hour certificate, an extended hours order or he observes hours under a general order of exemption, or he is subject to a restriction order, a notice must be kept posted in some conspicuous place stating the effect of the order or the certificate which applies.

Notice of application for a new justices' licence, or for the ordinary or special removal of a justices' licence must be displayed upon the premises in respect of which the application is to be made.

Hotel Proprietors' Act 1956: In order to obtain the benefit of the reduced liability of £50 for one article or £100 in the aggregate, innkeepers must exhibit in a conspicuous part of the reception office or desk, or, if none, at the main entrance of the inn, a print of the notice set out in the Schedule to the Hotel Proprietors' Act, 1956.

Weights & Measures Act, 1963: A notice must be prominently displayed indicating the measure used for the sale of whisky, gin, rum and vodka. (See also 'Measures'.)

Prices: The law requires the prices of food and drink to be displayed in a way which allows the customer to see them clearly when he comes to the bar and chooses his food or drink. There is a limit on a number of prices which it is necessary to display. If there are fewer than thirty items of food and drink apart from table wine all of them must be listed. If there are more than thirty items then at least thirty must be displayed and priced in a reasonably balanced way. Where drink is sold in more than one quantity at prices which are in the same proportion to each other as the quantities only one price need be indicated. Where a mixed drink, such as gin and tonic, is sold the composite price need not be shown separately if the price is in fact the total of the individual items e.g. the gin and the tonic.

All prices must be inclusive of any V.A.T. chargeable and if there are any extra charges such as a service charge these must be clearly shown. If an item on a price list is no longer being sold it must be removed as soon as is reasonably practicable. If a public house has a separate restaurant or dining area the price list must be shown at or near the entrance to the restaurant section so that customers can see prices before they enter. If the restaurant has direct access from the street the price list must be on view at the street entrance so that people passing by can see it.

Obligations to Serve the Public

An innkeeper is bound by law to accommodate all travellers until his house is full (see 'Innkeeper'). It is a question of fact whether he is an innkeeper or not. The keeper of a public house, which is not an inn, holds the same licence as an innkeeper but is at liberty to refuse to serve anyone he chooses, like any other shopkeeper. Justices may refuse to renew an old on-licence on the ground that the holder has persistently and unreasonably refused to supply suitable refreshment other than intoxicating liquor at a reasonable price. (See also 'Race Relations Act 1976'.)

Occasional Licences

An on-licensee can obtain occasional licences to enable him to sell intoxicating liquor on premises for a particular occasion, such as a cricket ground on the occasion of a match, or a public hall on the occasion of a dance. The granting of an occasional licence is not limited to specific functions but it has been held by the High Court that it refers to the existence of circumstances which give rise to the need for a licence to sell liquor at premises other than those for which the applicant holds a licence. Application for these licences, which may extend over a period not exceeding three weeks, must be made to a petty sessional court, at least 24 hours' notice having been given to the chief officer of police, or in the Metropolitan Police District the Commissioner of Police. The notice must state the name and address of the applicant, the place and occasion in respect of which the licence is required, the period for which it is to be in force and the hours to be specified in the justices' consent.

An application for an occasional licence may also be made in writing on giving at least one month's notice to the clerk of the justices.

Occasional licences cannot be granted for Christmas Day, Good Friday, or any day of public thanksgiving or mourning. An occasional licence is a different licence from the parent licence and therefore not subject to conditions applicable to the latter.

It is important to emphasise that the occasional licence is granted to a licensee and only authorises sale by that licensee. The holder of the occasional licence is responsible under the Licensing Act for the proper conduct of the licence and the premises at which the function is being held are regarded under the Act as being licensed premises while the occasional licence is in force. The licence holder will therefore be responsible for making sure that the relevant provisions of the Act are observed: for example he must not permit drunkenness or gaming and he must see that there is no sale to or consumption by persons who are under eighteen.

Occasional Permissions

The licensing justices may at a licensing sessions grant an Occasional Permission to the officer of an organisation or a branch of it. The organisation must not be carried on for purposes of private gain and it may not be granted in a licensing district more than four permissions in any period of 12 months. A permission gives the officer authority to sell at a function held by the organisation or branch in connection with its activities during a period not exceeding 24 hours.

The justices must be satisfied as to the suitability of the applicant and of the place where the function is to be held and also that the sale of intoxicating liquor is not likely to result in disorderly conduct or in disturbance or annoyance being caused to local residents.

Protection Order

A protection order gives authority to a person to carry on business on licensed premises pending the grant of a transfer at licensing sessions. It remains in force until the end of the second licensing sessions begun after the date of the order and until the disposal of any application made at the sessions for a transfer of the licence. The protection order ceases to have effect on the coming into force of a licence by way of transfer or removal or the coming into force of a further protection order.

The applicant must, at least one week before the holding of the court, serve on the chief officer of police, or in the Metropolitan Police District the Commissioner of Police, written notice specifying the full name, addresss and the occupation for the preceding six months of the person in whose favour the protection is sought.

In case of urgency, this notice may be waived if the court considers that such notice to the police had been given as was reasonable under the circumstances.

Where a licensee dies or is adjudged bankrupt the personal representatives, or trustee in bankruptcy, are in the same position as regards carrying on the business under the licence as if they had been granted a protection order on the death or bankruptcy.

Race Relations Act 1976

The Act makes it unlawful to discriminate against a person on racial grounds. Such grounds mean grounds of colour, race, nationality or ethnic or national origins. To discriminate against a person on racial grounds means to treat someone on those grounds less favourably than other people. The Act covers many situations such as applicants for jobs, employees, house buyers, tenants or prospective tenants, members or prospective members of clubs and the provision of goods, services or other facilities.

The Commission for Racial Equality set up under the Act has a duty to work towards the elimination of discrimination and promoting equality of opportunity and good relations between different racial groups. The Commission has powers to undertake investigations necessary for any purpose connected with its duties. Where discrimination is found the Commission can issue a Non-Discrimination Notice requiring the discrimination to cease. It can also bring proceedings where persistent discrimination is found and in certain other cases. It also has power to advise persons complaining that they have been discriminated against. A person alleging discrimination in the provision of goods, facilities or services may, subject to the provisions of the Act, bring proceedings in the appropriate county court. The court's powers include the award of damages and an injunction. The court also normally awards costs against the unsuccessful party.

The Act neither alters a licensee's duty to maintain order in his premises nor his right to refuse service for a proper reason without having to give his reasons at the time.

Renewals

After 4th April 1989 licences will run until the expiration of the current licensing period or if the licence is granted in the last three months of that period until the end of the next licensing period. The licensing period is a period of three years from the 5th April 1989 and every three years thereafter.

Restaurant and/or Residential Licences

A restaurant licence is a justices' on-licence subject to the condition that the sale or supply of intoxicating liquor is confined to persons taking table meals and for consumption as an ancillary to such meals.

A residential licence is a justices' on-licence subject to the condition that the sale and supply of intoxicating liquor shall be confined to residents and their private friends *bona fide* entertained by them for consumption on the premises or with a meal supplied at but to be consumed off the premises.

A restaurant and residential licence is a justices' on-licence subject to the conditions applying both to restaurant licences and residential licences.

The grant or renewal of such licences can only be refused on the following grounds:

(a)   the applicant is not a fit and proper person,
(b)   where the premises are not structurally adapted and *bona fide* used or intended to be used for the purpose of habitually providing main meals and/or board and lodging in conformity with the above conditions,
(c)   the premises are premises for which a justices' on-licence has been forfeited or they have been ill-conducted,

(d)   the conditions of an existing licence relating to seating accommodation or as to the availability of non-intoxicating drinks have been habitually broken,

(e)   a large proportion of the customers or residents, as the case may be, are under 18,

(f)   where it is intended that intoxicants shall be provided by self-service,

(g)   in the case of a restaurant or restaurant and residential licence where the provision of table meals does not form a substantial part of the trade,

(h)   where after reasonable steps have been taken to do so the premises have not been inspected by the local authority, the fire authority or the police.

Justices refusing such licences must give their reason in writing. There is, as in the case of other justices' licences, a right of appeal to the crown court against the decision of the justices.

Transfer

On application for the transfer of a licence the justices may compel both the holder of the licence and the person to whom it is to be transferred to attend in person before the justices at transfer sessions and may require the production of the agreement or other assurance under which the licence is to be transferred.

Twenty-one days' notice of intention to apply for transfer must be served on the holder of the licence, the clerk to the justices and the chief officer of police, or in the Metropolitan Police District the Commissioner of Police and the appropriate officer of the local authority. In London the local authority will be the London borough and outside London the district council. If the premises are in a parish notice must be given to the proper officer of the parish council or where there is no parish council to the chairman of the parish meeting. If the premises are in a community where there is a community council notice must be given to the proper officer of that council. It must be signed by the applicant or his authorised agent and set forth the name, address and occupation for the preceding six months of the transferee. A transfer can only be made in cases falling within the table following and the justices must be satisfied that the transferee is a fit and proper person to be the holder of the licence as well as being a person coming within the table.

The justices may make regulations determining the time which must elapse after the hearing of one application for transfer before another is made in respect of the same premises but they may in any particular case dispense with observance of such regulations.

Cases in Which and Persons to Whom a Transfer May be Granted:

Death of the holder of the licence.	The representatives of the holder of the licence or the new tenant or occupier of the premises.
Incapacity of the holder of the licence to carry on business under the licence owing to sickness or other infirmity.	The assigns of the holder of the licence or the new tenant or occupier of the premises
Bankruptcy of the holder of the licence.	The trustee of the bankrupt or the new tenant or occupier of the premises.
Occupation of the premises given up by the holder of the licence or his representatives.	The new tenant or occupier of the premises, or the person to whom the representatives or assigns have, by sale or otherwise, *bona fide* conveyed or made over the interest in the premises.
Wilful omission or neglect of the occupier of the premises who is about to quit the premises to apply for a renewal of the licence.	The new tenant or occupier.
Cases involving forfeiture or disqualification where the owner of the licensed premises or some person on his behalf has obtained temporary authority to carry on business until the conclusion of the second licensing session begun after the date of the authority and application for a transfer is made not later than that session.	The owner or any person applying on his behalf and the transfer may be granted as if the licence to be transferred was notwithstanding forfeiture, still valid.

[Further cases relating to licences in suspense are provided for in Sections 138 and 145 of the Licensing Act 1964.]

Wine Bars, Beerhouses etc.

If any person who holds a licence restricted to certain types of intoxicating liquor has in his possession on the licensed premises, without reasonable excuse, any kind of intoxicating liquor which he is not authorised to sell, he may be fined £100 beyond any excise penalty to which he may be liable and he forfeits the liquor. If he sells such liquor he is liable on conviction to imprisonment for a term not exceeding six months or to a fine not exceeding £1,000 or both. For a second or subsequent conviction he will also forfeit his licence. In addition he may be disqualified from holding a justices' licence – on a second conviction for a term not exceeding five years and on subsequent conviction for any terms of years or for life.

Where a beer, wine or beer and wine 'on' licence was in force on 3rd August 1961 and has been continuously renewed since that time the licensee may apply to the licensing justices for the licence to be varied to include other types of liquor. If the justices are satisfied that the application is made with the consent of the owner they must grant it. However, in a new town the consent of the licensing planning committee or new town committee is required. A licence varied in this way is not treated as an old 'on' licence within the meaning of the Licensing Act 1964. On the variation of such a licence the justices have power to impose conditions and these may be in addition to or in place of previous conditions. It is considered that this power does not enable conditions to be imposed which would effectively nullify the variation.

If a licensee wishes to add additional types of liquor to his licence and he does not come within the above paragraph then he must apply for a new licence.

The following sections, which are *not* taken from 'An ABC of Licensing Law', cover amusement machines (already treated briefly on page 51) and bar hygiene.

AMUSEMENT MACHINES IN LICENSED PREMISES

Machine Types and Licensing

Amusement machines provide a source of entertainment to customers, and a valuable source of income to the licensee and the brewery company concerned. (In a free house the following conditions would not apply, because the proprietor would either own the machine or pay rental for it, and the proceeds would be his own.) Coin-operated machines may only be installed with the prior agreement of the brewery company machine controller. Those in general use are as follows:–

A.W.P. (Amusements With Prizes – Fruit Machines)
S.W.P. (Skill With Prizes – Quiz Games)

Coin-operated Phonographs (Juke Boxes)
Pool Tables
Ancillary Games (Video, Pin Tables etc.)

Fruit Machines: These are the most popular gaming machines in public houses. At present the maximum payout prize is £4 in tokens or £2 in cash, the price of play being 10p. The legal requirements governing the supply of A.W.P. machines are a permit and a Customs and Excise licence.

The permit is granted in the name of the licensee by the local magistrate's court at a cost of £25.00, and must be obtained before the machine is installed. Each ingoing licensee must apply for this permit. The number of A.W.P.s allowed on any one site is regulated by the local authorities; the usual maximum is two. Permits are normally valid for three years.

The licence is a Customs and Excise requirement, and can only be obtained if a valid permit is submitted with the application; the licence itself must be displayed in the public house. The cost of a licence is at present £375.00 per year for each piece of equipment having a maximum payout of £4. The fee is normally paid by the supplying company, who then claims back the money through rent (each machine has a fixed rent, which is collected at regular intervals). In some cases the brewery, the supplying company and the licensee split the fee three ways.

To ensure maximum income from the machine(s) and to maintain customer interest, suppliers are instructed to change machines on a regular basis. Machine activity is also monitored by the brewery company machine controller.

The current (1988) licence fees are as follows:–

		Per annum
Licence for 5p play	Amusements With Prizes Fruit machine	£150.00
Licence for 5p play	Fruit Machine Maximum payout £4.00	£375.00
Licence for 10p play	Fruit Machine Maximum payout £4.00	£375.00
Licence for 10p play	Jackpot (Registered clubs only, and maximum of two)	£960.00

Juke Boxes: These pieces of equipment, if carefully monitored and regularly serviced and programmed, provide another effective source of income. Suppliers are instructed to ensure that an adequate supply of records is available.

Licences are required from the P.R.S. (Performing Rights

Society), which protects the copyright interest of composers and authors, and the P.P.L. (Phonographic Performance Ltd), which represents the makers of sound recordings.

Pool Tables: The popularity of pool tables in public houses has grown rapidly over the past ten years, and customer interest is further stimulated by the availability of league competitions and in-house promotions.

Tables are available in various sizes, the most popular being 6ft by 3ft and 7ft by 4ft. Cues, balls, chalk etc. are supplied with the tables. Suppliers are instructed to ensure that regular valeting and servicing are carried out to maintain customer interest.

Ancillary Machines: These are all available from the machine companies on the list of authorised suppliers whom the brewery company allows its licensees to deal with. A machine company wishing to appear on this list must meet the brewery company's standards, and will be thoroughly investigated before being included on the list. The following points would be considered:–

1. Experience: the company must demonstrate a satisfactory operational performance.
2. Financial status: the company must produce and file its latest or current audited accounts.
3. Legal status: the company must hold all the necessary Gaming Board Certificates, and must never have been prosecuted by the Board.
4. Operational status: the company must operate from premises suitably located.
5. Insurance: the company must carry full Public Liability Insurance.
6. Security: the company must operate an approved electronic data retrieval system, utilising meter reconciliation.

The brewery company will also list the conditions they expect their suppliers to comply with, to ensure that their premises are always supplied with up-to-date machines.

1. Machine injection: the rate of new machines must not be less than a certain percentage per month.
2. Rent lists: these must be received every three months, and issued no later than a specified time before their date of effect.
3. Machine changes: the site life of machines should not exceed thirteen weeks. Collection should be monitored weekly, and machines should be changed within seven days of any adverse performance.
4. Section 34 Gaming Permit: the supplier is responsible for renewing each permit.

5. Customs and Excise Licence: the supplier is required to renew this within twenty-one days of the due date.
6. E.D.C. (Electronic Data Capture): all A.W.P. machines must be fitted with acceptable E.D.C. units.
7. Tokens: the supplier must ensure that all machines are fitted with a dedicated token system.
8. Security:
    (a) The supplier must ensure that losses are minimised.
    (b) Keys (other than token refill keys) must never be in the possession of personnel other than those the supplier employs.
    (c) Payment of unsupported claims over £2 and supported claims over £4 must be reported to the machine controller.
    (d) Adequate security/safety measures must be taken to protect equipment sited in high-risk areas.
9. Break-ins: all break-ins must be reported in writing to the brewery company machine controller within twenty-four hours of the incident.

V.A.T. on Amusement and Gaming Machine Takings

Value Added Tax is now an important part of any business, and very few people who are in business or who are self-employed are exempt from paying V.A.T.

To say that a certain amount of confusion exists, as to who pays the V.A.T. on gaming machines, is an understatement; but according to Customs and Excise officials, the person who supplies the use of the machine to the public must account for the V.A.T.

V.A.T. Rating: The takings from amusement machines and gaming machines are liable to V.A.T. at the standard rate. The latter applies to all types of machines which are constructed or adapted for amusement or for playing a game of skill, chance, or chance and skill combined, where the machine is of a kind normally played by inserting a coin or token. Examples of machines in this category are Jackpot and Fruit Machines, 'One-armed Bandits', 'Amusements With Prizes' machines, 'Penny Back', 'Free Go' and 'Crane Grab' machines, Pin Tables, Video Games, and Juke Boxes.

Site Rentals: Site rentals are generally exempt from V.A.T., unless they relate to permission to site a machine in a hotel, inn, boarding-house or similar establishment, in which case they are taxable at the standard rate.

Who Pays Tax on Machine Takings?: The person who supplies the use of the machine to the public must account for the V.A.T. on the takings. If the occupier of the premises on which the machine is located owns, hires, or rents the machine, he is supplying the taxable service to the public and he must account for the V.A.T. on the whole of the taxable take.

If, on the other hand, there is no hire or rental agreement, but there is either a written or an oral agreement to share the profits on a percentage basis, the owner of the machine is supplying the service to the public and he must account for the V.A.T. on the whole of the taxable take.

The Taxable Take: V.A.T. must be accounted for on the taxable take of a machine, the total amount which players have put into the machine less only the amounts returned as winnings to players (except winnings returned to the payer of the tax or persons acting on his behalf).

The following must not be deducted from the taxable take:–

1. Any hire or rental charge paid to the company which owns the machine.
2. Any share of the profits or other charge due to another person (e.g. a brewer sharing the proceeds of the machine with a tenant).
3. Any payments made out of takings, such as those under a maintenance contract.
4. Any V.A.T. on any of the above charges or payments; and any payments of gaming machine licence duty.

Tokens: When the taxable take is being calculated, tokens should be treated as follows:–

1. A replayable token (i.e. one which can be used to play a machine) should be treated as having its recognised cash value – for example, if a machine can be played with either a 10p coin or a token, the value should be taken as 10p.
2. If the token is non-replayable (i.e. cannot be used to play a machine), but can be exchanged for cash or for goods sold on the premises, it should be treated as having the same value as the cash or goods for which it can be exchanged.
3. If the token is not replayable, and can only be exchanged for prizes which are goods not sold on the premises, it must be treated as having no cash value.

Claiming the V.A.T. Due: The taxable take is regarded as tax-inclusive; that is to say, it includes the V.A.T. which is payable. The amount of V.A.T. must be calculated by applying the 'V.A.T. fraction' to the taxable take. With the standard rate at 15%, the V.A.T. fraction is 3/23rds.

Some forms used by operators are misleading in that they enter the total take as the net figure. The total take should in fact be gross, and becomes net only after V.A.T. has been deducted.

BAR HYGIENE

Bar hygiene is vitally important, not only because the law requires it, but also because many customers will not use premises which they consider to be unclean.

Staff

Presentation is all-important, and where possible staff should be supplied with uniforms which convey total cleanliness. If this is not the policy of the establishment, then they should be encouraged to wear clothes which are pleasing to the eye as well as being fresh and spotless. Hands must be perfectly clean, without nicotine stains, and nails must be buffed and properly cut. Hair should be well cared for and free from scurf and excessive grease. Staff must always wash their hands after using the toilet; and should remember that their own personal standards of hygiene will, if creditable, reflect credit on the premises, and thus help to bring trade to that particular establishment.

Infections are spread by careless practices and dirty habits. Particularly to be avoided are nose-picking, uncovered infected wounds and cuts, sneezing, dirty handkerchiefs, dirty glass clothes, dirty roller towels and messy habits.

Food must never be handled, and coughing and sneezing over glasses or food must at all times be avoided. Infected cuts and skin infections should be covered by water-proof dressings and not by dirty pieces of bandage. Illness should be reported immediately to the employer.

The Bar

Bar counters must be kept both clean and dry. Drinks are inevitably spilt, but customers are annoyed if they have to pick up change from a wet surface. Ashtrays should be provided, and must be kept clean and ready for use; the provision of these discourages customers from stubbing out cigarettes on the counter or floor.

Dirt settles on the necks of bottles, so each should be washed before being displayed, to ensure that no dirt mixes with the liquor as it is being poured into a glass. Finger-prints can be left on glassware, so it is sensible to hold glasses either near the base or in the middle, but never never round the rim.

Glass cloths must be perfectly clean and and as dry as possible. A dirty cloth can carry all types of infection, and many publicans and hoteliers believe that it is better for glasses to be left to drain off without being wiped or dried. It is generally thought, however, that customers like to see a bright shining glass, and this can only be achieved by the use of a glass cloth; so there should always be a plentiful supply, and those used for drying glasses should never be used for any other purpose.

Counter cloths can inevitably become heavily infected, and should never be rinsed out in sinks where glasses are to be washed. If there is no separate sink, it is better that they should be kept in a bowl containing some suitable detergent. Draining-boards need to be frequently swilled down with clean water and wiped with a cloth kept specially for that purpose. It is a good idea to keep cloths of specific colours and distinct types for different needs.

In busy premises, glass-washing can be a considerable problem. Rapid circulation of glasses is essential, and in an effort to solve this problem, many premises have installed glass-washing machines; but opinions differ as to their merits. The two-sink method has distinct advantages. The first sink contains clean hot water to which a detergent has been added, and is used for the preliminary wash, while the second, filled with very hot water, is used for rinsing. Properly used, the method should ensure a sterile glass; but many barmen allow the water to go cold, or to become full of slices of lemon, left-over drink etc. The detergent used must be added in the right quantity at every change of water: too strong a solution can destroy the head on a pint of beer, and an inadequate mix can result in the glasses not being properly sterilised. Detergents must be carefully selected, and effective: they must not alter the taste of the beer, must not foam, and (most importantly) must not smell. Much research has been carried out in this particular area, and detergents are continually improving.

Bar Food

Most establishments now serve food in the form of bar snacks. The proprietors usually do this to attract custom and to supplement their beer sales; but to succeed in it, they must display their food in an attractive and prominent fashion. The food must at all times look fresh, and scrupulous attention should be given to the cleanliness of all cooking appliances, and to the washing of plates and cutlery. Like that of bartenders, the personal hygiene of staff preparing and serving food is extremely important, and no-one in bad health should be employed in the food industry unless with the approval of a medical practitioner. Sandwiches and snacks should be covered, not only to keep them fresh, but also to prevent their being coughed or breathed upon by customers. Tongs must always be used, and special cloths set aside for polishing any plates or cutlery prior to their being used.

Refuse and waste bins should be provided with tight-fitting lids. These should always be in a good state of maintenance, and thoroughly cleaned and washed daily. It is preferable not to site bins in the bars themselves, as they can attract infestation by rats and mice, which in turn causes contamination.

Adequate hand-washing and toilet facilities must be provided for all staff. There must be separate lavatories for the sexes, and these must be situated in a place where food and drink are not stored, prepared or sold. Flooring must be kept clean and tidy and washed daily, and damaged floors and lino repaired instantly.

All premises serving food or drink are subject to regular inspections by the Environmental Health Department; and if standards are not maintained, licensees are quite likely to be refused their licence at the next hearing. Specific guidelines are laid down; and it is the responsibility of all caterers and bar staff to adhere strictly to these regulations, and of employers to insist that their staff maintain high standards.

Smoking must never be allowed where food or drink is being prepared or served, and domestic pets should not be permitted to enter these areas.

THE MANAGEMENT OF LICENSED PREMISES: SUMMARY OF
GUIDELINES FOR LICENSEES

1. Monitor all purchases, and put them under lock and key as
    soon as possible. Do not make inexperienced staff responsible
    for this function.
2. See that all stockrooms and bars are kept properly locked up
    when not attended, and that locks are changed on a regular
    basis.
3. Do not allow excessive stock to be kept behind the bar, and
    only allow responsible people to issue it from cellars or stores.
4. Make sure that cellar requisitions are given for all transfers.
    There should be no loans or I.O.U.s.
5. Only use experienced staff, and make sure that they work as
    instructed.
6. Make sure that all staff are properly trained, and know what
    measure to use for every drink available on the premises.
7. Where lined glasses are in use, make sure that staff do not
    overfill; where they are not used, make sure that employees
    know up to what level to fill each container.
8. Ensure that unauthorised staff do not serve drinks 'on the
    house', and eliminate any credit.
9. Ensure that all allowances or any free drinks are properly
    recorded.
10. Watch wastages and breakages. Keep an account of them, in
    the same way as for bottles and cases.
11. Make sure that all income is efficiently recorded, and that it is
    properly allocated: drinks served with bar meals, for example,
    must go to 'liquor' and not to 'food'.
12. Have a cash register in each bar and watch its operation –
    ensure that customers can see what is rung up. Spot-check tills
    on a regular basis.
13. See that each bar has a current price list, which is comprehen-
    sive and visible to both staff and customers.
14. Inform the barman immediately of any price changes, prefer-
    ably in writing.
15. If applicable, ensure that the recipes of any cocktails or
    made-up drinks are available behind the bar, and that such
    drinks are charged properly.
16. Where there is an occasional bar, a record should be kept of
    what goes in and what is returned. This will enable spot checks
    to be made, in the event of anomalies.

17. Do not permit overcharges on banquets. This can be detrimental to the business.

18. Have regular stocktaking carried out by a member of the Incorporated Society of Licensed Trade Stocktakers, so that you know whether you are being defrauded and what gross profit you are achieving. Do not wait for your accountant to tell you at the end of the year.

SECTION II
STOCKTAKING

CHAPTER 4
LIQUOR STOCKTAKING: THE YIELD, THE PHYSICAL COUNT

STOCKTAKING

Extended Reports

A Stocktaker will produce for his clients either trading accounts, or extended reports, or both.

The former are detailed quite extensively on page 124, and are of use to a client when he wants to know what gross profit he is making, but is not particularly interested in acquiring more complex or useful information about his operation.

Extended reports vary considerably in the amount of information they give. Most are now produced on computers, by the use of programs designed to suit individual Stocktakers' requirements. All Stocktakers should, nevertheless, thoroughly understand the system and be able to extend reports manually when required. This may quite often be necessary, particularly if clients have problems and require immediate results, or if there has been a computer break-down, with consequent delays.

When deciding how much information to give a client, the Stocktaker must be careful to restrict print-outs to useful and informative facts, without reams of superfluous figures. Most clients like short, concise and easy-to-read reports. The most useful head-ings are listed on page 113, and it is important for the Stocktaker to understand the meaning of each and the method by which the figures are obtained.

It is preferable, when doing regular stocktaking, to prepare the record sheets before the visit. This will save considerable time on site, look much more professional, and enable the Stocktaker to update his sheets on a regular basis. He will also have access to his opening stock (last time's closing stock), with which comparisons can be made.

If extended results are being prepared manually, columns for each of the following will normally be needed.

1. The commodity, its size and unit.
2. The opening stock, which will be the previous closing stock.

3. Purchases – a wide column is usually required, in which to enter all purchases individually, from delivery notes, invoices or the Goods Received Book.
4. Total of purchases.
5. Closing stock – a wide column in which to enter separate stock counts, of which there might be several.
6. Total closing stock.
7. Total sales of each item. This is calculated by adding purchases less any returns to the opening stock, and deducting the closing stock.
8. Cost price, excluding V.A.T.
9. Consumption at cost price, i.e. total sales multiplied by the cost price.
10. Valuation – this is the closing stock figure, extended at cost price.
11. Selling price, including V.A.T., of each item (see page 86).
12. Consumption at selling price, i.e. total sales multiplied by the selling price.

Similar stock should never be counted as one unit; for example, different brands of whisky should not be grouped together, even though the bottles are of the same size. Not only does separation enable the client to see the different gross profit being achieved on each brand, it also allows tighter control by the Stocktaker, who will not have to count too many bottles etc. of any one variety. Further, it highlights overstocking of particular items, and in some instances may help to detect fraud or dishonesty. Procedures for counting the stock are explained on page 96; and it is only by using these proper procedures, and by thorough concentration, that the Stocktaker will achieve a correct final result. He must check for irregularities, and ensure that all prices marked on optics, pumps and shelves are the same as those shown on the tariff board. He is responsible to the client or company, and accordingly should never hesitate to report any discrepancies he finds, or any suspicions he has. He will note the dates of any price changes, so that he can make the necessary adjustments (see page 133), and in general audit the entire liquor operation, leaving the premises only when he feels sure that he has done a satisfactory job, and has acquired all the information which he is likely to need.

As far as spirits, vermouth, sherry, liqueurs etc. are concerned, the Stocktaker must gauge amounts in terms of tenths of a bottle. The ability to do this will come only with experience. The use of this method does require special care when large bottles are being dealt with: whatever the size of the bottle, its contents must be gauged in tenths of that size, and it is only when working out the selling price

PRICES CHARGED IN THIS ROOM

SPIRITS (all ⅙th gill)

WHISKY		*BOTTLED BEER*	
WHISKY	87	SWEET STOUT	70
DE LUXE WHISKY	1.00	GUINNESS	70
MALT WHISKY	95	EXPORT	70
CANADIAN CLUB	95	CARLSBERG PILSNER	70
OLD GRANDAD	95	CLAUSTHALER	70
SOUTHERN COMFORT	95	DANSK	70
JACK DANIELS	95	HOLSTEN PILS	95
		CARLSBERG SPECIAL	95
GIN	87	BUDWEISER	95
		BECKS BIER	95
VODKA	87		
		MINERALS	
RUM		BABY MIXERS	40
BACARDI	92	COCA COLA	50
DARK	87	GINGER BEER	50
		FRUIT JUICE	50
COGNAC ETC.		APPLETISE	60
3-STAR	1.10	HI JUICE ETC.	60
V.S.O.P.	1.50	DASH CORDIAL	10
CORDON BLEU	2.20	LEMONADE DASH	10
ARMAGNAC	1.20	LEMONADE GLASS	40
X.O.	4.00		
		PERRIER	
APERITIFS ETC. (all ⅓rd gill)		SMALL	70
		MEDIUM	90
VERMOUTHS	80	LARGE	1.20
DUBONNET	80		
CINZANO	80	*WINE BY THE GLASS*	
NOILLY PRAT	80	125 ml	90
ALL SHERRY	80	175 ml	1.25
CAMPARI	1.10		
ADVOCAAT	1.00	*PORT (⅓rd gill)*	
GREEN GINGER	50	RUBY/TAWNY	80
PIMMS NO.1 CUP	1.50	LATE BOTTLED	1.10
BEER			
BITTER, 1 PINT	1.06	*LIQUEURS (all ⅙th gill)*	
BITTER, ½ PINT	53	LIQUEURS	1.00
LAGER, 1 PINT	1.06	PERNOD	90
LAGER, ½ PINT	53	MALIBU	90
CIDER, 1 PINT	1.06	TEQUILA	90
CIDER, ½ PINT	53		
TOBACCO		*BAR SUNDRIES*	
HAMLET	30	CRISPS	17
CASTELLAS	60	SALTED NUTS	30

ALL PRICES INCLUSIVE OF V.A.T. AT 15%

that the Stocktaker will need to be aware of the number of measures obtainable from each.

If a Stocktaker gauges the contents of a bottle as half full, he will in effect be saying that it contains $5/10$; and since the 10 would be recurring each time, he would simply write $5/$. Though they are counted in dozens, the same procedure would apply for beers and minerals. Many Stocktakers have now changed to the decimal system: they generally count the bottles in dozens, and then enter their total count in decimals, using the table shown on page 95.

Prices – Retail and Cost

To produce an extended result (see page 83), the Stocktaker must have accurate cost and retail prices. Cost prices present no major problems, because they can be extracted from invoices at regular intervals. Retail prices are much more complex, and require extreme accuracy, if correct results are to be produced.

By law, a current price list similar to the one shown on page 85 has to be displayed in each bar.

Invoices generally show cost prices, and when the Stocktaker is dealing with these, he must ensure that he uses the same format as for retail prices. In other words, if the retail price is per dozen, then so must be the cost price; with the retail price for cigarettes being per packet, the cost price must be per packet also. The only difference will be that the retail price includes V.A.T., whereas the cost price does not. Invoices must be checked by the Stocktaker on each visit, and any changes in cost prices noted. If invoices are not available price lists can be obtained from suppliers, but some customers do have very preferential terms and receive substantial discounts, so it is always best to insist on sight of invoices.

Before the selling prices are entered on the stock sheets, two important factors must be established: (1) the unit selling price, (2) the yield, or number of measures expected from a container.

Counting and Pricing Table

Category	Counting method	Pricing
Cask Beer	In gallons	Per gallon
Bottled Beer, Minerals, Soda Water	In dozens and twelfths	Per dozen
Cordials	In single and part bottles (to the nearest 1/10th)	Per bottle
Bulk Cordials, Postmix Minerals	In gallons (or litres) (to the nearest 1/10th)	Per gallon (or litre)
Spirits, Liqueurs, Ports, Sherries, Vermouths etc.	In single and part bottles (to the nearest 1/10th)	Per bottle
Cask Sherry	In gallons (to the nearest 1/10th)	Per gallon
Wine (sold by the glass)	In single and part bottles (to the nearest 1/10th)	Per bottle
Other table wine (1/2s, 1/4s etc.)	In single bottles	Per bottle
Crisps, Nuts etc.	In dozens and twelfths	Per dozen
Confectionery, Sundries	In dozens and twelfths	Per dozen
Cigars, Whiffs	In singles	Per single cigar
Cigarettes	Individually or per packet	Per packet or per hundred

THE YIELD

Cask or Keg Beer

All draught beer is measured in gallons, irrespective of size of container; so the Stocktaker would multiply the (pint) selling price by 8 to obtain the unit retail value.

The capacities of the traditional casks are as follows:–

Butt	108 gallons	864 pints
Puncheon	72 gallons	576 pints
Hogshead	54 gallons	432 pints
Barrel	36 gallons	288 pints
Kilderkin	18 gallons	144 pints
Firkin	9 gallons	72 pints
Pin	4.5 gallons	36 pints

Metal casks came into the trade at the time of metrication, so there is now, besides the traditional range, a completely new one which is still being added to. Currently, the most common sizes are:–

100 litres   22 gallons   176 pints
 50 litres   11 gallons   88 pints
 45 litres   10 gallons   80 pints

Most of the old wooden casks have now disappeared, having been replaced by aluminium or stainless steel types.

Cordials and Lemonade

Cordials are not normally dispensed by measure, but are simply poured into the glass, either to complement a beer or spirit or to make a long drink, with the addition of water. In some cases, where beer or lager is dispensed in brim glasses (i.e. those which the exact measure fills to the top), an inbuilt surplus can occur when the cordial which displaces the beer is also charged for; this will not of course happen if the cordial is added to a metered pint.

The generally accepted method of pricing cordials or squash is by using the large or one-third gill dash. (Many Stocktakers prefer to cost them by the pint or half-pint, or even by the bottle. This is perfectly acceptable, provided care is taken.) Thus, if a dash of cordial is sold at £0.08, the following calculations would apply:–

From a 25 oz bottle, 15 measures at £0.08   = £1.20
From a litre bottle, 21 measures at £0.08   = £1.68
From a gallon container, 96 measures at £0.08   = £7.68

To produce a selling price based on dozens, the individual unit price would have to be multiplied by 12.

Lemonade is much more difficult to price because it can be sold in so many different ways: by the litre, by the pint, by the dash, and sometimes with beer to make shandy. The Stocktaker must establish the most common selling unit and then work out a compromise price, but if he is unable to do this, the lower price should be adopted. In some cases lemonade is free, so would be shown on the stock sheets at no retail charge.

Premix and Postmix Minerals

The basic difference between premix and postmix syrups is that the former are delivered ready for use, normally in 18 or 18.75 litre canisters, whereas the latter come in concentrated form, the mix and the size of container varying considerably.

Before metrication, the capacity of a premix canister (i.e. 18 or 18.75 litres) was expressed as 660 fluid ounces or 33 pints; the figure

A dipstick is a useful accessory for the gauging of postmix syrup containers (the Bruntsfield Hotel, Edinburgh).

Care must be taken when looking for the 'wet mark' after dipping cask-conditioned beer (The Greenmantle, Nicholson Street, Edinburgh).

of 33 would be multiplied by the price of a pint of lemonade to obtain the retail price of the full container.

Postmix is automatically mixed with water at the point of dispense. It comes in a variety of pack types, sizes and strengths: there are rigid poly packs (4.5 litres or 5 litres), 'bag in box' packs (10, 18 or 20 litres), and canisters (10, 18.5 or 18.75 litres). The most common types are the 5 litre packs which are used to top up the large canisters, and the sealed containers themselves from which the mix is dispensed. Dilution rates include 9 to 1, 7.5 to 1, 6 to 1, 5 to 1, 4 to 1, and 3 to 1. Given this variability, it is important for the Stocktaker to establish the exact mix of each brand – most major suppliers show it on the label, but some of the smaller manufacturers do not. The most common dilution rate is 5 to 1; a formula for obtaining the selling price (per litre) for a bar price of £0.30 per half-pint is as follows:–

£0.30 ÷ 10   (the number of ounces in a half-pint)
            = £0.03 per ounce;
£0.03 × 35   (the number of ounces in a litre)
      × 6   (the dilution factor)
            = £6.30 per litre.

An alternative calculation is as follows:–

35   ounces = 3½ × 10   oz   (half-pint);   3½ × 6   (the   dilution factor) = 21;
21 × £0.30 = £6.30 per litre.

For a 3 to 1 mix, the calculation would follow the same pattern:–

35   ounces = 3½ × 10   oz   (half-pint);   3½ × 4   (the   dilution factor) = 14;
14 × £0.30 = £4.20 per litre.

One of the common errors of inexperienced Stocktakers is to assume that a 5 to 1 mix necessitates multiplication by 5 rather than 6: the actual equation indicates 5 parts water and 1 part syrup.

Because postmix syrups, like bottled lemonade, are sold in a variety of ways, great care should be taken in the assessing of their selling prices.

Strength of Mix

The automatic mixing valves on postmix containers sometimes fail to work correctly, and it is therefore good policy to have them checked at least once a quarter or, where particularly large quantities of postmixes are involved, once a month. The retail price of the contents of these containers is quite considerable, and any malfunction can affect stock results very considerably, sometimes by up to hundreds of pounds.

Equipment exists which checks the strength of postmixes; it is called a Brix meter or, more accurately, a refractometer, but it is extremely difficult to obtain, and certainly not available on the open market.

Because of the compactness of the equipment and the high profit margins available, postmixes and premixes are popular within the trade; but for the Stocktaker, it is very difficult to assess an accurate potential yield for postmixes and even more difficult to maintain consistency. It is the Stocktaker's responsibility to achieve yields as close as possible to the exact figure, and to advise his clients to have the mix checked at regular intervals.

Fruit Juices and Machines

Because fruit juice is imported from distant countries such as Brazil, it is common practice to transport it in concentrated form. This is done by removing most of the water and freezing the remainder. On arrival at its destination, it is processed back into juice of whatever concentration is required. If it is reconstituted to its original strength, it may according to the Fruit Juice Regulations of 1977 be called '100% fruit juice', but if more water is added, then it must be called a 'fruit juice drink'. The lowest juice content is 5% (referred to as 'squash') and the highest is 40% (referred to as 'hi fruit').

There is a growing market for fruit juice dispensing machines, and several varieties are available.

1. *Straight Dispense:*   5, 10, 18 or 20 litre bags of pure fruit juice may be dispensed through a cooling system, in the same way as premixed cola or lemonade; but they must be stored in a cold cabinet similar to that used for bulk milk. The Stocktaker will either weigh the container, or assess the level of juice in the box.

    Advantages: Since no mixing is involved, there is little waste and less chance of error or wrong mixing ratios.

    Disadvantages: Because the mixture is thin, the fleshy parts of the juice tend to sink to the bottom of the bag and be dispensed first. If the volume of sales is high, bags have to be changed fairly frequently.

2. *Postmix (Manual Mix):*   The juice is supplied in either 1 litre Tetrapacks or 40 oz cans, to which water is added. Dilution rates are stated on the containers or on the delivery notes; they are usually either 4 to 1, 5 to 1 or in some instances 6 to 1. It is fairly simple to work out the volume of fruit juice obtainable from each container, applying the same principle as for postmixes (see page 89). The tank has an agitator which keeps the juice properly mixed, and it is usually also fitted with a cooling

system. It is now becoming quite common for equipment to be supplied which enables the juice to be kept in the cellar and dispensed through a tap at the bar counter. The system works in exactly the same way, except that the tank is not on public display.

For stocktaking purposes it is usually best to have the container marked at the level of one complete mix of juice, so that the Stocktaker will be able to work out his closing stock without too much difficulty.

Advantages: The juice can be quickly and easily mixed. Good profit margins are achievable, and the system is ideal for busy outlets.

Disadvantages: The machines must be regularly cleaned, and any juice not sold within thirty-six hours should be discarded. The taste of the fruit juice may be affected by the tap water added to the mixture.

3. *Postmix (Machine Mix:)*   This is generally supplied in either 5 or 10 litre 'bag in box' containers, or 12 or 18 litre canisters. It is mixed in exactly the same way as postmix concentrates. The dilution ratio is stated on the box or delivery note, and the actual mix is usually set by the supplier's fitter. Recently, a number of companies have begun to install their equipment under the bar counter; if this is done, the juice generally comes in a 5 litre container with a 4 to 1 dilution rate. The Stocktaker will calculate his selling price by using the procedure previously described.

Advantages: The system involves no manual mixing and little or no waste, is useful in large outlets, and produces good profits.

Disadvantages: Mixer jets can become blocked, upsetting the dilution ratio. Unless regular checks are carried out, wastage – and consequently stock problems – may occur.

Spirits, Liqueurs, Ports, Sherries, Vermouths etc.

The number of nips to a bottle of spirit obviously depends upon the size of the bottle and of the measure being used. It is advisable for the Stocktaker to remove the bottle from the optic, turn it upside down or on its side, and then assess the volume of liquid in it. (Because certain varieties of bottle have concave bottoms, it is much easier to gauge the contents to the accuracy required, i.e. to the nearest tenth, if the bottle is laid on its side.)

The measures used in this country are based on Imperial units, whereas bottles now tend to come in metric sizes. The most common sizes of measure are one-third, one-quarter, one-fifth and one-sixth gill. The gill is a quarter-pint (five ounces); thus one-sixth of a gill equals five-sixths of an ounce which equals 0.833 ounces.

Since the standard spirit bottle contains 26.4 ounces (75 cl), the yield must be that divided by 0.833, which equals 31.69. As the yield is slightly below 32, most Stocktakers base their calculations on 31 or 31.5.

Liqueurs are generally served in one-sixth measures. Most bottles are 70 cl, but a few (such as Drambuie) are the same size as spirit bottles, so great care must be taken to gauge the correct yield. In smaller sizes, both 50 and 48 cl bottles are available. In some cases liqueurs are served in one-fifth gill measures; the table gives projected yields for both. (This and the following yield table show figures rounded off to whole numbers; a table of exact figures can be seen on page 282.)

Liqueurs		6 Out	5 Out	4 Out
35 fl oz	1 lt	42	35	28
26⅓ fl oz	75 cl	32	26	21
24⅔ fl oz	70 cl	30	25	20
24 fl oz	68 cl	29	24	19
20 fl oz	57 cl	24	20	16
17½ fl oz	50 cl	21	17	14
17 fl oz	48 cl	20	17	13

Sherry and ports are normally served in sherry glasses or by the double-sixth (one-third) measure; there is a difference between the two, so the Stocktaker must ascertain the method of dispense and work out his yield accordingly. In the case of vintage port the figure would be reduced by at least one measure, to allow for sediment. By the glass, the yield of port or sherry per 70 cl bottle would be 13; by the one-third measure, it would be 15.

Vermouth is generally served through the optic in one-third gill measures, giving a yield of 16 on a 75 cl bottle or 32 on a magnum. The Stocktaker must ascertain the measure being used before he assesses the selling price.

The following table indicates the number of yields which might be expected from bottles of various sizes. In some cases a tolerance would be allowed to cover such things as leaking optics, wastage, wrong pours etc., but no Stocktaker should do this on his own initiative: it requires the full consent of the client, to whom it should also be made clear that such action will decrease the estimated gross profit percentage figure.

Bottle Yield Table

Spirits Old Unit	Size in Imperial units	Size in Metric units	No. of measures		
			6 Out	5 Out	4 Out
Gallon (6 bottles)	160 fl oz	4.54 lt	192	160	128
US Gallon (5 bottles)	133⅓ fl oz	3.78 lt	160	133	106
New Size (3 lt) (4 bottles)	105 fl oz	3 lt	126	105	84
Half Gallon (3 bottles)	80 fl oz	2.27 lt	96	80	64
New Size (2 lt)	71 fl oz	2 lt	84	70	56
Half US Gallon	66⅔ fl oz	1.9 lt	80	66	53
New Size (Magnum) (2 bottles)	53 fl oz	1.5 lt	63	53	42
40 oz	40 fl oz	1.13 lt	48	40	32
New Size (1 lt)	35 fl oz	1 lt	42	35	28
New Size (e.g. Whisky)	26½ fl oz	75 cl	32	26	21
Continental (e.g. Brandy)	24 fl oz	68 cl	29	24	19

Ports, Sherries and Ginger Wine			3 Out	2½ Out	2 Out
Litre	35 fl oz	1 lt	21	17	14
Bottle	26⅓ fl oz	75 cl	16	13	11
Bottle	24⅔ fl oz	70 cl	15	12	10

Vermouth and Dubonnet

Magnum	53 fl oz	1.5 lt	32	26	21
Litre	35 fl oz	1 lt	21	17	14
Bottle	26⅓ fl oz	75 cl	16	13	11

Cask Sherry

This is usually measured in gallons or litres to the nearest tenth. The Stocktaker can use his beer dipstick to gauge quantities, but it is better for him to carry a short stick specially adapted for this purpose. Sherry is generally served in either 2 or 2½ oz measures, so his yield per gallon would be either 80 or 64.

Wines

The new code of practice for the dispensing of still wines by the glass was introduced in 1984, and may eventually become mandatory. Each establishment can choose two measures from the range of eleven listed below. They must be either metric or Imperial, and not one of each; the difference in capacity between the two must not be less than 50 millilitres or 2 fluid ounces. The Stocktaker must ascertain the size of glass being used, and work out his yield accordingly.

Size in Metric units	Size in Imperial units	No. of measures (to the nearest half-glass)			
		70 cl	100 cl	150 cl	200 cl
100 ml		7	10	15	20
	4 fl oz	6	8.5	13	17.5
125 ml		5.5	8	12	16
	5 fl oz	5	7	10.5	14
150 ml		4.5	6.5	10	13
	6 fl oz	4	6	9	12
175 ml		4	5.5	8.5	11.5
	6⅔ fl oz	3.5	5	8	10.5
200 ml		3.5	5	7.5	10
	8 fl oz	3	4	7	9
250ml		3	4	6	8

Confusion can occur when bottles are sold at a rate different from that applying when they are dispensed by the glass. To avoid this problem, clients should be encouraged to sell bottles of wine at prices corresponding to the appropriate multiple of the price per glass. For wines sold by the glass, the price of the bottle should be divided by the appropriate number from the above table. If necessary, bottles of different sizes can be stocked – one size for sale as a full unit, and another for sale by the glass.

Many establishments are now dispensing wine from 3, 5, 10 or 20 litre packs. As with postmix, the container can be weighed, or the Stocktaker can gauge the quantity left in it by feel and estimated weight.

Cigarettes

Cigarettes, which are seldom sold individually, are generally counted in hundreds and tenths thereof, so that 260 would be entered as 2.6. The yield from a unit would be 5, and the selling price per unit would be 5 times the price of a packet of 20. Some Stocktakers prefer to count in packets, and in this case the yield would be 1 and the selling price would be the price per packet. Examples of both methods are shown below.

Cost price   £1.24 per 20 (V.A.T. excluded)
Retail price £1.53 per 20 (V.A.T. included)

On an extended stock report, by the first method the cost price would be £6.20 (£1.24 × 5) and the retail price £7.65 (£1.53 × 5).

Cost	Retail	Sales	Consumption at Cost	Consumption at Retail
£6.20	£7.65	8	£49.60	£61.20

By the second method (i.e. counting in packets), the figures would be calculated as follows:–

Cost	Retail	Sales	Consumption at Cost	Consumption at Retail
£1.24	£1.53	40	£49.60	£61.20

Small Cigars

It is always beneficial to count these as single units: even where packets are involved, it is generally easier to write down the number of cigars rather than the number of packets. The reason for this is that staff very often open packets and sell individual cigars. This would create difficulties in stocktaking, and because particular brands are often sold not only as individual cigars but also in packets of several, it is likely that the Stocktaker would have to hold two lines for each product. When special discounts are in operation, the Stocktaker should open a special line, or make an allowance under 'cheap sales'.

Beers, Minerals, Crisps, Nuts and Confectionery

These are all sold in dozens, so the selling price would be 12 times the unit charge. A useful table for the conversion of twelfths to decimals is given below.

No. of twelfths	Decimal equivalent
1	0.083
2	0.166
3	0.25
4	0.333
5	0.416
6	0.5
7	0.583
8	0.666
9	0.75
10	0.833
11	0.916
12	1.0

The packaged snacks here referred to – crisps, nuts, confectionery etc. – are sold in most bars; in clubs, they are often owned and purveyed by the steward, but in most cases they are part of the bar stock, and must be controlled in the same way as wet stock.

Sometimes this is done on a monetary basis: the value of the deliveries, at cost, is added to the previous value, and the present value is then deducted to give a consumption amount. To produce an expected retail sales figure, a mark-up percentage is then applied. The main reasons for using this method are that sundries often comprise a complex variable array of items but are a relatively small part of the total bar turnover, and that many of the delivery notes involved are lacking in detail and clarity, e.g. '4 Scratchings' instead of '4 × 20 × 18p Scratchings'.

The drawback with the monetary method is that the mark-up on different types of goods varies considerably: chocolate and sweets have an average mark-up of 25%, children's 1p and 2p sweets about 33⅓%, and crisps 42%. A further complication is that many of the lines involved are zero rated for V.A.T. The 'crisp' type of snack, usually boxed in 48s, are divided in this respect: in general, the principle is that items made from potatoes are subject to V.A.T., but those based on maize, other cereals or cheese are zero rated. Other V.A.T.-free items include unsalted nuts, nuts and raisins, pork scratchings, poppadums, shellfish, pickled eggs, cheese and biscuits, and popcorn.

The most accurate method of stock control for sundries is to list them by type, like any other category of bar stock. An exception may be made for chocolate: if there are several types of bar, these may be listed by price rather than by brand – this will save space, and any difference in mark-up will be minimal. (With conventional listing, a single common brand might require four separate lines, for temporary special offers create continual fluctuations in the price of chocolate.)

Matches, cigarette papers and other smokers' sundries can be included in this section, as the mark-up on these is much closer to that for sundries than to that for the tobacco items with which they are sometimes listed.

THE PHYSICAL COUNT

It is always best to take stock while the premises are closed, and before the start of the day's business. This enables the Stocktaker to establish a clear cut-off date, and to proceed with his work unhampered. As far as possible, he should plan his count beforehand, and where practicable follow the same routine on every visit. In larger establishments, it is always advisable to check if a private function is being held which might prevent entry to a particular bar for a particular period, or if any deliveries are anticipated. The Stocktaker must co-operate with management, and if a change in routine is requested or suggested, he should comply.

If the stock is being taken during the afternoon, or during trading hours, the Stocktaker must be careful to monitor activities within the premises. For instance, if after he has counted the cellar stock the barman removes a bottle of whisky from there, the Stocktaker will probably count it again when he comes to the bar; so the movement of stock should not be permitted until the physical count is completed. If a delivery is made while stock is being taken, it will either be included or set aside for inclusion in the next stocktaking.

In such circumstances it would be best, unless otherwise instructed, to cover the work in the following order:–

1. Bottle and case deposits.
2. Cellars, including full containers of beer.
3. Bars not in use.
4. The bar in use, left if possible until it has closed.
5. Draught beer in use.

If the bar remains open, a cut-off point will have to be arranged as the time at which the till is read. Any money taken during the day can be added on to the takings figure, with a reminder being made to adjust that figure on the next visit; or it can be converted to stock, so that income is not interfered with and a proper cut-off point (i.e. as at close of business the previous night) is established. If £241 is recorded for the day so far, the Stocktaker will add to his closing stock goods whose value totals that figure at retail price. If whisky costs 70p per one-sixth gill, he would – assuming a yield of 31 – add 11.1 to his bottle count. This procedure is not ideal because, although the final gross profit figure will be correct, that applied to each group of items will be incorrect, and so will sales ratio figures. For this reason, many Stocktakers prefer to add the amount read at the cut-off point to their income figure, making a note to deduct the same amount at the next stock.

Bars

The Stocktaker should always be methodical, usually starting with the optics and working from left to right. Each shelf should be dealt with in turn; bottles should never be deliberately missed out and left for later consideration. The Stocktaker must check back fittings; and always ensure that he has completed each section before moving on to the next.

Reflections in mirrors can be misleading, as can empty or dummy bottles used as display stock. Cigars, matches and cigarettes are often stacked on or near the till, so particular attention should be paid to that area.

Before moving on to the bottle shelves, the Stocktaker should check the walls for nuts, crisps or other saleable products, and the counter for cordials, syphons or lemonade. Checking under the sink, opening all drawers and cupboards, and asking if any stock is kept elsewhere are all advisable measures: time spent in checking can save many anxious moments.

After counting the bottle shelves, again from left to right and using a torch if necessary, he should carefully scan the entire bar and ensure that nothing has been missed. If asked to do so, he should check the till and take a note of cash in hand. Before leaving the area, he should check the stock sheets to see if any item for which there is an opening balance is without a closing stock.

Draught Beer Cellar

It is extremely difficult to gauge beer accurately, particularly when bigger casks are involved. Each container must be physically inspected.

The normal method of measuring the contents of traditional beer casks is by using a dipstick supplied by the manufacturers. This can vary according to the make of cask, and is usually calibrated to measure any size from a pin to a hogshead. Specially adapted dipsticks, marked 'S.T.', are available for measuring the contents of casks standing up; those marked 'L.Y.' are made especially for those lying on the stillion. When measuring real ale, great care must be taken not to disturb the beer, as it often takes up to forty-eight hours to resettle and may in some cases have to be returned to the brewer. If sedimented beer is dispensed under top pressure, it is advisable for the Stocktaker to protect himself by asking the client to turn off the gas and prepare the cask for dipping. When a measurement is being taken on a stillion, the dipstick should always be kept at right angles to the cellar floor.

There are various methods of measuring sealed containers, but experience will generally enable the Stocktaker to gauge with a reasonable degree of accuracy the amount of beer left in a keg. He will, if possible, lift the container, or failing that tilt it and either find the point of balance or find the level by the wash. In some cases it may be possible to tap the side of the container and use the changes in resonance to assess the contents.

Draught beer awaiting return should be counted into stock. A note should be made of the label, cask and gyle numbers so that it can be identified when collected or credited. Full gas cylinders should be counted if a valuation is being prepared.

A torch provides useful assistance, in the gauging of tank beer (the Bruntsfield
Hotel, Edinburgh).

The weight and the wash help to indicate the contents of this keg of Guinness
(The Greenmantle, Nicholson Street, Edinburgh).

Bottled Beer and Mineral Stores

The Stocktaker must satisfy himself that bottled beers and minerals are stacked in full cases with part-full ones on top. He should satisfy himself that each stack contains the same, and that empty cases are not stored under full. (Again, if a valuation or extended result is required, all cases should be counted, whether empty or full.)

Beers and minerals are traditionally counted in dozens and twelfths, but vary in the number per case. Most British beers and minerals come in quantities of 1, 2, 3 or 4 dozen, but Continental beers can be delivered in cases of 16 or 20, so the Stocktaker must ensure that he knows the quantity per case for each product. It is customary for all 'baby minerals', i.e. bitter lemon, ginger ale, tonic etc., to be counted as one unit under the heading 'baby mixers'. The same procedure would apply to fruit juices; but if cost prices differed (because of purchasing from different suppliers), a separate line would have to be set up for each brand.

Postmixes and Premixes – Gauging of Canisters

The breaking of a seal on a canister is not advisable because the suppliers, if there is a problem, may refuse to grant credit on both the contents and the container, on account of 'customer interference'. The best method of gauging is to weigh a full container and assess part canisters by comparison with that figure. By subtracting the empty weight from the full weight and dividing the result by the capacity in litres (usually 18), a weight per litre can easily be obtained. This method would also be applicable to the 'bag in box' type of container. If scales are not available, the Stocktaker would probably have to gauge the volume of liquid within the container. Doing this accurately comes only with experience, but the skill is a crucial one: even a small degree of error can prejudice the result of the stock quite considerably.

Canisters that are not sealed, including premixes, can be opened once the CO_2 gas has been turned off, and gauged either by eye or by the use of a dipstick. Some companies do make stainless steel dipsticks for use with their own canisters, but these are very difficult to obtain, and more often than not the Stocktaker has to produce his own.

Before he leaves the cellar, the Stocktaker should check all shelves and cupboards for stock, and the state of gas or cooling systems (which he may have turned off); it is his responsibility to ensure that everything is left as found. Again, stock sheets should be checked for gaps; and a final visual inspection should be made of the area.

Spirits, Wines, Tobacco and Dry Goods

It is standard practice to start at the top left-hand corner of a spirit store, and work along the shelves towards the floor. Clients should be encouraged to maintain consistency, if possible, by keeping their stock in the same order as it appears on the Stocktaker's sheets, and their wine in the same order as is used on the wine list. All cases should be checked, and where they appear intact the Stocktaker should verify that the seals are secure on both top and bottom. He should test the seals on all bottles, and open cigar tins to ensure that they are full.

Other Locations

It is important for the Stocktaker to check, before completing his count, that no stock is kept elsewhere. In some instances, white wine may be kept in the kitchen refrigerator, cigars in a humidor in the restaurant, or crisps and nuts in the food store or office. During particularly busy periods such as Christmas, or when special promotions are in operation, stock is often kept in living quarters. Any keys given to the Stocktaker must be kept securely and handed over to a responsible person as soon as possible.

Bottle and Case Deposits

It is not always considered necessary to count empty bottles and cases when preparing an extended stock result. It is recommended, however, that an accurate count be taken on each visit because:–

1. it enables the client to know exactly how much stock he is holding;
2. it allows the Stocktaker, when producing an extended result, to exercise some control over purchases and returns, for example by pinpointing short deliveries.

If they are included as a line item on the extended report, any losses will affect the gross profit. A separate entry would have to be made, as shown in the example, and the Stocktaker would have to be extremely careful to extract all purchases and credits for deposits from the delivery notes or invoices.

In the example, any deposits received have been entered in the 'purchases' column, and any returned to the suppliers shown as a credit. While this example does not show a loss at retail value, the client may request it to be incorporated into the final result. It sometimes happens that a check on the area where empties are kept will lead to the discovery of stock which should have been counted.

It is essential always to include deposits in year-end or changeover valuations. All cases, deposits and empties must be accurately

ITEM	UNIT	O S	PURCHASES	TOTAL	C.S.	TOTAL	SALES	COST PRICE	CONS AT COST	VALUATION	SELLING PRICE	CONS AT RETAIL	COST OF PURCHASE
BOTTLES SMALL	DOZ	120	20(60)40(10)30	20	136	136	4	0·52	2·08	70·72			
BOTTLES PINT	DOZ	8	4(6)6(4)4	4	12	12	—	0·73	—	8·76			
CASES AT 50p	IND	21	30(30)	—	21	21	—	0·50	—	10·50			
CASES AT 1.00	IND	66	10(30)20(5)15	10	70	70	6	1·00	6·00	70·00			
BOTTLES FURSTENBERG	DOZ	6 9/.	5(34/)10(6⁸/.)	5	10	10	18/	·84	1·40	8·40			

counted, and the cost of full bottles must also be included. The headings would be as shown, but the Stocktaker would be responsible for ensuring accurate cost prices. Some bottles do not have a deposit value, and therefore care must be taken not to include these as part of the valuation.

Many establishments have cases or bottles which have been there for a considerable length of time, and it may well be that the company which originally supplied them is no longer in business, or that the particular premises have changed their suppliers. In either case, it would not be advisable to include them in the valuation, as it is unlikely that the purchaser (if the premises are being sold) would be able to recoup any money from them. Similarly, at a year-end valuation, the client should be informed that they have not been included, and advised either to discard them or use them for other purposes, as they are not likely to warrant any credits in the future.

Most premix and postmix containers have a deposit value, as do certain kegs; it is the responsibility of the Stocktaker to ensure that he knows what has a deposit value and what has not.

If a Stocktaker does not wish to show deposits on the main report, but he is required to monitor them, he will be able to do a separate trading account which will show a monetary loss or gain on this particular commodity. This will appear as follows:–

Deposit values 1/1/89	£354.46	Deposit values 3/2/89	£297.80
Purchases less credits	(£56.66)	Income	nil
Gross loss/gain	nil		

or:–

Deposit values 1/1/89	£354.46	Deposit values 3/2/89	£273.80
Purchases less credits	(£56.66)	Income	nil
Net loss	£24.00		

Price Differences and Changes

It is becoming more common for the same prices to be charged throughout premises, but in many establishments, particularly larger hotels, bars will vary in their price structures. This not only creates difficulties for staff moving from one bar to another, but also necessitates stronger controls, particularly by the Stocktaker. Ideally a cellar control system (see page 21) will operate; but if it does not, the Stocktaker will have to prepare for each bar a price adjustment figure, often referred to as an 'uplift' or 'surcharge' (see page 136).

To avoid adjustments for price increases which have occurred in the middle of a stock period, it is advisable to encourage clients to increase prices, where possible, on the day of stocktaking only.

CHAPTER 5

LIQUOR STOCKTAKING: THE STOCK REPORT

'Unit', 'Cost Price', 'Selling Price' and 'Opening Stock' Columns (see stock sheet, page 104)

The Stocktaker will arrive on site with prepared sheets, usually showing each item with its 'Unit', 'Cost Price' and 'Selling Price'. The 'Opening Stock' will be the previous time's closing figure. Cost prices which have been extracted from invoices will exclude V.A.T., whereas selling prices will include it. Selling prices will be calculated as follows:–

	£	£
Harp Lager (gal.)	1.05×8 (per gallon)	= 8.40
Barbican (btl.)	$.70 \times 12$ (per dozen)	= 8.40
Guiness (pt)	1.10×12 (per dozen)	= 13.20
Minerals (baby)	$.40 \times 12$ (per dozen)	= 4.80
Lemonade (75 cl)	$.10$ per dash $\times 12$ (per dozen) $\times 15$ dashes per bottle	= 18.00
Grouse Whisky (150 cl)	$.80 \times 63$ (per 150 cl bottle)	= 50.40
Bells Whisky (40 oz)	$.80 \times 48$ (per 113 cl bottle)	= 38.40
Antiquary (btl.)	$.95 \times 32$ (per 75 cl bottle)	= 30.40
Bristol Cream (btl.)	$.70 \times 15$ (per 70 cl bottle)	= 10.50
Sweet Martini (150 cl)	$.65 \times 32$ (per 150 cl bottle)	= 20.80
Creme de Menthe (50 cl)	1.00×21 (per 50 cl bottle)	= 21.00
Drambuie (75 cl)	1.00×32 (per 75 cl bottle)	= 32.00
Tequila (70 cl)	1.00×29 (per 70 cl bottle)	= 29.00
Hirondelle Wine (150 cl)	$.90 \times 10$ (glasses per 150 cl bottle, using 150 ml glasses)	= 9.00
Crisps (doz.)	$.15 \times 12$ (per dozen)	= 1.80
Benson and Hedges (pkt)	1.50×1 (per packet)	= 1.50

On the stock sheets which follow, the sequence of headings is not necessarily that used by all Stocktakers: each will select his own procedure, and possibly include more information.

For further information on pricing, see page 86.

ITEM	UNIT	O S	PURCHASES	TOTAL	C.S.	TOTAL SALES	COST PRICE	CONS AT COST	VALUATION	SELLING PRICE	CONS AT RETAIL	COST OF PURCHASE
Harp Lager	Gall	78					3.60			8.40		
Barbican BTL	Doz	6 6/.					3.80			8.40		
Guinness PT	Doz	2 1/.					6.00			13.20		
Minerals Baby	Doz	38 4/.					1.60			4.80		
Lemonade 75 cl	Doz	7/.					2.10			18.00		
Grouse Whisky	1.5	18 4/.					14.80			50.40		
Bells Whisky	40 oz	7 3/.					11.06			38.40		
Antiquary	Btl	2 1/.					8.80			30.40		
Bristol Cream	Btl	3 7/.					3.97			10.50		
Sweet Martini	1.5	1 9/.					4.40			20.80		
Creme de Menthe	50 cl	6/.					5.10			21.00		
Drambuie	75 cl	12/.					9.98			32.00		
Tequila	70 cl	3 6/.					7.10			29.00		
Hirondelle Wine	1.5	8 4/.					4.00			9.00		
Crisps	Doz	14 6/.					1.06			1.80		
Benson & Hedges	Pkt	18					1.20			1.50		

'Closing Stock' Column (see stock sheet, page 106)

The Stocktaker will count the stock in the way already described, and enter his figures in the 'Closing Stock' Column. In the case of Harp Lager, he will have found three 11-gallon kegs full and one part-full, containing (in his opinion) 9 gallons. He will have counted bottled beer in full dozens and twelfths, and spirits, sherry, liqueurs etc. in tenths. With Bells Whisky, for example, he will have found two part-bottles, one half-full and the other a little under. There will also have been two areas where he has seen full bottles, perhaps three on the cellar shelf and six still boxed.

'Purchases' Column (see stock sheet, page 107)

From the delivery notes, the Stocktaker will check all entries in the Goods Received Book and enter these on the stock sheets (see page 3). He will ensure that all his entries are correct, and that he has used exactly the same format as he did for the closing stock. Spirits will always be numbered to full bottles, but the Stocktaker must ensure that he also knows the number of units per case. If there is any difficulty, the information will probably be available either from the invoice or from the box, on which the number of bottles is generally clearly shown.

Bottled beers and minerals do come in cases of various sizes, and delivery notes differ: some show cases, whereas others indicate dozens. The Stocktaker must make absolutely sure that he has obtained the correct purchase figure, for otherwise his final result will be wrong.

Had there been any returns, he would either have noted them in a special column (headed 'Credits'), or reduced the 'Purchases' accordingly.

Some Stocktakers may prefer to use the first 'Total' column on the stock sheet to show the total of the opening stock and purchases. On these sample sheets, it has been used to show the purchases total only, which facilitates calculation if the purchase price is to be extended.

'Sales' Column (see stock sheet, page 108)

The 'Sales' figure represents the actual amount of each item sold during the stock period. The Stocktaker will total his 'Purchases' and 'Closing Stock' columns, and will arrive at his 'Sales' figure by using the following formula:–

Opening stock + purchases – closing stock = Consumption;

e.g.   Harp Lager –

78 + 66 – 42 = Sales of 102 gallons.

ITEM	UNIT	O S	PURCHASES	TOTAL	C.S.	TOTAL	SALES	COST PRICE	CONS AT COST	VALUATION	SELLING PRICE	CONS AT RETAIL	COST OF PURCHASE
Harp Lager	Gall	78			33·9			3.60			8.40		
Barbican BTL	Doz	6%/			9/. 18/. 4			3.80			8.40		
Guinness PT	Doz	2/.						6.00			13.20		
Minerals Baby	Doz	38%/			4/. 1%/ 6³/ 8. 24.			1.60			4.80		
Lemonade 75 cl	Doz	7/.			4/. 1.			2.10			18.00		
Grouse Whisky	1.5	18 4/			9/. 1. 7.			14.80			50.40		
Bells Whisky	40 oz	7³/			5/. 4. 3·6			11.06			38.40		
Antiquary	Btl	2 /.			%/. 2			8.80			30.40		
Bristol Cream	Btl	3 /.			4/. 6/. 2			3.97			10.50		
Sweet Martini	1.5	1 9/.			7/.			4.40			20.80		
Creme de Menthe	50 cl	6/.			6/.			5.10			21.00		
Drambuie	75 cl	1 ²/.			1·2·			9.98			32.00		
Tequila	70 cl	3 6/.			³/. 2·			7.10			29.00		
Hirondelle Wine	1.5	8⁴/			6/.12			4.00			9.00		
Crisps	Doz	14 6/.			1·3·12			1.06			1.80		
Benson & Hedges	Pkt	18			26			1.20			1.50		

ITEM	UNIT	O S	PURCHASES	TOTAL	C.S.	TOTAL	SALES	COST PRICE	AT COST	VALUATION	PRICE	RETAIL	PURCHASE
Harp Lager	Gall	78	11·33·22		33·9			3.60			8.40		
Barbican BTL	Doz	6/.	2		9/18/.4.			3.80			8.40		
Guinness PT	Doz	2/.			18/.			6.00			13.20		
Minerals Baby	Doz	38 4/.	12·20		4/14/.63/8·24.			1.60			4.80		
Lemonade 75 cl	Doz	7/.	3		4/·1·			2.10			18.00		
Grouse Whisky	1.5	18 4/.	6·6		10/1·7			14.80			50.40		
Bells Whisky	40 oz	7 3/.	12·		5/1 4/·3·6·			11.06			38.40		
Antiquary	Btl	2 4/.			4/·2			8.80			30.40		
Bristol Cream	Btl	3 7/.			4/·4/·2			3.97			10.50		
Sweet Martini	1.5	19/·1·			7/·			4.40			20.80		
Creme de Menthe	50 cl	6/·			6/·			5.10			21.00		
Drambuie	75 cl	17/·	3·3		1·2			9.98			32.00		
Tequila	70 cl	3 6/·			3/·2·			7.10			29.00		
Hirondelle Wine	1.5	8 4/·	6·6·		10/·12			4.00			9.30		
Crisps	Doz	14 6/·	12·		1·3·12			1.06			1.30		
Benson & Hedges	Pkt	18	20·		26			1.20			1.50		

ITEM	UNIT	O S	PURCHASES	TOTAL	C.S.	TOTAL	SALES	COST PRICE	CONS AT CCST	VALUATION	SELLING PRICE	CONS AT RETAIL	COST OF PURCHASE
Harp Lager	Gall	78	11·33-22	66	33·9	42	102	3.60			8.40		
Barbican BTL	Doz	6⁴⁄	2	2	6/ 18/ 6/	6²	2⁴⁄	3.80			8.40		
Guinness PT	Doz	2⁴⁄			18/	18/	5/	6.00			13.20		
Minerals Baby	Doz	38⁴⁄	12·20	32	4/ 16/ 63· 8·24	40⁄	30³⁄	1.60			4.80		
Lemonade 75 cl	Doz	7/	3	3	4/ 1·	14⁄	2³⁄	2.10			18.00		
Grouse Whisky	1.5	18⁴⁄	6·6	12	9/ 1-7	8⁄	21⁸⁄	14.80			50.40		
Bells Whisky	40 oz	7³⁄	12·	12	5/ 4/ 3·6·	9⁹⁄	9⁴⁄	11.06			38.40		
Antiquary	Btl	2⁄			1/ 2	2⁄		8.80			30.40		
Bristol Cream	Btl	3⁄			4/ 4/ 2	3	7/	3.97			10.50		
Sweet Martini	1.5	1⁹⁄	1	1	7/	7/	2²⁄	4.40			20.80		
Creme de Menthe	50 cl	6/			6/	6/	6/	5.10			21.00		
Drambuie	75 cl	1²⁄	3·3	6	1·2·	3	4²⁄	9.98			32.00		
Tequila	70 cl	3⁶⁄			3/ 2	2³⁄	1³⁄	7.10			29.00		
Hirondelle Wine	1.5	8⁴⁄	6·6	12	4/ 12	12⁶⁄	7⁸⁄	4.00			9.00		
Crisps	Doz	14⁶⁄	12	12	1·3-12	16	10⁴	1.06			1.80		
Benson & Hedges	Pkt	18	20	20	26	26	12	1.20			1.50		

ITEM	UNIT	O S	PURCHASES	TOTAL	C.S.	TOTAL	SALES	COST PRICE	CONS AT COST	VALUATION	SELLING PRICE	CONS AT RETAIL	COST OF PURCHASE
Harp Lager	Gall	78	11·33·22	66	33·9	42	102	3.60		151·20	8.40		237-60
Barbican BTL	Doz	6¼	2	2	6/.8/.4/..	6¼	2¼	3.80		23·43	8.40		7-60
Guinness PT	Doz	2¼			18/.	18/	6/	6.00		10-00	13.20		
Minerals Baby	Doz	38⁴/	12.20	32	4/.16/.63/.8.24.	40¼	30³/	1.60		64·13	4.80		51-20
Lemonade 75 cl	Doz	7/.	3	3	4/.1.	14/	2³/	2.10		2·80	18.00		6-30
Grouse Whisky	1.5	18⁴/	6·6	12	6/.1.7.	8⁶/	21⁸/	14.80		127·28	50.40		177-60
Bells Whisky	40 oz	7³/.	12·	12	5/.4/.3·6	9⁹/	9⁴/	11.06		109-49	38.40		132-72
Antiquary	Btl	2⁷/.			1/.2	2¹/.		8.80		18·48	30.40		
Bristol Cream	Btl	3⁷/.			4/.6/.2	3	7/.	3.97		11-91	10.50		
Sweet Martini	1.5	1⁹/.	1	1	7/.	7/	2²/	4.40		3·08	20.80		4-40
Creme de Menthe	50 cl	6/.			6/	6/		5.10		3·06	21.00		
Drambuie	75 cl	1⁴/.	3·3	6	1.2.	3	4⁴/	9.98		29·94	32.00		59-88
Tequila	70 cl	3⁶/.			3/.2	2³/	13/	7.10		16·33	29.00		
Hirondelle Wine	1.5	8⁴/.	6·6·	12	6/.12	12⁴/	7⁸/.	4.00		50·40	9.30		48-00
Crisps	Doz	14⁴/.	12/	12	1·3·12.	16	10⁶/.	1.06		16·96	1.30		12-72
Benson & Hedges	Pkt	18	20.	20	26	26	12	1.20		31·20	1.50		24-00

ITEM	UNIT	O S	PURCHASES	TOTAL	C.S.	TOTAL	SALES	COST PRICE	CONS AT COST	VALUATION	SELLING PRICE	CONS AT RETAIL	COST OF PURCHASE
Harp Lager	Gall	78.	11.33.22	66	33.9	42	102	3.60	361.20	151.20	8.40	856.80	237.60
Barbican BTL	Doz	6⁹/.	2	2	6/.18/.4	6²/.	2⁴/.	3.80	8.87	23.43	8.40	19.60	7.60
Guinness PT	Doz	2/.			18/.	18/.	5/.	6.00	2.50	10.00	13.20	5.49	
Minerals Baby	Doz	38⁴/.	12.20	32	4/.14/.6²8.24	40¹/.	30³/.	1.60	48.40	64.13	4.80	145.20	51.20
Lemonade 75 cl	Doz	7/.	3	3	4/.1	1⁴/.	2³/.	2.10	4.73	2.80	18.00	40.50	6.30
Grouse Whisky	1.5	18⁴/.	6.6	12	4/.1.7	8⁶/.	21⁸/.	14.80	322.64	127.28	50.40	1098.72	177.60
Bells Whisky	40 oz	7³/.	12	12	5/.4.3.6.	99/.	9⁴/.	11.06	103.96	109.69	38.40	360.96	132.72
Antiquary	Btl	2/.			1/.2.	2/.	-	8.80		18.48	30.40		
Bristol Cream	Btl	37/.			4/.6/.2	3	7/.	3.97	2.78	11.91	10.50	7.35	
Sweet Martini	1.5	1⁹/.	1.	1	7/.	7/.	2²/.	4.40	9.68	3.08	20.80	46.76	4.40
Creme de Menthe	50 cl	9/.			6/.	6/	-	5.10		3.06	21.00		
Drambuie	75 cl	1²/.	3.3.	6	1.2	3	4⁴/.	9.98	41.92	29.94	32.00	134.40	59.88
Tequila	70 cl	3⁴/.			3/.2	2³/.	1³/.	7.10	9.23	16.33	29.00	37.70	
Hirondelle Wine	1.5	8⁴/.	6.6	12	6/.12	12⁶/.	7⁸/.	4.00	31.20	50.40	9.00	70.20	48.00
Crisps	Doz	14⁹/.	12.	12	1.3.12.	16	10⁶/.	1.06	11.13	16.96	1.80	18.90	12.72
Benson & Hedges	Pkt	18	20	20	26	26	12	1.20	14.40	31.20	1.50	18.00	24.00

In these sample stock sheets, spirits are still expressed in tenths, and cigarettes in single packets. Beers, minerals and crisps have been calculated in dozens; but many Stocktakers prefer, having taken their physical count in dozens, to convert the total into tenths by using the table shown on page 95. Either method is acceptable; the system used depends on the individual concerned.

'Valuation' and 'Cost of Purchases' Column (see stock sheet, page 109)

The 'Valuation' figure is arrived at by multiplying the cost price of the particular product by the closing stock figure. It is this figure which would ultimately be entered on a Certificate of Valuation. The 'Cost of Purchases' is reached in the same way, and is the cost price multiplied by the total purchase figure.

e.g.   Drambuie –

Valuation figure £9.98 × 3 = £29.94 (excluding V.A.T.);
Cost of purchases £9.98 × 6 = £59.88 (excluding V.A.T.).

'Consumption at Cost' and 'Consumption at Retail' Columns (see stock sheet, page 110)

This is the volume of stock sold at both cost and retail price.

e.g.   Hirondelle Wine –

(a)   Calculating sales at cost price:
        7.8 × £4.00 (cost price per bottle excluding V.A.T.) = £31.20;
(b)   Calculating sales at retail price:
        7.8 × £9.00   (retail   price   per   bottle   including
        V.A.T.) = £70.20.

Gross Profits

From the figures entered, the Stocktaker will now be able to work out any gross profits which he requires. The formula used is as follows:–

Gross Profit = Retail price (excluding V.A.T.) – cost price. Gross profit percentage is the above figure divided by the retail price, excluding V.A.T., and multiplied by 100.

Gross profits per item would be as follows:–

	Cost Price £	Retail Price £	Retail Price (excl. V.A.T.) £	Gross Profit %
Harp Lager (gal.)	3.60	8.40	7.30	50.7
Barbican (btl.)	3.80	8.40	7.30	48.0
Guinness (pt)	6.00	13.20	11.48	47.7
Minerals (baby)	1.60	4.80	4.17	61.7
Lemonade (75 cl)	2.10	18.00	15.65	86.6
Grouse Whisky (150 cl)	14.80	50.40	43.83	66.2
Bells Whisky (40 oz)	11.06	38.40	33.39	66.8
Antiquary (btl.)	8.80	30.40	26.43	66.7
Bristol Cream (btl.)	3.97	10.50	9.13	56.5
Sweet Martini (150 cl)	4.40	20.80	18.09	75.7
Creme de Menthe (50 cl)	5.10	21.00	18.26	72.0
Drambuie (75 cl)	9.98	32.00	27.83	64.1
Tequila (70 cl)	7.10	29.00	25.22	71.8
Hirondelle Wine (150 cl)	4.00	9.00	7.83	48.9
Crisps (doz.)	1.06	1.80	1.57	32.4
Benson and Hedges (pkt)	1.20	1.50	1.30	8.0

If the Stocktaker is advising the client about what he needs to charge, per unit measure, to maintain specified percentages, he would use the following formula:–

$$\frac{\text{Cost price}}{(100 - \text{specified percentage})} \times (100 + \text{V.A.T. percentage})$$

$$= \text{Selling price.}$$

The following examples, relating to Harp Lager and Grouse Whisky, assume a V.A.T. rate of 15%.

To achieve 50.7% profit from Harp larger –

$$\frac{3.60}{(100 - 50.7)} \times (100 + 15) = \frac{3.60}{49.3} \times 115 = 0.073 \times 115$$

$$= \text{£8.40 per gallon.}$$

If a client wished to increase his gross profit to 55% on this particular product, his calculation would be as follows:–

$$\frac{3.60}{(100 - 55)} \times (100 + 15) = \frac{3.60}{45} \times 115 = 0.08 \times 115$$

$$= \text{£9.20 per gallon}$$

$$\text{or } \frac{9.20}{8} = \text{£1.15 per pint.}$$

If he wished to increase his gross profit on spirits to 70%, his calculation on Grouse Whisky would be as follows:–

$$\frac{14.80}{(100-70)} \times (100+15) = \frac{14.80}{30} \times 115 = 0.493 \times 115$$

$$= £56.70$$

$$\text{or } \frac{56.70}{63} = 90\text{p per measure.}$$

PROGRESSING AND UNDERSTANDING THE REPORT

From the calculations already prepared on the stock sheet, the report can be completed as shown on page 114.

As already indicated, the format of stock reports varies considerably. Some are computerised, and others are calculated manually, showing no more than the surplus or deficit figure. Each Stocktaker sets his own standards and clients, similarly, must decide just how much information they want and need. Almost any amount can be produced manually or by computers; below are listed some of the more common headings, with explanations.

Sales Mix and Ratio

'Sales mix' refers to the quantity of each item sold in relation to the quantities of others. It is the mix of products, and is generally shown as a sales ratio figure. If, on total sales of £2,859.58, draught beer income was £856.80, that would mean that the percentage ratio of sales was 29.9%, i.e. $(856.80 \div 2,859.58) \times 100$. If the gross profit on draught beer was only 40% and the sales ratio in excess of 50%, then the Stocktaker would be able to explain to his client that because 50% of all his sales were only returning a 40% gross profit, he would never be likely to achieve high profitability. Sales mix is particularly important if reasons are being sought for fluctuating gross profits. In the stock report shown on the preceding pages, draught beer sales represent just under 30% of total sales, while spirits represent 51%. If this position were to be reversed, the overall gross profit would be considerably reduced, because of the different profit margins attainable on spirits and on beer. If Customs and Excise maintain that the premises should be achieving a certain figure, it may be possible to prove (in favour of the client) that because of sales-mix ratios, this anticipated gross profit is unobtainable.

Gross Profit – Actual and Estimated

Unless income is recorded separately for each individual item, it is not possible to produce an actual gross profit for every commodity;

INCORPORATED SOCIETY OF LICENSED TRADE STOCKTAKERS

NAME: _Society Hotel_

STOCKTAKING SUMMARY PERIOD FROM: ___3 / 9 / 88___ TO: ___9 / 10 / 88___ (incl)

	CONSUMPTION AT COST PRICE	CONSUMPTION AT SELLING PRICE	SECTION GROSS PROFIT %	SALES MIX RATIO %	STOCK VALUATION	VALUE OF PURCHASES
Draught Beer	367 – 20	856 – 80	50·7	29·9	151 – 20	237 – 60
Bottled Beer	11 – 37	25 – 09	47·9	·9	33 – 43	7 – 60
Minerals	53 – 13	185 – 70	67·1	6·5	66 – 93	57 – 50
Spirits	426 – 60	1459 – 68	66·4	51·1	255 – 25	310 – 32
Port and Sherry	2 – 78	7 – 35	56·5	·2	11 – 91	
Vermouth	9 – 68	45 – 76	75·7	1·6	3 – 08	4 – 40
Liqueurs	51 – 15	172 – 10	65·8	6·0	49 – 33	59 – 88
Wines	31 – 20	70 – 20	48·9	2·5	50 – 40	48 – 00
Tobacco	14 – 40	18 – 00	8·0	·6	31 – 20	24 – 00
Crisps/Nuts	11 – 13	18 – 90	32·3	·7	16 – 96	12 – 72
Container Deposits						
Sundries						
Total	978 – 64	2859 – 58	60·6	100·0	669 – 69	762 – 02
Allowances						
Total	978 – 64	2859 – 58				

ESTIMATED GROSS PROFIT		ACTUAL GROSS PROFIT		SURPLUS/DEFICIT	
Consumption at retail (excl. VAT and allowances)	2486·59	Income (excl. VAT)	2417·53	Income (incl. VAT)	2780·16
Less consumption at cost	978·64	Less consumption at cost	978·64	Less consumption at retail	2859·58
Estimated GP	1507·95	Actual GP	1438·89	Deficit	£ 79·42
Estimated GP percentage	60·6%	Actual GP percentage	59·5%	Deficit percentage	2·8%

so estimated ones have to be prepared by using cost and retail extensions. Actual gross profits can only be calculated on the total figure, as shown below:–

Income (excl. V.A.T.)	£2,417.53	
Consumption at cost	£978.64	
Gross Profit	£1,438.89	(59.5% of Income)

The estimated gross profit is the figure, after the deduction of allowances and V.A.T., which the premises would have achieved had there been no surplus or deficit. For this calculation, 'income' is replaced by 'consumption at retail', thus:–

Sales at retail value (excl. V.A.T.)	£2,486.59
Allowances (excl.V.A.T.)(see page 118)	£104.52
Consumption at retail (excl. V.A.T.)	£2,382.07

Then –

Consumption at retail (excl. V.A.T.)	£2,382.07
Consumption at cost	£978.64
Estimated Gross Profit	£1,403.43 (58.9% of Consumption at retail)

The actual gross profit is based on the exact income figures, whereas the estimated one is based on the retail value of sales. The difference between the two will be caused by a surplus or deficit figure: if there is a deficit, the actual gross profit will be lower than the estimated one, and *vice versa*. In this example, the actual gross profit is greater than the estimated gross profit. There is, therefore, a surplus: £1,438.89 − £1,403.43 = £35.46 (excluding V.A.T.) (see page 118).

By using this information, the Stocktaker will be able to tell his client what gross profit he has achieved, what he would have made had there been no surplus or deficit, and what percentage profit his prices are geared to produce on the existing sales mix, without allowances. To calculate this percentage, he would divide the difference between the value of sales at retail (less V.A.T.) and the cost of sales, by the former (see section on '"Consumption at Cost" and "Consumption at Retail" Columns'), and multiply by 100.

Days Stockholding

This information is sometimes given to clients as a guide as to whether they are holding the correct levels of stock. The number of days stockholding of each item is normally produced, but in some instances this information is only given for each category of item (e.g. beers, wines or spirits). Depending on the location of the premises, it is usual to recommend that two to three weeks' requirements be held in stock at any one time. If the establishment is remote and supplies are not easy to obtain, then obviously the number of days stockholding would increase accordingly.

The information is not difficult to produce. If, over a six-week stock period, a client uses 62 bottles of whisky and has left in stock 38, his days stockholding would be 25.8:–

$62 \div 42 = 1.47$ bottles per day;
$38 \div 1.47 = 25.8$ days stockholding.

Using the same formula with the draught beer figures on the sample stock sheet (scc page 110), the result would be 14.8 days stockholding:–

102 (sales) $\div 36$ (days in period) $= 2.83$ gallons per day;
42 (stock in hand) $\div 2.83 = 14.8$ days stockholding.

Reference should be made to the section on 'Overstocking' (page 30). Stock levels should be kept to an absolute minimum, for money in the bank is preferable to stock of the same value which is unlikely to sell for some time.

It is only sensible to take advantage of special offers when the product will sell quickly: if one free case is on offer against the purchase of three, it is not worth participating if all four will lie in the cellar for many months afterwards.

If days stockholding figures are being produced on a group basis (e.g. spirits or minerals), some items such as liqueurs or wines will frequently show up as being grossly overstocked. This happens because of the range which has to be kept, so many items of which rarely sell. There is little the Stocktaker can do, other than advise his client of the reason for this high stockholding.

Stock on Hand

The term 'stock on hand' relates to goods on the premises at the time of stock. A valuation should include all empty bottles, cases and full CO_2 cylinders, together with any other chargeable containers. On the basis of his count of full bottles, the Stocktaker will have to add the value of such bottles as are chargeable to the valuation; those which do not have a deposit value should of course be excluded.

If a year-end valuation is required, it may not always be possible for the Stocktaker to be present on the actual day. If this is the case, he will have to make an adjustment to the valuation (see page 139).

Cumulative Figures

Sometimes, for internal reasons, a client requires the Stocktaker to maintain cumulative figures. A date has to be established, usually the year end, and the procedure is for successive stocks regularly to be added to the previous ones. Thus, at any given time, the client would know his gross profit to date and his overall surplus or deficit figure for the year. It is normal practice to clear this figure at the end of each financial year, and recommence for the next.

Consumption at Cost and Retail

To produce an overall estimated gross profit, the Stocktaker will adopt exactly the same procedure as he did to establish gross profit figures for individual items. He will require both the 'consumption at cost' and the 'consumption at retail' figures – the latter because they are based on selling prices inclusive of V.A.T., which he must remove before he makes his calculations. On a stock report, if consumption at cost is £978.64 and at retail £2,859.58, the gross profit will be 60.6%, calculated as follows:–

£2,859.58 less V.A.T. at 15% = £2,486.59;

$$\frac{2,486.59 - 978.64}{2,486.59} \times 100 = 60.6\%.$$

Purchases

The purchase figure shown on the stock report should be much the same as the invoice totals. There will, however, be small discrepancies because of charges and credits relating to containers, if these are not included in the Stocktaker's figures.

Surplus or Deficit

Known by some Stocktakers as 'overage or shortage', this figure at the end of a stock report indicates whether sufficient money has been taken to cover the retail value of sales. If during a stock period ten bottles of whisky have been sold at 80p per dash, the Stocktaker (assuming the use of a one-sixth gill measure) will expect the business to have recouped £256.00. He makes a comparable calculation for every single item on the premises, and finds a retail value of sales which should agree with the cash taken. If the cash figure is higher, there is a surplus; if lower, a deficit. The percentage either way is calculated by dividing that (surplus or deficit) figure by the income including V.A.T.

On the sample stock sheet (page 114) there is a deficit of £79.42, but no allowances have been taken into account, and the introduction of these could considerably change the end result. (Allowances are discussed in detail on page 126.) At the conclusion of this report, a figure of £120.20 has been taken into account, and the new report (on page 119) clearly indicates the difference in the estimated gross profit figure. Further, the entering of the allowances figure has turned what was a deficit into a small surplus of £40.78. The actual gross profit figure is not altered, because this is the figure actually achieved on the premises without any other factors being taken into account.

A commonly-used alternative method of showing the surplus or deficit figure is as follows:–

Consumption at retail	£2,859.58
Allowances	£120.20
Estimated sales	£2,739.38

Then –

Income (incl. V.A.T.)	£2,780.16
Estimated sales	£2,739.38
Surplus	£40.78

The result can be affected by other factors, such as surcharges or transfers included in the main body of the report, and these would all be incorporated as necessary. Full details are given on page 129.

ADDITIONAL PROCEDURES

Proving the Result

It is possible to prove that gross profits are correct by using the basic trading account (see page 124). It is normal practice to take the purchase information from the invoice totals, excluding the deposit element if empty bottles and cases have not been included. For this particular exercise, the cost of purchases has been extended on the stock sheets.

Opening stock	£886.32	Closing stock	£669.69
Purchases	£762.02	Income	£2,417.53
Gross Proft	£1,438.88		
	£3,087.22		£3,087.22

Gross Profit	59.5%

Allowances Deducted at Cost

In some instances, particularly in larger units where internal controls are maintained, transfers are recorded at cost and the Stock-

INCORPORATED SOCIETY OF LICENSED TRADE STOCKTAKERS

NAME: _Society Hotel_

STOCKTAKING SUMMARY PERIOD FROM: 3/9/88 TO: 9/10/88 (incl)

	CONSUMPTION AT COST PRICE	CONSUMPTION AT SELLING PRICE	SECTION GROSS PROFIT %	SALES MIX RATIO %	STOCK VALUATION	VALUE OF PURCHASES
Draught Beer	367−20	856−80	50·7	29·9	151−20	237−60
Bottled Beer	11−37	25−09	47·9	·9	33−43	7−60
Minerals	53−13	185−70	67·1	6·5	66−93	57−50
Spirits	426−60	1459−68	66·4	51·1	255−25	310−32
Port and Sherry	2−78	7−35	56·5	·2	11−91	
Vermouth	9−68	45−76	75·7	1·6	3−08	4−40
Liqueurs	51−15	172−10	65·8	6·0	49−33	59−88
Wines	31−20	70−20	48·9	2·5	50−40	48−00
Tobacco	14−40	18−00	8·0	·6	31−20	24−00
Crisps/Nuts	11−13	18−90	32·3	·7	16−96	12−72
Container Deposits						
Sundries						
Total	978−64	2859−58	60·6	100·0	669−69	762−02

Allowances
Pipe Cleaning		30−00
Wastage		24−00
Kitchen		66−20
Total	978−64	2739−38

ESTIMATED GROSS PROFIT		ACTUAL GROSS PROFIT		SURPLUS/DEFICIT ▲	
Consumption at retail (excl. VAT and allowances)	2382·07	Income (excl. VAT)	2417·53	Income (incl. VAT)	2780·16
Less consumption at cost	978·64	Less consumption at cost	978·64	Less consumption at retail	2739·38
Estimated GP	1403·43	Actual GP	1438·89	Surplus	£40·78
Estimated GP percentage	58·9%	Actual GP percentage	59·5%	Surplus percentage	1·5%

INCORPORATED SOCIETY OF LICENSED TRADE STOCKTAKERS

NAME: *Society Hotel*

STOCKTAKING SUMMARY PERIOD FROM: 3/9/88 TO: 9/10/88 (incl)

	CONSUMPTION AT COST PRICE	CONSUMPTION AT SELLING PRICE	SECTION GROSS PROFIT %	SALES MIX RATIO %	STOCK VALUATION	VALUE OF PURCHASES
Draught Beer	367−20	856−80	50·7	29·9	151−20	237−60
Bottled Beer	11−37	25−09	47·9	·9	33−43	7−60
Minerals	53−13	185−70	67·1	6·5	66−93	57−50
Spirits	426−60	1459−68	66·4	51·1	255−25	310−32
Port and Sherry	2−78	7−35	56·5	·2	11−91	
Vermouth	9−68	45−76	75·7	1·6	3−08	4−40
Liqueurs	51−15	172−10	65·8	6·0	49−33	59−88
Wines	31−20	70−20	48·9	2·5	50−40	48−00
Tobacco	14−40	18−00	8·0	·6	31−20	24−00
Crisps/Nuts	11−13	18−90	32·3	·7	16−96	12−72
Container Deposits						
Sundries						
Transferred to Kitchen	(22−68)	(66−20)				
Total	955−96	2793−38	60·6	100·0	669−69	762−02

Allowances

Pipe Cleaning   30−00
Wastage   24−00

Total	955−96	2739−38

ESTIMATED GROSS PROFIT		ACTUAL GROSS PROFIT		SURPLUS/DEFICIT	
Consumption at retail (excl. VAT and allowances)	2382·07	Income (excl. VAT)	2417·53	Income (incl. VAT)	2780·16
Less consumption at cost	955·96	Less consumption at cost	955·96	Less consumption at retail	2739·38
Estimated GP	1426·11	Actual GP	1461·57		
Estimated GP percentage	59·8%	Actual GP percentage	60·4%	Surplus	£40·78
				Surplus percentage	1·5%

taker is required to show these transfers within the main body of the report rather than as an allowance. It is not always possible to credit the purchases column, because stock is often transferred by measures. In the case of food, the chef may requisition a single brandy or a double port, or a large sherry for making trifle. When this happens, the value of the stock at retail will be totalled, but the cost of the stock will not be determined in detail: it will be calculated from the retail price by the application of a standard cost of sale.

What the Stocktaker is in fact doing, on the sample Stocktaking Summary (page 120), is to remove the £66.20 from the allowances section, and to credit his sales at selling price by the same amount and his sales at cost by £22.68. The latter figure is the full retail value less V.A.T., multiplied by the cost of sale which in this case is 39.4% (the difference between the anticipated gross profit and 100%). If all the transfers had been of spirits, the Stocktaker might elect to use a different cost of sale percentage, in this case 33.6%; he would use his initiative in deciding on the most accurate alternative.

Once these two figures have been established, they must both be removed from the stock sheets. This is done quite simply, by setting up another line with the appropriate heading (e.g. 'transferred to Kitchen') and the figure 1 shown in brackets (i.e. minus) in the purchases column.

The final stock report would now be as shown on page 120.

Because allowances have been reduced, the estimated and actual gross profit figures have changed; but the overall deficit/surplus figure is as before. The allowance figure of £22.68 has now been extracted at cost, and should be entered in the Goods Received Book (Food) (see page 163).

VALUATIONS AND TRADING ACCOUNTS

Valuations

A valuation of stock on hand is quite simply a statement indicating the value of goods held at particular premises at a given time. It might be required for a change of ownership, or (more often) for use by the accountant, who will incorporate it into his accounts at the end of a trading period. In either instance, the procedure remains the same.

Stock would be counted in the manner described on page 96, and entered under one of eleven or more categories. Bottles (including full ones) and cases do have considerable value, so these should be included and would form part of the Certificate of Valuation (see page 123). Up-to-date cost prices must be used; and the analysis should be prepared exclusive of V.A.T.

STOCK VALUATION AT COST

ITEM	UNIT	COUNT	TOTAL	COST	VALUATION
Mild	Gall	11·36·4	51	3.80	193·80
Lager	Gall	14·54·18	86	3.93	337·98
					£531·78
Newcastle Pts	Doz	6/. 94/. 8/.	10.5	6.80	71·40
Guinness ½ pt	Doz	13/. 5/. 11/.	2·583	4.10	10·59
Cider Cans	Doz	87/. 12/. 3/.	10.0	6.66	66·60
					£148·59
Lemonade Ltr	Doz	8/. 4. 7/.	5.25	3.50	18·37
Fruit Juices	Doz	58·64/. 3/.	64.583	2.38	153·70
Post Mix	Ltr	10. 18. 7	35	3.60	126.00
					£298.07
Grouse Whisky	1.5	8/. 16/. 12.	14·4	15.40	221.76
Bacardi	Half	18. 12.	30.	4.90	147.00
Canadian Club	Bt	10. 1/. 7/.	10.8	8.92	96.33
					£465.09
Bristol Cream	Bt	8/. 1/. 12	12.9	4.20	54.18
Ruby Port	Bt	7. 3/. 18/.	9.1	5.01	45.59
					£ 99.77
Vermouth	1.5	37/. 15. 3/.	19	4.92	93.48
Green Ginger	Bt	8/. 3. 1/.	3.9	3.00	11.70
					£105.18
Drambuie	Bt	8/. 3/. 9	10.1	10.90	110.09
Benedictine	Bt	3/. 8/. 6	7.1	11.47	81.43
					£191.52
Wine 20 Ltr	Ltr	5.20.4	29	3.15	91·35
Beaujolais	Bt	126/. 7.	19.6	3.50	68.60
					£159.95
Hamlet	Ind	18.6.100	124	0.28	34.72
Matches	Doz	12. 8/. 6	18.666	0.61	11.38
					£46.10
Crisps	Doz	18.44/. 6	28.333	1.30	36.83
Dry Roasted Nuts	Doz	6. 3/. 9	15.25	1.88	28.67
					£65.50
Cases	Ind	8.80.6	94	1.00	94.00
Bottles	Doz	120.8.672/.	195.166	0.52	101.49
					£195.49

This information can now be entered on a Certificate of Valuation.

The eleven most usual headings are shown below. There is no fixed order: this varies from one Stocktaker to another.

1. Draught beer
2. Bottled and canned beer
3. Minerals
4. Spirits
5. Sherry and port
6. Vermouth and apéritifs
7. Liqueurs
8. Wines
9. Tobacco
10. Sundries (nuts, crisps etc.)
11. Containers

A condensed extended stocktaking sheet, and the final Certificate of Valuation, are shown in the accompanying examples.

Certificate of Valuation
Society Stocktaking Services Ltd.

Premises ....

We certify that a fair valuation of stock on hand at the above premises cost value excluding V.A.T. after close of business on Saturday 31st December 1988 would be Two thousand three hundred and seven pounds and four pence made up as follows

Draught beer	531.78
Bottled/canned beer	148.59
Minerals	298.07
Spirits	465.09
Sherry/port	99.77
Vermouth/apéritifs	105.18
Liqueurs	191.52
Wines	159.95
Tobacco	46.10
Sundries	65.50
Containers	195.49
Stock on hand (excl. V.A.T.)	£2,307.04

Stocktaker's signature ....

The style of this certificate will vary considerably from one Stocktaker to another, but it will usually contain both a breakdown of stock and the date, and be signed by a responsible person as being true and accurate. Additional lines can be added for other items, such as food, cleaning materials etc. If the stock is not done on the due date, an adjustment may have to be made; for further information, see page 139.

Trading Accounts

Trading accounts simply indicate to a client the gross profit figure and percentage that he has made over a given period. They do not tell him what he should have made, and supply far less information than does the extended stock result (see page 83). However, many clients do request them; and if the Stocktaker is asked to prepare one, he should proceed as follows:–

1. Count the stock on hand and value it – this becomes the opening stock.
2. At the end of a given period, re-count the stock and again value it – this becomes the closing stock.
3. Extract from invoices all purchases relative to the period. If the invoices have not yet been received, the cost must be calculated from delivery notes, and deposits and containers both received and returned during the period must be taken into account.
4. Deduct any returns, credits or discounts from the purchase figure.
5. Establish the income figure for the period. Ensure that it is exact.
6. Calculate as follows:–

Period 1 January 1988–31 January 1988

Opening stock	£2,307.04	Income	£6,103.79
Purchases	£3,081.52	Less V.A.T.	£796.15
	£5,388.56		£5,307.64
Less closing stock	£2,727.66	Less stock used	£2,660.90
Value of stock used	£2,660.90	Gross Profit	£2,646.74

or, as a percentage:–

$$\frac{\text{Gross Profit} \times 100}{\text{Net income}} = \frac{2,646.77 \times 100}{5,307.64} = 49.87\%.$$

The only unknown quantity in this equation is the 'Gross Profit' figure; but it can be arrived at by a simple subtraction.

An alternative and perhaps more usual method of setting out the trading account is as follows:–

Opening stock	£2,307.04	Closing stock	£2,727.66
Purchases		Income	
(excl. V.A.T.)	£3,081.52	(less V.A.T.)	£5,307.64
Gross Profit	£2,646.74		
	£8,035.30		£8,035.30

or, as a percentage – 49.87%.

To summarise:–
Income + closing stock – opening stock – purchases = Gross Profit;
Gross Profit ÷ income (less V.A.T.) × 100 = Gross Profit percentage.
For examples including allowances, see page 131.

CHAPTER 6
ALLOWANCES AND ADJUSTMENTS

Whatever the size of his premises (multi-bar, or single unit), every licensee should keep and show to the Stocktaker an accurate record of allowances, analysing all items which have left the bar – whether as wastage, gift or promotion – either without payment, or at a price lower than the normal retail one. The following are some examples of items for which allowances should be made.

Pipe Cleaning

As draught beer already in the lines has to be 'pulled off' before the pipes are cleaned, a loss occurs. In most cases, it is left to the manager or proprietor to assess the number of pints which are wasted, and often the amount given to the Stocktaker is inflated. It is normal for pipes to be cleaned on a weekly basis; but sometimes it is done every second week, or even once a month. It is important for the number of pipe cleans to be recorded, so that an accurate assessment of wastage can be made. Where actual figures are not kept, the following table will assist the Stocktaker in working out a fair and reasonable allowance.

$\frac{3}{4}$ inch piping – one pint per   6.5 feet
$\frac{5}{8}$ inch piping – one pint per   9.4 feet
$\frac{1}{2}$ inch piping – one pint per 14.7 feet
$\frac{3}{8}$ inch piping – one pint per 26.1 feet
$\frac{1}{4}$ inch piping – one pint per 58.8 feet
$\frac{3}{16}$ inch piping – one pint per 104.7 feet
$\frac{1}{8}$ inch piping – one pint per 247.5 feet

Small-bore pipes are generally installed from the cooler to the dispensing equipment only, and in an average bar the volume of beer in these would be as follows:–

flash cooler to head   – $\frac{1}{3}$ pint
dual flash cooler to head – $\frac{2}{3}$ pint

In some cases, an overall allowance (incorporating both pipe cleaning and wastage) is made at a rate of 3% of total draught beer sales,

126

or 1 gallon in every 36. This 'rule of thumb' assessment is unlikely to be accurate, given the variability of lengths of piping.

Ullage or Wastage

'Ullage' originally referred to the amount of liquor needed to fill up a cask which was not quite full – hence the need for an 'ullage allowance'; its more common use today is as a general term for all items that are considered unsaleable. It might apply to bottles with necks broken when decapped, corked wines, drinks returned, beer in drip trays at the end of the day, or general wastage and spillage. All such items should be recorded by staff, and details should be given to the Stocktaker. Occasionally a fixed allowance is given, but it is always a good idea to insist on records being maintained, even if only to keep staff aware of the high costs involved in wastage.

Staff Drinks

In some premises it is customary, at the end of an evening, to provide staff with a free drink before going home. Each must be accurately recorded at full retail value, so that the necessary allowance can be made.

Kitchen Drinks

To compensate for the effects of heat in a kitchen, chefs are often permitted to have free beer. This is commonly known as a 'sweat pint', and would be treated in the same way as staff drinks.

Kitchen Transfers

It is always best, where there is a substantial volume of liquor used in the kitchen, to buy in on a totally separate invoice, thus divorcing the transaction from the liquor operation. Where this is impracticable, the procedure for internal transfers (described on page 129) should be applied.

If the Stocktaker is producing results for liquor only, and if he is aware that there are transfers which are not being allocated to the kitchen, he should normally transfer them out at retail only. The liquor gross profit would thus be less than anticipated, and the catering operation would (at least in theory) show a compensating increase. This method would however ensure that gross profits were kept in line with those produced by the accountant at the end of the year.

Alternatively, if the transfer is allowed at full cost and retail without the cost being charged to the kitchen, the gross profit shown on the liquor operation will be correct, but will differ from that produced by the accountant.

Promotions

Promotions play an important part in the licensed trade, and whether they are internally or externally operated, full records must be maintained so that proper allowances can be given. For a promotion that is undertaken by a company marketing a product, losses incurred by the establishment will be recouped either in stock or cash (see page 135). Where internal promotions take place, a note of any loss in normal income should be retained and given to the Stocktaker. Unless proper controls operate, it is likely that high surpluses or deficits will occur.

'Happy Hours'

'Happy hours', which are becoming more and more popular in licensed establishments, inevitably place demands upon the Stocktaker's expertise in calculating adjustments for 'losses'. In many cases, 'happy hour' prices are exactly half the normal selling ones, so that all the Stocktaker has to do is to allow 100% of the takings for the 'happy hour' period. It is imperative that a till reading be taken at both beginning and end, or that lines be drawn on the till roll at the appropriate times, so that takings at reduced prices can be assessed. In some cases, the 'happy hour' prices are merely reduced, and it is up to the Stocktaker to work out the best way to assess the allowance. With the help of itemised till rolls, it is possible to calculate the amount of pints of beer or nips of whisky sold at reduced prices (see page 23); without this facility, however, it would be advisable to work on a percentage system, as shown under 'Uplifts for Price Differences' (see page 136), using the method described but treating the difference as an allowance rather than a surcharge.

Management/Personal Consumption

Full allowances at retail must be given for any stock consumed personally by the management or proprietor, unless it is being internally transferred at cost value to personal use.

Cheap Sales

If a customer purchases a bottle of whisky over the bar counter, it is probable that he will pay the off-sales price. As the Stocktaker will calculate his selling price at full retail value, he will need to allow for any difference, or a deficit will occur. Bottles of sizes not sold by the measure would generally be entered on the extended stock report at off-sales prices, so it is important to keep a note of any products, including wine, for which the full retail price is not obtained.

Presentation of Allowances

Allowances represent a figure for stock which has in effect been used, but for which a reduced income or no income has been received. The gross profit is affected because, although the stock has been purchased through the business, no retail price has been paid. So that the client can monitor and control his allowances, the Stocktaker is advised to show them in detail and under appropriate headings, for example:–

Pipe Cleaning	£46.80
Ullage	£39.00
Kitchen	£2.86
Promotions	£12.40
Happy Hour	£123.57
Management	£8.60
Cheap Sales	£10.00
Staff	NIL
Total:	£243.23

Stock Transfers (Internal)

Transactions entailing allowances generally relate to the liquor operation, and because the cost figure is not affected, the allowances will only be deducted from consumption at retail. However, in large establishments stock is often transferred between departments, and such movement is recorded through the bookkeeping system. If these transfers were substantial but were only being allowed against consumption on the retail side, the actual gross profit would be reduced quite considerably.

If stock is being charged to another department at cost, the Stocktaker will be able to deduct it from his figures at both purchase and retail price (see page 130). As a result, the overall gross profit on liquor will not suffer, and true percentage profits will be obtained for the other departments.

It is up to the Stocktaker to establish the system being operated by his client, and to adjust his figures in a compatible manner: if their systems are not the same, the figures produced by the accountant at the end of the year will differ considerably, and the client will lose confidence.

Typical areas for liquor transfers are listed below, and the subsequent examples show the different results obtained, first without, and then with, the transfers being taken into account.

Kitchen — Where brandy, wine etc. are used in the preparation of dishes;

Promotions   – Where goodwill drinks are given free of
              charge to generate new business;
Conferences   – Where mineral water, cordials etc. are put on
              tables for delegates attending meetings;
Housekeeping – Where miniature bottles of spirit or sherry are
              left in guests' rooms;
Management   – Where liquor is taken for the personal
              consumption of the management or the clients
              they entertain.

Result without transfers:–

Income excl. V.A.T.	£8,695	Income incl. V.A.T.	£10,000
Consumption		Consumption	
at cost	£4,960	at retail	£10,160
Gross Profit	£3,735	Deficit	£160
	(42.9%)		(1.6%)

Result with transfers as follows:–

	Cost value excl. V.A.T.	Retail value incl. V.A.T.
Transfer to Kitchen:		
1 × 40 oz Brandy	£16.00	£45.60
2 × bottle Port	£9.00	£19.40
	£25.00	£65.00
Transfer to Conference:		
10 doz. litres Cordials	£62.00	£105.00
5 doz. litres Perrier	£27.00	£72.00
	£89.00	£177.00

The result would now be calculated as follows:–

Income excl. V.A.T.	£8,695	Income incl. V.A.T.	£10,000
Consumption		Consumption	
at cost after		at retail after	
transfers	£4,846	transfers	£9,918
Gross Profit	£3,849	Surplus	£82
	(44.2%)		(0.8%)

If the £25.00 'to Kitchen' and £89.00 'to Conference' were not
transferred at cost, the gross profit for liquor would still be the
original 42.9% with a surplus of £82:–

Income excl. V.A.T.	£8,695	Income incl. V.A.T.	£10,000
Consumption		Consumption	
at cost	£4,960	at retail after transfers	£9,918
Gross Profit	£3,735	Surplus	£82
	(42.9%)		(0.8%)

This type of adjustment can also be made in reverse, with stock being transferred from other departments to the liquor operation. Items such as lemons, cherries, bulk peanuts or cream are quite often transferred from kitchen to bar, and if the cost of food purchases is being reduced by their value, then it should be included as a purchase on the liquor stocks. However, as these goods are usually given away at no charge, a retail value rarely applies. The following example shows how to incorporate transfers, both from and to the bar, into a result.

Stock transferred from kitchen to bar

6 jars Cherries	£30.00
2 boxes Lemons	£17.00
4 × 3 kg Salted Nuts	£24.00
	£71.00

Income excl. V.A.T.		£8,695	Income incl. V.A.T.		£10,000
Consumption			Consumption		
at cost	£4,960		at retail	£10,160	
Plus			Plus		
transfers in	£71		transfers in	Nil	
Less			Less		
transfers out	(£114)	£4,917	transfers out	(£242)	£9,918
Gross Profit		£3,778	Surplus		£82
		(43.4%)			(0.8%)

On the majority of occasions, transfers are not recorded as such and are treated as allowances which are deducted from the retail consumption figure only. It is sometimes useful, though, to add the cost amount of the items being allowed for to the gross profit, so as to estimate what this would have been had the goods not been given away, spilled, or sold at a cheaper price. Since most extended stocktaking systems have the facility to show the estimated gross profit figure both before and after allowances (see page 121), it is usually only when preparing a trading account that the Stocktaker is likely to have to provide this information, as in the following example:–

Gross Profit Trading Account

Opening stock	£5,000	Closing stock	£6,000
Purchases	£11,000	Income excl. V.A.T.	£20,000
Gross Profit	£10,000		
	£26,000		£26,000

Gross Profit 50%

If a record of allowances had been kept during this period which amounted to £800 at retail value, and this were treated as part of income, a theoretical gross profit could be calculated to show what the percentage would have been had this figure in fact represented income rather than allowances:–

Opening stock	£5,000.00	Closing stock	£6,000.00
Purchases	£11,000.00	Income	£20,000.00
Gross Profit	£10,000.00	Allowances	
Allowances	£695.65	£800 less V.A.T.	£695.65
	£26,695.65		£26,695.65

Gross Profit 51.6%

Thus, although the client has an actual gross profit percentage of 50.0%, his percentage would have been 51.6%, had there not been any allowances during the period.

When adjusting for allowances, the Stocktaker will work out the retail value and deduct it from the retail consumption figure, before calculating the surplus/deficit result.

MISCELLANEOUS ADJUSTMENTS

Adjustments Involving Cost Price Changes

The following examples assume that, during the stocktaking period, an increase of 14p has occurred in the cost price of a gallon of lager, from an old price of £3.65 to a new price of £3.79 (excluding V.A.T.). The Stocktaker will work out the volume of beer purchased at the new price; in this instance, he has established that out of total purchases of 264 gallons, 110 were delivered since the price increased.

Example 1

Opening Stock	Purchases	Closing Stock
121 gal.s	264 gal.s	121 gal.s

Because all the beer purchased at the higher price is still in stock and none has been consumed, no adjustment will be necessary. When preparing his valuation, however, the Stocktaker will have to take into account the remaining 11 gallons of old stock:–

121 gallons at £3.79 = £458.59 less 11 at £0.14 = £1.54
Net value £457.05
or 121 gallons at £3.65 = £441.65 plus 110 at £0.14 = £15.40
Net value £457.05

Example 2

Opening Stock	Purchases	Closing Stock
121 gal.s	264 gal.s	66 gal.s

In this instance, consumption includes 44 gallons of new stock, so a cost surcharge of £6.16 (44 × £0.14) will have to be applied. Because all the stock in hand will have been purchased since the price increase, the valuation will be worked out at the new rate, i.e. 66 × £3.79 = £250.14.

Similar calculations would be applicable to any products whose prices had increased during the stock period.

Adjustments Involving Retail Price Changes

Where computerised tills are in use, this adjustment will be more accurately calculated if the till is cleared on the morning of the change and at the stocktake. For the purpose of this demonstration, it is assumed that the price of spirits has been increased by 2p around the middle of the stocktaking period.

Example 1

Vodka – number of measures sold at the old price   780
      – number of measures sold at the new price   650

If the retail consumption is calculated at the old price, then a surcharge of £13.00 (650 × £0.02) would have to be applied. If it is calculated at the new price, then an allowance of £15.60 (780 × £0.02) would be necessary.

Example 2

Where computerised tills are not in use, the Stocktaker will take the income before and after the increase and work out the ratio of vodka sales from these figures, as follows:–

Income before increase = £6,000 = 54.5% of total sales (£11,000)
Income after increase = £5,000 = 45.5% of total sales (£11,000)

From his own records, he will see that the number of vodka sales during the period was 1,440, so that:–

54.5% of 1,440 = 785 measures sold at the old price
45.5% of 1,440 = 655 measures sold at the new price

Using this calculation, he will apply a surcharge of £13.10 (655 × £0.02) or an allowance of £15.70 (785 × £0.02), depending upon which selling price he is using.

In the above examples, the Stocktaker's figures show sales of 1,440 measures, as against the till figure of 1,430. This discrepancy could derive from the count, or be covered by allowances. If neither of these explanations applies, it may be proof of some dishonest activity.

Purchases Discounted or Free of Charge

Discounts are generally shown on invoices. In order to keep his gross profit margins correct, the Stocktaker must extract this information and incorporate it into his extended result. If he extracts discounts of £250.20, he will show this total as a credit against his costs; in other words, he will reduce his purchases by that amount.

Consumption at Retail	Consumption at Cost	Gross Profit	Gross Profit %
£16,000	£8,000	£8,000	50.0%
£16,000	£8,000	£8,250.20	51.5%
	− £250.20 (discount)		

The normal procedure, as shown in the example below, is to enter the discount as a 'cost only' item on a separate line with the heading 'discount', and to put in the 'purchases' column a minus figure, (1). If all the credit applies to draught beer, it can be allowed in that section, and similarly if applicable to any other single group. This enables the gross profit on each section to be maintained correctly.

Beer discount

Cost	Retail	Purchases	Sales	Consumption at Cost	Consumption at Retail
£250.20	nil	(1)	−1	−£250.20	nil

This calculation has the effect of reducing the purchases by £250.20, thereby improving the gross profit by a proportional amount. Because no stock has been delivered, the retail side will not be affected.

Wine and spirit suppliers frequently give discounts which depend upon the number of cases purchased. They tend to do this, though, in kind, for example by offering one free bottle for every case bought. This type of discount can be shown on a separate line with the normal retail price and no cost, i.e.:–

Whisky (free)

Cost	Retail	Purchases	Sales	Consump-tion at Cost	Consump-tion at Retail
nil	£16.80	1	1	nil	£16.80

Alternatively, it can be included with similar items and a discount shown, as set out in the following example:–

Twelve bottles of whisky are supplied plus one free of charge:

Whisky

Cost	Retail	Purchases	Sales	Consump-tion at Cost	Consump-tion at Retail
£7.10	£16.80	13	13	£92.30	£218.40
Free Spirits £7.10	nil	(1)	−1	−£7.10	nil

Thirteen bottles of whisky have been sold at full retail value, but one has been shown separately as a credit against cost, thereby maintaining the correct gross profit levels for that section.

Internal and External Promotions

It is quite common practice for a company to hold a promotion night at a client's premises. It might be that they are trying to boost their sales of a certain brand of vodka, and to encourage such sales they ask their client to sell that brand, for the night, at half-price; they in their turn will supply sufficient stock, free of charge, to cover any lost income. It often happens that the client benefits by this sort of promotion, as replacement stock can be more than expected; and unless the Stocktaker is informed, inflated surpluses will occur. In normal circumstances he will ignore the transaction, because there should be no loss or gain to the premises, as the following example demonstrates:–

Normal retail price of vodka	80p
Special promotion price	40p
Loss per measure of vodka	40p

If the client sells 12 × 40 oz bottles by one-sixth gill measures, he will take £230.40, which would produce an equivalent loss as far as his stock is concerned. The promoting company would be expected to supply, free of charge, 6 × 40 oz bottles of vodka, thus adding £230.40 to his stock at retail value (6 × 48 measures × £0.80).

Uplifts for Price Differences

A Stocktaker is sometimes requested to give an overall result for premises where there are bars with different price structures. He will normally take the cheapest bar and apply surcharges; the following example assumes three bars, with the public bar prices being used to produce the overall report.

	Public	Lounge	Function	Total
Turnover for period	£8,000	£5,500	£2,650	£16,150
Percentage of total sales	49.53%	34.06%	16.41%	100%
Price differences				
Spirits	68p	70p	71p	
Draught Beer	88p	91p	92p	
Bottled Beer	60p	62p	63p	
Minerals	36p	38p	39p	

Total sales for period

Spirits	96.1 × 40 oz bottles	or 4,613 measures
Draught Beer	956 gallons	or 7,648 pints
Bottled Beer	140 dozen	or 1,680 bottles
Minerals	120 dozen	or 1,440 bottles

Lounge Bar	% of Sales		Price dif.	
Spirits	34.06% =	1,571 measures	@ £0.02 =	£31.42
Draught Beer	34.06% =	326 gallons	@ £0.24 =	£78.24
Bottled Beer	34.06% =	48 dozen	@ £0.24 =	£11.52
Minerals	34.06% =	41 dozen	@ £0.24 =	£9.84
Total Surcharge				£131.02

Function Bar	*% of Sales*	*Price dif.*
Spirits	16.41% = 757 measures	@ £0.03 = £22.71
Draught Beer	16.41% = 157 gallons	@ £0.32 = £50.24
Bottled Beer	16.41% = 23 dozen	@ £0.36 = £8.28
Minerals	16.41% = 20 dozen	@ £0.36 = £7.20
Total Surcharge		£88.43

It would be normal for each group of surcharges to be raised in its own section; under 'Spirits', therefore, a new line would be entered with the heading 'Lounge and Function Surcharge'. There would be no cost price, but a retail one of £54.13, with a purchase of 1. Application of the same procedure to each section would maintain the correct profit margin for each group of items.

Spirit surcharge

Cost	Retail	Purchases	Sales	Consumption at Cost	Consumption at Retail
nil	£54.13	1	1	nil	£54.13

If the Stocktaker does not consider it necessary to make calculations as precise as those given above, he can work out the percentage difference in prices between the bars, and apply that figure as a surcharge at the end of his report. He may calculate that the lounge bar is 2.5% dearer than the public bar, and the function bar 3.5% dearer:–

$$£5,500 \times 2.5\% = £137.50$$
$$£2,650 \times 3.5\% = £92.75$$

Total Surcharge   £230.25

There is a difference of £10.80 between the total obtained above (£131.02 + £88.43 = £219.45) and this second figure (£137.50 + £92.75 = £230.25). The former is more precise; if the latter method is used, the percentages must be carefully calculated to make the surcharges as accurate as possible.

Loaned or Borrowed Stock

If goods have been borrowed from other premises and not returned before the stocktaking, the Stocktaker has two options:–

1. To include them as purchases, with a reminder that they should be treated as credits at the next stocktake after they have been returned.
2. To exclude them from the closing stock count. This can only be done if supplies have arrived during the intervening period, or if the borrowed stock has not been used in the meantime.

If stock has been loaned and not returned, it can either be treated as a credit purchase and debited at a later date, or be added to the closing count.

To cover himself against charges of supplying inadequate information, a Stocktaker should always enclose details of any loans or borrowings with his report, so that the proprietor is made aware of them.

Returned Beer

It is normal policy for breweries to give full credit on any beer that is returned, and in such instances the Stocktaker should credit it against the purchases on his stock report. If the beer is out-of-date, or below standard because of poor cellar management, the brewery is under no obligation to give credit, but should give a refund on any duty paid. According to current Customs and Excise legislation, any cask containing in excess of 3% of its capacity should receive credit when returned, provided the beer is in good condition. However, some breweries still adhere to previous legislation, and refuse to give credit for anything less than indicated below:–

6 gallons per hogshead
4 gallons per barrel
3 gallons per kilderkin (or 100-litre keg)
2 gallons per firkin (or 50-litre keg)

Or, for beers which contain yeast:–
12 pints per hogshead
 8 pints per barrel
 4 pints per kilderkin
 2 pints per firkin

If a full 11-gallon keg of bitter is returned to the supplier and full credit is anticipated, the Stocktaker will either deduct 11 gallons from the purchases or create a separate line to show the return, as set out in Example 1.

	Purchases	Cost Price	Selling Price	Consumption at Cost	Consumption at Retail
Example 1					
Bitter	(11)	(£3.71)	(£7.60)	(£40.81)	(£83.60)
Example 2					
Bitter	(11)	000	(£7.60)	000	(£83.60)

Example 1 has the effect of crediting the consumption both at cost and at retail; but if, ultimately, credit is not given, some Stocktakers would follow Example 2, giving no credit at cost but allowing it in full at retail. Others would either show it as an allowance or not at all, attributing the consequent deficit to bad management (and covering themselves by explaining, in a letter, why the shortfall has occurred).

YEAR-END ADJUSTMENTS

Most year-end valuations are scheduled for close of business on the last day of a month. This is usually the busiest time for a Stocktaker, the one when he can least do with an additional workload. Because he cannot be everywhere on the same day, he will have to make adjustments to valuations which may have been taken several days before or after the exact date.

The procedure differs according to when the valuation is done. Basically, the Stocktaker must either add or subtract the value of purchases for the intervening period, and the reverse procedure applies to the cost element of the income. For example:–

Stock Taken as at Close of Business on 27 December 1988

Purchases in period (incl. deposits and V.A.T.)	£1,473.20
Income for intervening period (incl. V.A.T.)	£2,610.87
Valuation at nearest stocktake to year end	£12,347.18
Normal gross profit percentage	57.6%

Year end 31st December 1988

Valuation as at 27.12.88	£12,347.18	Income for period (excl. V.A.T.)	£2,270.32
Less cost of sales	£962.61	Cost of sales	42.4%
	£11,384.57		
Add purchases for period (excl. V.A.T.)	£1,281.04		
Amended valuation	£12,665.61		

Stock Taken as at Close of Business on 4 January 1989

Purchases in period (incl. deposits and V.A.T.)	£637.05
Income for intervening period (incl. V.A.T.)	£7,792.71
Valuation at nearest stocktake to year end	£10,346.43
Normal gross profit percentage	57.6%

Year end 31st December 1988

Valuation as at 4.1.89	£10,346.43	Income for period (excl. V.A.T.)	£6,776.27
Plus cost of sales	£2,873.14	Cost of sales	42.4%
	£13,219.57		
Less purchases for period	£553.96		
Amended valuation	£12,665.61		

PREMISES

Year end adjustment sheet   COB 31/7/88

Date of last stocktake	4 / 8 / 88
Valuation at that time	£ 12,306 – 12
Cumulative G.P. percentage	53·6 %
Number of days	3

PURCHASES
Details of Invoices (Incl. VAT)

DATE	No.	COMPANY	AMOUNT
2/8/88	1076	J. Swan	240 – 73
2/8/88	21371	G. Andrews	36 – 80

Total (Excl. VAT)	£ 241 – 33
Total A (Excl. VAT)	+ 1208 – 56
Total B (Excl. VAT)	+ 16 – 32
Total C (Excl. VAT)	– 11 – 12
PURCHASES FOR PERIOD	£ 1455 – 09

INCOME (Incl. VAT)

DATE	INCOME	DATE	DRAWINGS
1/8/88	428 – 32		
2/8/88	317 – 11		
3/8/88	453 – 29		

Total income (Ex. VAT)	£ 1042 – 37
Less Gross Profit percentage	53·6 %
Cost of sales	483·66
Valuation at last stock	12306 – 12
Plus/Minus purchases	– 1455 – 09
Plus/Minus cost of sales	+ 483 – 66
Year end valuation	£ 11334 – 69

If the year end occurs after the stocktake, add purchases and deduct cost of sales. If before, then reverse the procedure.

PURCHASES

Details of delivery notes
Invoices not yet received

Date

D/N No.	ITEM AND QUANTITY		UNIT PRICE	EXT. PRICE
JOHNS+CO 010037	Pils	2 doz	5·26	10·52
2/8/88	Export	6 doz	3·60	21·60
	Lager	8 doz	3·54	28·32
	Export	6 × 11	3·96	261·36
	Lager	4 × 36	4·02	578·88
	Gas cylinders	2	4·00	8·00
Cr	Cases	8	1·00	
Cr	Bottles	6	·52	
SNEDDON+CO. 20076	Grouse	6 × 1.5	15·20	91·20
3/8/88	Tio Pepe	× 3	4·40	13·20
	Drambuie	× 3	9·96	29·88
	Smirnoff	12 × 1·5	13·80	165·60
Total A				£ 1208·56

Deposits

Purchases	Credits
16 – 32	11 – 12

Total B	Total C
16 – 32	11 – 12

In the examples shown, the average profit achieved is 57.6%, so the cost of sales will be the difference between that and 100%. All figures exclude V.A.T.

If the stock is taken before the year end:–

DEDUCT COST OF SALES AND ADD PURCHASES.

If the stock is taken after the year end:–

ADD COST OF SALES AND DEDUCT PURCHASES.

On the analysis (page 140), all purchases for which no invoice has yet been received are listed on the right-hand side, together with their extended price (exclusive of V.A.T.). Invoices and details of income are shown on the left, and the final adjustment is made in accordance with the previous calculations.

If the Stocktaker is making a year-end adjustment in premises with which he is not familiar, he will have to obtain from his client either previous accounts or Stocktaker's reports, so that he can estimate a realistic gross profit figure. If this information is not forthcoming, he will have to calculate a figure by using his own experience, or by referring to the tariff board to estimate achievable figures; but in these circumstances, particularly if the valuation is high, he should always qualify his certificate by stating what gross profit figure he has used.

CHAPTER 7
BROKERS, STOCKTAKERS AND CHANGEOVERS; GENERAL STOCKTAKING

BROKERS, STOCKTAKERS AND CHANGEOVERS

England and Scotland differ considerably in their procedures for a tenancy change (where one tenant takes over from another). In Scotland, a tenancy change often involves furnishings and fittings, and a price is agreed by the brewery or an independent valuer, which both parties are then expected to accept. There is little room for negotiation, but both sides do know exactly where they stand some time before the date of the changeover. In England, it is the 'broker' (middleman) who plays an active part in the preliminaries, and ensures the smooth running of the tenancy change by arranging and managing the change day.

The majority of brewers employ brokers to find them tenants. This involves advertising, sending out details about the public house concerned, and interviewing prospective tenants, which in itself can take a considerable amount of time. The broker will short-list the best applicants, and put their names forward to the brewery.

Once the tenant has been selected, the outgoing valuer will prepare a trade inventory, which will be sent to the other side to value. The brewery are only involved to the extent of ensuring that furnishings or fittings belonging to them are not included in the valuation. In England, however, where it is usual for there to be two inventories, a 'Trade Inventory' and an 'Optional Inventory', some brewers have the right to decide which items shall appear on which list; and thus they have the right to approve the final inventory(ies).

The respective valuers for both parties, together with other interested bodies, will agree a convenient change date. The ingoing valuer will prepare notices for the transfer of licence, which normally involves a protection order which can be obtained with seven days' clear notice both to the police and to the Clerk to the Court. (In an emergency, and provided the authorities agree, this can be procured at considerably shorter notice.) This protection order merely allows a third party to run the house under the previous tenant's licence. The General Magistrates' Bench can hear a protection order application, and the principal requirement at law is that 'he or she [the prospective licensee] is a fit and proper person'. The full transfer hearing needs twenty-one clear days' notice before the application can be heard before the licensing justices themselves. If there is sufficient time, a protection order can be avoided by direct application to the transfer sessions, although the choice of change date will then be restricted by the limited number of transfer sessions available throughout the year.

In addition to preparing notices to protect the licensing situation, the ingoing broker must ensure that he will have the money from the incoming tenant in good time for the change, principally so as to guarantee that the transaction can actually take place. It tends to be an unwritten rule, among brewers, that the monies should be received by the broker at least fourteen days prior to the date of the change. If the ingoing broker has the full amount of the change monies in his client's bank account, he will at the end of the morning discharge the various demands for money as they come in from the brewery, the outgoing valuer, and the Stocktaker.

If the ingoing valuer has not received his client's money by the day of the change, he must ensure that he can obtain a banker's draft by that morning. This should be for the full amount; if it is not, either he must have cash from his client, or the transaction will have to be cancelled. Unless the full purchase price has been deposited, any payment by the broker out of his client's account would be a criminal offence.

The Change Day

On the morning of the change, the date of which generally coincides with the court hearing, all those involved arrive at about nine o'clock. The Stocktakers agree the valuation and are paid at the end of the day by the brokers, who themselves tie up loose ends by taking stock of the glass, checking the inventory to ensure that all items are there and in working order, and making sure that all electrical and mechanical appliances are working satisfactorily.

The completion of the change, obviously, depends very much on the passage of the court hearing itself; in most contracts of sale, there is a clause which states that the whole transaction is subject to the granting of a licence.

Before cheques are actually exchanged by the brokers, the ingoing broker will ensure that he has the keys to the premises and that they all fit. This is very important, because the cost of replacing locks can be prohibitive and might, technically, be the broker's responsibility. The final task undertaken by the broker acting for the outgoing tenant is to ensure that all meters (gas, electricity etc.) have been read by the appropriate authorities.

The Valuation

The person valuing the furnishings and fittings on behalf of the broker will price them on a 'going concern' basis. He will not be putting a realisable value on them, nor will he be valuing them at replacement price; he will assess their worth to that particular business, and for this reason it is not normal for antiques to be listed at their true worth, unless with the prior agreement of the ingoer. If the value involved was out of proportion to any related return from the business, it would certainly not be appropriate to use it in the valuation, where the value given should reflect the value of an item for its obvious purpose, its life expectancy, and its cost of replacement.

If the two valuers are unable to agree the valuation of furnishings and fittings, an independent arbitrator will be called in. The valuation must be reasonable, because neither the brewer nor the ingoing tenant wants excessive figures; at the same time, however, the outgoing tenant wants a fair price for the furnishings and fittings which he paid for when he took over the tenancy, and for the items which he has subsequently purchased.

The valuer must from the first be absolutely certain about what the brewery regard as belonging to them. In some cases fitted seating is included in the inventory, in others it is not. In general terms, anything that is movable would be regarded as an asset; but whereas washhand basins etc. would not be included, cookers, ovens and bain marie units would. Outgoing tenants may argue about the inclusion of certain items, but the brewery will have a clear policy which will be available to the valuer.

The inventory is a list of all the furnishings and fittings on the premises. It is an entire package, a collection of good, bad and useless goods: the vendor does not have the right to choose to sell or not to sell, nor the purchaser the right to refuse to buy items he considers too expensive (unless they are optional). A 'bundle of goods' is being sold, and a collective price is being obtained; generally, this price represents substantially more than their value outside a public house. Individual items could perhaps be sold for more than the inventory price; but conversely, many more items might not even find a purchaser, were they not included in the trade inventory.

Where individual items have unusual or substantial values, it is wise to notify one's client of their worth. Some brokers think it advisable to tell their client the value of the inventory before they discuss it with the other valuer. They inform him of major items of value, and normally have no objection to notifying him of individual prices. It is unusual to give a totally priced inventory; if this is requested, the broker must decide whether to give the valuation as it stands before the valuers' meeting, after it, or on both occasions. A request for a priced inventory is probably not a valid request: it is, rather, an indication of lack of trust.

Taking the Inventory

An inventory is a detailed listing of furniture, fixtures, fittings and all other effects of the premises. To prepare a proper inventory, the valuer will need to describe individual items so that they can be easily identified.

Of the following examples of inventories, the first is inadequate in style, whereas the second is more informative and accurate.

	Carpet as laid
3	Circular top tables
4	Rectangular top tables
	Fixed seating
12	Chairs
6	Stools
10	Prints
4	Wall lights
2	Pairs curtains on runners
2	Chandeliers

	Leaf-patterned Axminster carpet as planned with underlay 25 sq. yds.
3	Oak stretcher-framed tables with 24″-diameter grained formica tops
4	Oak refectory-style tables with pegged-end supports 4′ × 2′
	Polished hardwood-framed fixed boxed-base seating with foam-cushioned seat and back covered in buttoned tan vinyl 15′
12	Elm wheelback chairs with fish-tail supports
6	Oak 20″-high stools with foam-cushioned seats covered in studded tan vinyl
6	Hogarth-framed and glazed country scene prints
4	Framed and glazed village scene prints
2	Easy-glide curtain railways
2	Pairs of lined Sanderson coaching scene curtains
4	Brass twin electric wall-brackets with fluted-edge glass shades
2	Brass triple-branch electric chandeliers with fluted-edge glass shades on chained suspensions

The second, correct version of the inventory is much more detailed than the first, and is less likely to cause any argument between the parties; for it would be almost impossible to remove items and replace them with others of lower value, without detection.

Inventories are usually required for free house transfers, as they are integral to contracts; but in these instances they would not normally need to be priced.

There are several types of valuation:–

1. Insurance – The valuer would assess the stock at replacement cost, and the client would be encouraged to increase cover at periodic intervals.
2. Probate – If the business has ceased to trade, the stock will be valued at what is thought to be a realistic price for the whole (probably a low valuation); but if the business is still trading, the same procedure as for a transfer will be adopted.
3. Stock at valuation – A fair price will be sought for both the vendor and the purchaser.
4. Bankrupt stock – The valuation will be made in the same way as for probate.
5. Dissolution of partnership – This will require a simple valuation, as for a changeover, usually with one valuer acting for both parties.

It is common practice for a valuer, when preparing priced inventories, to relate his calculations to a ten-year depreciation period; but each will have his own system, and work accordingly. Items over ten years old are not automatically written off; the valuer will use his discretion, and price each according to its age, condition and life expectancy. He will also take account of whether or not the new tenant will utilise the particular item.

It is quite common for a valuer to find items which are on lease or loan, subject to rental or hire purchase payments, or the personal property of the outgoing tenant. It is normal practice to list such items on the inventory, clearly indicating that they are not part of the assets and are therefore not included in the valuation. (In some cases, items on hire purchase are included in the valuation if the valuer for the outgoing party has given an undertaking, in writing, to settle the amount outstanding under the H.P. agreement.) The broker would also cover himself by obtaining a signed document from the outgoing tenant, confirming that these assets were his personal property or responsibility.

THE STOCKTAKER AND CHANGEOVERS

The Stocktaker will be called in to act either for the ingoing tenant, or for the outgoing one, or, in some cases, for both. Whatever his role, the Stocktaker's task will be a difficult one: he must be fair not only to the client, but also to himself, and in a situation where one party is looking for a bargain and the other for more than the stock value, his job will not be easy.

If the Stocktaker has worked regularly at the premises, he will have advised his client to ensure that all stock is 'in date'; and his task for the day will be a little easier, because he knows the lay-out of the premises, the way in which stock levels have been maintained, and the extent to which a proper rotation has been effected. If he is new to the premises, he will need (irrespective of which party he is working for) to check every bottle (where applicable) for 'sell by' date, and to lift down every case to make sure that those beneath are full and contain the same product as the one on top. It is unusual for vendors to attempt deliberately to 'outsmart' the Stocktaker, but it does happen, and it is up to the latter to ensure that the job he does is both thorough and accurate.

If he is acting purely for the purchaser, the Stocktaker must take extra care; for in the same way as a customer would not buy inferior or out-of-date stock from a supermarket, there is no reason why he should purchase poor-quality produce from the vendor.

The procedure at changeovers does vary in different parts of the country. In Scotland it is fairly informal, usually with only the two parties and the Stocktaker in attendance; up to fourteen days may elapse before any money is paid for the stock, and the transaction would then be dealt with by the two solicitors. In England, the situation is more complex: not only would both sides be present on the day of a tenancy change, but in all probability brokers would be there too, one to represent each party. They would take the agreed valuation from the Stocktaker, and enter it on their final statements.

In the event of a free house change, the Stocktaker may well be left to deal with the entire transaction. The Stocktaker acting for the ingoing tenant, having agreed the valuation with his opposite number, will present a copy to his client; the latter will make out a cheque and hand it to the Stocktaker, who will give it to the vendor's Stocktaker to pass on to his client. The Stocktaker acting for the purchaser should always take his client round the premises, indicating exactly what stock has been counted, where it is kept, and what has not been included in the valuation, and highlighting any other relevant points.

As the stock is being counted, each area should be locked as soon as it has been completed, and the key taken by the Stocktaker acting for the purchaser. On no account should keys be passed to anyone else without the authority of that person. No 'bottling up' should be done while the stock is being counted; it is the duty of the Stocktaker acting for the vendor to ensure that all the stock is intact, static and ready for valuation, and for this reason he should endeavour to arrive before his opposite number.

Beers and Minerals

Nearly all bottled beers and minerals are dated, either on the cap or on the label, and it is the responsibility of the Stocktaker to ensure that everything is 'in date'; if he finds any beers or minerals past their best, he should set them aside and notify both parties that this stock has not been included in the valuation. If the vendor elects to remove it from the premises, he may, provided he does so under the supervision of the Stocktaker; but if he elects to leave it on the premises, then the value of any deposits must be included in the final Certificate of Valuation.

Draught Beer

Keg beer is normally recognised to be 'in date' if it is within six weeks of the brew date, which should be clearly marked on the top of the container. Cask-conditioned beer is generally acceptable within a three- to four-week period. If a 'best before' date is not shown, clarification can be obtained from the brewery concerned, should difficulties arise.

Beer awaiting return can create problems, and it is always in the interest of the vendor to ensure that returns are made before the date of sale. Except with the mutual consent of both parties, the Stocktaker should not include any such ullage within his valuation. He should make it clear to the purchaser that he has excluded it, and then it is up to the vendor to ensure that any credits given for that produce go direct to his account.

Spirits, Vermouths etc.

Part-bottles should be measured in exactly the same way as for an extended stock, but the Stocktaker acting for the purchaser would be well advised to carry out spot checks with his hydrometer (see page 274), to ascertain proof, and he should also make sure that all full bottles are properly sealed. All full cases should be opened and carefully checked. Stock which is obviously very old, or has torn and damaged labels, should not be included in the valuation, but the vendor should always be given the opportunity to remove this stock if he wishes to do so.

In all cases, it is up to the Stocktaker acting for the ingoing client to ensure that the stock levels are not excessive on any one line. He may well need to discuss this with his client, or with the Stocktaker acting for the other side, and suitable discounts on price should be made if necessary.

At a changeover, the Stocktaker is often under pressure to complete his task, and this may cause him to rush his calculations and make errors. It is vitally important that he takes his time, and remembers that the actual calculations are just as important as taking the stock. If possible, he should have an assistant with him to check the extensions; failing this, every column and every calculation must be double-checked. At the end of the stock, all full bottles must be converted to deposit value and included in the relevant section of the final Certificate of Valuation (see page 156).

In certain instances, a limit will have been fixed beforehand beyond which the value of the stock must not pass. In the case of a tenancy, this may have been fixed by the brewery; if a free house is involved, it would be normal practice for the purchaser's solicitors to have this limit written into the contract of sale. If, after the valuation, the limit is found to have been exceeded, the purchaser should be asked if he is prepared to accept this; and if he agrees, he would probably expect some concession, either in the form of a discount or of extra time in which to pay the excess value. If he is not prepared to cover the extra cost, the vendor must accept the situation and arrange for the removal of the excess stock, either by him personally or by the suppliers.

At all changeovers, the Stocktaker is responsible for representing his client, and it is his responsibility to ensure that all stock is good and consumable. If he is acting for both parties, or for the purchaser only, he will ensure that all stock is of excellent quality and within date. He will keep the ingoing client informed of any irregularities, and notify him of any stock which he considers should be purchased within the very near future. If he is acting for the vendor, he will try to obtain as much money as possible for his client, and will leave it to the purchaser's representatives to highlight overstocking, out-of-date stock, and damaged goods.

Food

The food stock would be taken in exactly the same way as indicated on page 160, but extreme care must be taken if the premises are changing ownership. Except in special circumstances, only full containers should be included in the valuation, and then only if the Stocktaker is absolutely sure that their quality is good and that, if frozen, they are not 'freezer-burnt' or old. Meat should only be included if in good condition; and it might be acceptable for a price to be put on all the stock, e.g. gâteaux, cheese etc., which is currently in use. Food should be listed in detail, so that the purchaser is fully aware of what he is buying. Home-made dishes should be carefully analysed, and omitted from the valuation if they appear to have been prepared some time beforehand. If lids or doors on freezers do not close properly, this could indicate that stock has not been properly looked after, and special attention should be given to anything inside those particular freezers. Unusually expensive produce should be listed separately and shown to the purchaser.

There are three methods of valuing wines, and these are described below.

The Open Market Valuation

This is the price that a bottle of wine would fetch at an auction, and it would be extremely difficult for any Stocktaker to assess this figure. However, some auctioneers specialising in the sale of wines do produce current lists of anticipated prices, and it might be possible to procure one of these.

The Current Replacement Value

If wines were laid down when bottled, at a time when they were not ready for drinking, the Stocktaker would have to estimate their value at maturity. For example, Château Lafite 1961, which bought at auction in 1971 would have cost £175 per dozen, would be worth £2,300 eight years later, having matured over that period. This type of valuation is often required for insurance purposes.

Transfer of Stock

This is the type of valuation required when a business is changing hands. The wine would be listed, and current cost prices would be extracted either from invoices or from a trade price list. This procedure is perfectly acceptable as long as the Stocktaker makes allowances for damaged labels, and makes himself aware of any fine wines and their vintages. He must be extremely careful in the manner in which he handles such wine.

If there is a large stock of fine wines on the premises, the Stocktaker would need to establish whether they had been purchased through a recognised supplier, at an auction, or 'en primeur' in France prior to bottling. The method of storage would also affect the overall price; and if he does not have an adequate knowledge of wine, the Stocktaker would be wise to seek professional advice. Clients will appreciate his honesty, and will be glad to acknowledge that the business is of such importance that expert advice is thought necessary.

Wines brought 'en primeur' are usually Château-bottled clarets, and the price tends to vary considerably. (It will usually be given in French francs, and will have to be converted into sterling.) Such wine also increases in value from the time of purchase to the time of bottling, and the Stocktaker should add 30% to the cost price to allow for this, together with insurance, freight, duty (see end of this section) and V.A.T. charges.

If wines are bought at auction, the true price is the 'hammer' price plus a buyer's premium of 10%. There is also a clearance fee (currently £4.00 per case), and there are handling charges and insurance in transit.

As demonstrated, quite considerable problems can arise in the valuing of fine wines; and without a proper knowledge of the trade, the Stocktaker may find himself out of his depth to the extent of producing an incorrect valuation, which will cause all sorts of problems at a later date.

The presence of a heavy sediment is not a good sign in white wines, and can mean that the product is past its best. There are exceptions, however: some good white Burgundies can be extremely long-lived and produce a sediment which is not detrimental to the wine. Many German wines are best drunk within three to four years, but age can in a few cases improve the product, so that a great vintage Beerenauslese may lie for fifteen years without harm. Similarly, most Loire wines should be drunk young, so that a wine of four years or more is considered 'over the hill'; the exceptions here are Sancerre and Montlouis.

Red wines are more difficult to price because different shippers can and do command different prices. Château-bottled clarets vary in price from year to year and area to area, but are the wines best documented in reference books. Burgundy wines are the most difficult to price, as their value depends on the domain or section of the vineyard from which the wine has come, along with details of the shipper.

Most red wines should have, as a natural feature of their production, a sediment which is not detrimental to the wine. They may also have a scattering of tartrate crystals (also visible in white wine); these are harmless, and guarantee that the wine has a good backbone and body, but they should have been discarded while the wine was in 'bulk', prior to bottling.

It is extremely difficult for the Stocktaker to value wines unless they appear in current price lists. He can, for instance, include a 10-year-old Auslese German wine, but not a 10-year-old Liebfraumilch; he can transfer 20-year-old Château clarets, but not a similar Mouton Cadet. Beaujolais is best drunk young, but individual vineyards can produce wine which is good for up to five or seven years, which means that a 5-year-old Moulin-à-Vent could be transferred, but not a 1-year-old Beaujolais Nouveau.

A damaged label can reduce the value of a wine, and in such instances the Stocktaker is advised to discuss the matter with both the purchaser and the vendor. If the damage is caused by metal wine racks, but the name is still identifiable, the bottle may well be acceptable. Damp and discoloured labels probably indicate poor storage conditions, and the value of such wines will be substantially decreased. In many circumstances, wines with damaged labels will be treated as house stock and charged accordingly. This means that the purchaser will be able to sell the contents by the glass, and thereby not lose any money on his purchase.

Duty Rates

The current (1988) average rates of duty are as follows:–

Red and white table wines, from E.E.C. countries, not exceeding 15% vol.
75 cl bottles – 9.00 litres per case, £9.22 per case
73 cl bottles – 8.76 litres per case, £8.97 per case
70 cl bottles – 8.40 litres per case, £8.60 per case

For wines from outside E.E.C. countries, £0.80 per case is payable in addition to the above.

Champagne and sparkling wines of E.E.C. origin
75 cl bottles – 9.00 litres per case, £15.22 per case

Sherry, Port and Madeira not exceeding 18% vol.
75 cl bottles – 9.00 litres per case, £15.88 per case
70 cl bottles – 8.40 litres per case, £14.83 per case

Sherry, Port and Madeira exceeding 18% vol. but not 22% vol.
75 cl bottles – 9.00 litres per case, £18.33 per case
70 cl bottles – 8.40 litres per case, £17.11 per case

Sherry, Port and Madeira exceeding 22% vol.
75 cl bottles – 9.00 litres per case, £19.75 per case
plus £1.42 per case for every 1% above 23%

GENERAL STOCKTAKING

Fuel, Oil and Gas

Stocktakers are often requested, particularly at changes of ownership, to value fuel, oil, gas or other substances. Basically the procedure is simple, and generally all that has to be done is for the meter to be read and that figure multiplied by the unit cost. In the case of petrol which, for safety reasons, is generally stored underground, the manhole cover should be lifted to expose the large round cap which, when unscrewed, gives access to a dipstick, which

A garage dipstick is essential for assessing the quantity of petrol (Crewe Toll Service Station, Edinburgh).

A good cellarman, with a knowledge of his stock, can be of immense help with fine wines (the Caledonian Hotel, Princes Street, Edinburgh).

will indicate the amount of petrol left in the tank. Because the liquid is light-coloured it can be difficult to read the level, but if the dipstick is first rubbed with chalk, the mark left by the petrol will be much easier to see.

Oil tanks often have a gauge, a clear plastic tube at the side which shows the level of liquid, or a calibrated pole. This reading should not automatically be taken as correct, and if the Stocktaker is in doubt, he should remove the breather cap and dip the tank with any suitable implement. It is sometimes necessary to know the capacity of the tank; clients frequently do not know what this is, but the undernoted example will enable a Stocktaker to work it out for himself.

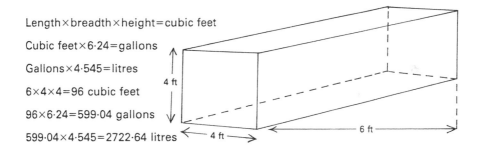

Length×breadth×height=cubic feet

Cubic feet×6·24=gallons

Gallons×4·545=litres

6×4×4=96 cubic feet

96×6·24=599·04 gallons

599·04×4·545=2722·64 litres

Gas is more complicated. Full containers would have to be counted and then valued from recent invoices, but the Stocktaker must remember that containers do have a deposit value. A hire charge per container has to be paid on initial delivery so that, in theory, a vendor will be entitled to claim that money back from a purchaser. However, to cover depreciation, the owning company will reduce the value of the containers on a sliding scale (after one year, for example, they are worth only 70% of the original cost).

Because of the intricacies of this aspect of stocktaking, it is advisable for the Stocktaker to contact the suppliers themselves, who may give the seller a refund of what he is due and then charge the purchaser the current market price for hire of the existing containers. This takes the onus off the Stocktaker, and ensures an accurate and fair transaction for both parties. For year-end valuations, the Stocktaker will need either to see the contract for the containers or to liaise with the owners.

Large bulk gas containers generally have a meter which indicates the percentage volume of gas inside. Though the Stocktaker can work out the value himself, he would be wise to give the meter reading to the suppliers, who will give him a valuation. They know the size of the tank and also the current market price, and can normally give a figure immediately. If it is necessary to assess the size of a cylindrical tank, the following formula would apply:–

$\frac{22}{7}$×Radius squared×length of tank in feet=cubic feet

Cubic feet×6·24=gallons

Gallons×4·545=litres

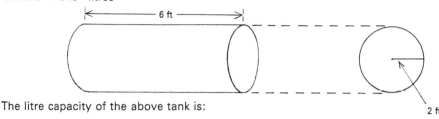

The litre capacity of the above tank is:

$\frac{22}{7}$×(2×2)×6=75·43 cu ft

75·43×6·24=470·68 gallons

470·68×4·545=2139·24 litre capacity

It is a good idea, after taking a reading on any type of tank, to check when the last delivery was. This would indicate the approximate level that might be expected, and could help to corroborate the Stocktaker's figure.

Cleaning Materials

If the valuation is required for a change of ownership, it is general policy to value full containers only. The Stocktaker should make a list of everything he is shown, and extract costs from invoices or current price lists. He must be careful not to include old or damaged stock, unless agreement has been reached between the purchaser and vendor (in which case, a special price will probably be applied). Some cleaning materials, particularly dish-washing powders, can be very expensive, so extreme care must be taken in the count and valuation.

Stationery

Stationery is counted and valued in exactly the same way as cleaning materials. It can sometimes be difficult to find cost prices, particularly where items such as brochures have been specially printed, and it is normal in such circumstances for a compromise price to be agreed between the two parties. Where the vendor's name or V.A.T. number is shown, it is unlikely that the stationery will be of any use to the purchaser; but provided the situation is discussed, it may be that a nominal value can be applied. The vendor should be informed of any stock which is not being charged for, and given the opportunity to remove it from the premises.

Miscellaneous Items

The sale contract may state that other items such as maintenance material, coal or light bulbs are to be included in the valuation. The standard principle would apply, with any good stock being counted and listed.

Glasses

If glassware is to be included in the valuation, it may apply only to full boxes, which would be priced at cost value; but if glasses in use are to be included, a percentage discount may be given which takes account of usage.

Floats

Usually, the purchaser and vendor will agree the amount of cash in hand themselves, and the former will hand over a cheque at the time. If asked to include it in the valuation, the Stocktaker should count the money and agree the sum with both parties before adding it to his certificate. If the purchaser and vendor have themselves agreed the amount, there is no need for a further check.

CHANGEOVERS: FINAL CERTIFICATE OF VALUATION AND STATEMENT OF SETTLEMENT

At a change of ownership, it is always advisable to ask the client for a copy of that part of the contract which relates to the stock valuation; this saves confusion, and enables the Stocktaker to proceed with his work unhampered. (For a year-end valuation, all the stock can be counted, unless any is obviously obsolete; inclusion would be according to the client's instructions.) In any type of stocktaking, a prepared stocksheet is always an asset, and will save both time and confusion when the stock is being counted.

The total value of the stock in each section would be added to the

Certificate of Valuation and presented in the usual manner, as shown in the following example.

Certificate of Valuation
Society Stocktaking Services Ltd.

Premises ....

We certify that a fair valuation of stock on hand at the above premises cost value excluding V.A.T. after close of business on Saturday 31st December 1988 would be Three thousand and eleven pounds and four pence made up as follows

Draught beer	531.78
Bottled/canned beer	148.59
Minerals	298.07
Spirits	465.09
Sherry/port	99.77
Vermouth/apéritifs	105.18
Liqueurs	191.52
Wines	159.95
Tobacco	46.10
Sundries	65.50
Containers	195.49

Total	£2,307.04
Cleaning materials	186.00
Coal	42.00
Calor gas	326.00
Subtotal	£2,861.04
Floats	150.00
Total	£3,011.04

Stocktaker's signature ....

Two examples of statements of settlement are shown on the following pages.

Statement of Settlement

at the Change of

The ....

Sold to .... by ....

	£	p.	£	p.
To Amount of Brewers Deposit	—	—		
" " " Valuation of Inventory				
" " " " " Optional				
" " " " " Glasses				
" " " Stock				
" " " Fixtures				
" " " VAT at % on £				
" " " Rates from to				
" " " Water Rate to				
Introduction Fee				
" Valuation Charges				
" Cost of Preparation of Inventory				
" Administration Fee				
" Stocktaking Charges				
" Paid Court Fees				
" Cost of Service of Notices				
" Cash in till				
" Attending and Effecting Change				
" Travelling and Out of Pocket Expenses				
"				
"				
"				
"				
" VAT at % on fees and charges				
Less Deposit Paid To Brewers £ }				
To Brokers £ }				
Proportion of Rates to				
" of Water Rates to				
Deficiencies in Inventory				
....				
....				
....				
....				
....				
Balance Due £				

Statement of Settlement

at the Change of

The ....

Sold by .... to ....

	£	p.	£	p.
By Amount of Brewers Deposit	–	–		
" " " Valuation of Inventory				
" " " " " Optional Items				
" " " " " Glasses				
" " " Stock				
" " " Fixtures				
" " " VAT at % on £				
" " " Rates from to				
" " " Water Rate to				
" Cash in till				
"				
"				
"				
"				
Less				
Dilapidations				
Brewers Trading Account and Rent				
Valuation fee				
Cost of Preparation of Inventory				
Administration Fee				
Stocktaking Charges				
Proportion of Rates from to				
" of Water Rates to				
Attending and Effecting Change				
Travelling and Out of Pocket Expenses				
Deficiencies in Inventory				
Retained Pending Full Transfer				
....				
VAT at % on fees and charges				
Balance Due			£	

CHAPTER 8
FOOD AND ANCILLARY STOCKTAKING

FOOD STOCKTAKING

Principal Reasons for Taking Food Stock

These may be summarised as follows:–

1. To ensure that profitability is maintained.
2. To control wastage, short deliveries, and costings.
3. To maintain a proper policy of portion control.
4. To eliminate, or at least control, pilferage.

The procedure for food stocktaking is quite different from that used in liquor control. An extended result is not normally produced, because it would be both time-consuming and impracticable, except in special circumstances. The stock on hand is valued at cost; and to produce a trading account, what is required is this figure, together with income, opening stock valuation, purchases and details of any allowances. The stock listing should be kept legible, in case the client requires a copy. Purchases are taken as a total figure, no analysis being necessary unless the client requests a breakdown of sales. However, sight of invoices and delivery notes is essential, both for stamping and for the ensuring of accurate prices.

It is in the Stocktaker's own interest to discourage the client from asking for extended results, because of the difficulties which would arise in a normal trading kitchen. Selling prices would have to be found for each individual item, and this would not be easy in the case of bags of flour, herbs, soup powders and other bulk items, particularly when the containers were part-full. He would also have to count individual butter, salt, pepper and sauce portions, and establish the number of measures left, for example, in a half-gallon jar of mustard. The only circumstance in which accurate extended results can be produced is where strict portion control is applied, and every item is delivered ready to serve. In this instance, all commodities would have a selling price; but the count would still be substantial, considering all the smaller items which would have to be included.

Taking the Physical Count

Every item of food within the kitchen must be listed. As in liquor stocktaking, it is advisable where possible to work from left to right and top to bottom, doing one area at a time. Ideally one would work through the kitchen in a logical manner, but this may not always be possible, because the chef may want certain areas done first; and within reason, the Stocktaker should always co-operate. The most difficult part of the operation is to identify meat, fish, and other fresh items, a skill which comes only with experience. If the Stocktaker does not know, then he should always ask, for in this way he will be better informed the next time. (Diagrams of the more common cuts of meat and of popular fish are shown elsewhere.) Deep freezes must be emptied; it is always more reliable to count the stock as it is being returned. A typical stock sheet is shown on page 162. Some Stocktakers do prefer to have ready-prepared ones; this is perfectly acceptable, but because of the large variety of sizes of container and types of food, the list could be very extensive.

Some Useful Guides for Physical Stocktaking of Food
Food Store: All food in this area would normally be found in full containers; but if it is not, it should be valued in parts thereof. If possible, obtain cost prices from the labels on the foodstuffs themselves, if only to save time later on. Check to the rear of shelves; put bad food to the side; and double-check the count. In the case of flour and sugar bins, estimates should be made. Tinned foods should be listed individually, together with their sizes. Cans were formerly graded on a scale from A1 to A10, the latter being the largest, but with the introduction of metrication, sizes are changing; the following table indicates comparisons:–

A10	3 kg
A5	1.25 kg
A2½	822 g
A2	540 g
A1	450 g

Deep Freezes: Pull everything out, organise it, and count it as it is returned. The contents of burst bags should not be counted. The chef can usually be consulted, if the Stocktaker has difficulty in identifying any food.
Walk-in Cold Room, or Refrigerators: All meat should be identified and weighed. The Stocktaker should work round the cold room in a logical manner, being sure to list everything as he sees it. It is generally acceptable to put a value on such things as sweet trolleys or cheeseboards (see page 149), but care must be taken to ensure

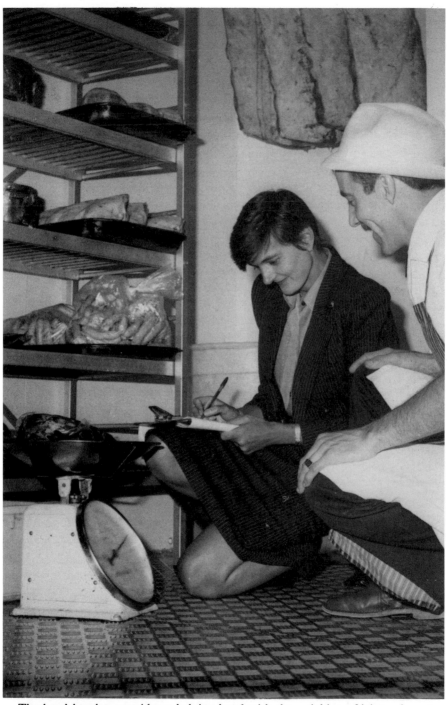

The hotel butcher provides a helping hand with the weighing of joints of meat (the Caledonian Hotel, Princes Street, Edinburgh).

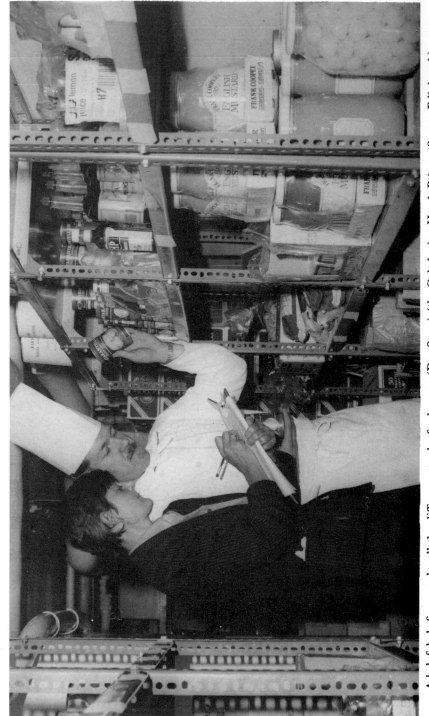

A helpful chef can make all the difference to the food count (Dry Store) (the Caledonian Hotel, Princes Street, Edinburgh).

accuracy. Where a limited amount of working stock is held in a small domestic refrigerator, the Stocktaker should consider the situation and decide if a single value will suffice.

Fruit and Vegetables: These are to be listed as seen, and by the appropriate unit of measurement, but mouldy or 'off' produce should not be counted. Fresh fruit and vegetables can cause difficulties because they are purchased in so many different ways – individually, or by the pound, box, punnet, chip, bag or bunch. It is only by examining the invoice that the Stocktaker will be able to ascertain the chargeable quantification of each item, but some of the more common ones are listed below:–

Pound	Small quantities of fruit or vegetables
Box	Apples, oranges, tomatoes, courgettes
Net	Onions, cabbages
Punnet	Strawberries, raspberries, cress
Chip	Mushrooms
Bag	Potatoes, carrots, cauliflowers
Bunch	Parsley, spring onions
Individual	Melons, cucumbers, avocados

Kitchen: The Stocktaker should always ask the chef if anything is cooking, and add it to his list. Count the stock as seen throughout the kitchen, and ensure that no area has been missed. Large bins may contain flour or sugar. Be particularly cautious with expensive items such as caviar, truffles, smoked salmon, lobster etc. All meat must be properly weighed and listed. Different cuts of the same animal can vary quite considerably in price. It is common practice to allow extra value on cooked meat because shrinkage occurs during the cooking process. In any kitchen, there are likely to be shelves or cupboards where the chef keeps his working stock; this normally consists of part-bottles or containers, and is known as 'mis-en-place'. It is generally acceptable to work out an estimated value for each area on site, and simply to write down that value on the working sheets. So that the Stocktaker knows, on successive visits, what he has valued, he should detail these estimates area by area. Before finishing his physical take, he should ensure that there is no stock kept elsewhere (in the restaurant, bars, pantries, lounges etc.).

Stocktakers must be fully aware of hygiene regulations, and adhere to them rigidly. Hands should be washed regularly, fresh food touched as little as possible, and appropriate dress (possibly a white coat) worn when food stocks are being taken.

Once he has completed his count, the Stocktaker will have a listing of all the consumable stock within the kitchen, a listing from which the following would be a typical extract:–

ITEM	UNIT	QUANTITY	TOTAL	COST	VALUE
Butter	lb	20½.3			
Flour (Plain)	1.5	12.1,30.6.			
Solid Pack Apples	A10	24			
Coffee Packs	3 oz	160.80.42			
Sirloin Cooked	lb	40.			
Sirloin Uncooked	lb	30.28.			
Sausages	lb	40.			
Pate Maison	lb	21.			
Strawberries	Pun	12.3.			
Mushrooms	Chip	6.4½			
Potatoes	Bag	3½			
Melon	Ind	12.8.			
Breaded Scampi	lb	28.12.			
Gourmet Scampi	lb	16.			
Dover Sole	lb	6.			
Trout	lb	20.6			
Mis en Place (Shelf 1)	£	6		1.00	
Mis en Place (Shelf 2)	£	14		1.00	

Food Stocktaking Sheet

ITEM	UNIT	QUANTITY	TOTAL	COST	VALUE
Butter	lb	20½.3	23½	1.28	30·08
Flour (Plain)	1.5	12.1.30.6.	49	.59	28.91
Solid Pack Apples	A10	24	24	1.36	32.64
Coffee Packs	3 oz	160.80.42	282	.60	169.20
Sirloin Cooked	lb	40.	40	3.40	136.00
Sirloin Uncooked	lb	30.28.	58	2.90	168.20
Sausages	lb	40.	40.	.60	24.00
Pate Maison	lb	21.	21	2.50	52.50
Strawberries	Pun	12.3.	15	.60	9.00
Mushrooms	Chip	6.4½	10½	2.40	25.20
Potatoes	Bag	3½	3½	3.20	11.20
Melon	Ind	12.8.	20	1.80	36.00
Breaded Scampi	lb	28.12	40	1.80	72.00
Gourmet Scampi	lb	16.	16	5.50	88.00
Dover Sole	lb	6.	6	4.80	28.80
Trout	lb	20.6.	26	1.40	36.40
Mis en Place (Shelf 1)	£	6	6	1.00	6.00
Mis en Place (Shelf 2)	£	14	14	1.00	14.00
					968.13

Food Stocktaking Sheet (extended)

FOOD GOODS RECEIVED SHEET

DATE	SUPPLIER AND REF.	ITEM	QUANTITY AND SIZE	PRICE	TOTAL	INVOICE TOTAL
8/8/88	J. Wilson	Sirloin	28 lbs	2·90	81·20	
	03868	fillet	30 lbs 8 oz	4·00	122·00	
		mince	20 lbs 4 oz	1·20	24·30	
		Sausages	10 lbs	·60	6·00	
		Back bacon	12 lbs	1·48	17-76	251-26
9/8/88	Kimberley Frozen Food	Scampi B	20 lbs	1·80	36-00	
		Prawns	20 lbs	3·40	68-00	
	06120	Whitebait	12 lbs	1·30	15-60	
		Chips	72 lbs	30	21-60	141-20
9/8/88	Petty Cash	Colourings	6 only	92	5·52	
		B.F. gateau	2 only	5·50	11·00	16-52
9/8/88	Bar	Brandy	1 Bottle	9·80	9·80	
		Sherry	1 Bottle	3·60	3·60	13-40
10/8/88	Hall Bros.	Pineapple Slices	6 × A10	1·96	11·76	
	7120	Soup Powder	2 × 3·5	12·40	24·80	
		Bouillon	4 only	7·80	31·20	
		Jam portions	2 × 144	7·20	14·40	82-16
10/8/88	J.W. Baker	Bread				
		w/ending				
		estimate		20·40	20·40	20·40

Valuing the Stock

The Stocktaker should take as many cost prices as possible from invoices, and extend the figures to give line valuations (see page 162). As far as V.A.T. is concerned, most foods are zero rated, but some items such as ice-cream and fruit juice are subject to tax; chocolate items, too, are generally standard rated.

It is advisable to insist upon a client's keeping a Goods Received Book (see example, page 163) in the same way as he would for liquor, so as to record any purchases or returns. Items like bread or milk, which are delivered daily but for which delivery notes or invoices usually arrive on a weekly or monthly basis, must also be entered. From this, the Stocktaker will be able to assess the value of the food bought during the period. It may well be that some of the more recent purchases are unpriced; in such cases, he will have either to contact the supplier or to estimate the value, making any necessary adjustment at the next stocktaking, once invoices have been received. He will also need to acquire from his client details of allowances and income for the period, which would be extracted in exactly the same way as liquor income; great care must be taken to ensure that the figure extracted is the correct one (see page 4).

Food Allowances

Basically, allowances are made for any food which goes out of the kitchen and for which no money is received. Food in this category might be for the proprietor, the management or the staff; for pool or darts teams; for 'complimentary' distribution; for transfer to the bar; or (if written-off) for disposal. The total value of the allowances would need to be calculated at full retail or cost price, and deducted as demonstrated.

If the Stocktaker is also doing liquor stocks, he may be asked to charge any food transferred to the bar (e.g. fruit, nuts etc.) through the bar and reduce his food purchases accordingly (see page 131).

Producing a Gross Profit

Exactly the same principle applies as in the calculation of a trading account within the liquor operation:–

(Income + closing stock) − (opening stock + purchases) = Gross Profit; to find Gross Profit percentage, divide by the income figure and multiply by 100.

When allowances at retail are taken into account:–

(Allowance (at retail) + income + closing stock) − (opening stock + purchases) = Gross Profit; to find Gross Profit percentage, divide by the income figure plus allowances and multiply by 100.

When allowances at cost are taken into account:–
(Allowances (at cost) + income + closing stock) − (opening stock +
purchases) = Gross Profit; to find Gross Profit percentage, divide by
the income figure and multiply by 100.

Food Trading Account

As will be seen from the previous formulae, there are three methods
of presenting a trading account: ignoring allowances, incorporating
them at retail, and incorporating them at cost. To demonstrate the
three methods, Ex. 1 to 3 below make use of the following figures:

Opening stock	£1,120.50
Closing stock	£968.13
Purchases (excl. V.A.T.)	£6,803.47
Income (excl. V.A.T.)	£13,150.20
Allowances at retail (excl. V.A.T.)	£480.00

Example 1
Trading account excluding allowances:–

	£		£
Opening stock	1,120.50	Closing stock	968.13
Purchases	6,803.47	Income	
Gross Profit	6,194.36	(excl. V.A.T.)	13,150.20
	14,118.33		14,118.33

Gross Profit 47.10%.

Example 2
Trading account taking in allowances at retail price:–

	£		£
Opening stock	1,120.50	Closing stock	968.13
Purchases	6,803.47	Income	
Gross Profit	6,674.36	(excl. V.A.T.)	13,150.20
		Allowances	480.00
	14,598.33		14,598.33

Gross Profit 48.97%.

Example 3
Trading account taking in allowances at cost price:–

	£		£
Opening stock	1,120.50	Closing stock	£968.13
Purchases	6,803.47	Income	
Gross Profit	6,439.35	(excl. V.A.T.)	13,150.20
		Allowances	244.99
	14,363.32		14,363.32

Gross Profit 48.97%.

or:–

	£		£
Opening stock	1,120.50	Closing stock	£968.13
Purchases	6,803.47	Income	
Gross Profit	6,439.35	(excl. V.A.T.)	13,150.20
Allowances	(244.99)		
	14,118.33		14,118.33

Gross Profit 48.97%.

Clients should always be given the actual gross profit figure, with any further details as auxiliary information.

Food Gross Profit

There are two methods of assessing profitability: as gross profit on sales, and as gross profit on cost, otherwise known as 'mark-up'. The examples in the previous section showed profitability as gross profit on sales, the method most commonly used in calculating food stock results. If a client achieves a 50% gross profit, then the amount he has made is identical to the cost of the food; if he achieves only 40%, then his food cost represents 60% of the total income. The calculations in the following section relate to gross profit on cost, or mark-up; the relationship between these two ways of measuring profitability can be demonstrated as follows:–

Gross Profit on Cost and Selling

Purchase price	£100
Selling price	£200
Profit	£100
Gross profit on selling	50%
Gross profit on cost, or mark-up	100%

Mark-up

If the client purchases food for £100 and sells it for £133, then his mark-up is 33%, or 25% gross profit on sales. To convert the former to the latter, calculate as follows:–

$$\frac{\text{Mark-up (percentage)} \times \text{cost}}{\text{Income}} = \text{Gross Profit on sales (percentage)}$$

In the example on page 169, where the client achieves a 34% gross profit result, he will in fact have made £51 profit on every £100-worth purchased:–

$$\frac{\text{Cost price} \times 100}{100 - \text{Gross Profit on sales (percentage)}} = \text{Selling price}$$

$$\frac{0.99 \times 100}{100 - 34} = £1.50$$

He purchased his goods for £0.99 and sold them at £1.50, so his mark-up is 51%:–

$$\frac{\text{Mark-up} \times 100}{\text{Selling price}} = \text{Gross Profit on sales (percentage)}$$

$$\frac{0.51 \times 100}{1.50} = 34\%$$

Failure to Achieve Projected Gross Profits

Unless the reason for lack of profitability is obvious, one would need to consider the various possibilities and advise the client accordingly. It is good policy to adopt the suggestions listed below as control guidelines.

Purchasing:

1. Plan your menu to suit the food available.
2. Take advantage of seasonal prices.
3. Buy competitively: 'shop around', don't overbuy.
4. Buy sensibly, and within a defined policy.
5. Buy in accordance with definite specifications – quality, weight etc.
6. Buy in bulk only if it is appropriate to do so.
7. Order perishables a little at a time.
8. Order daily goods (milk, rolls etc.) as needed, not by standing order.

Deliveries:

1. Check the weight of meat etc. on accurate scales.
2. Check quantities, sizes and counts of all goods.
3. Do not encourage deliverymen to enter the kitchen.

Storage of Food:

1. Keep stores tidy: put new items at the back, and use stock in rotation.
2. Where applicable, keep stores properly numbered and coded.
3. Keep accurate records, including cost prices.
4. Treat stores as carefully as a spirits cellar: allow only authorised access.

Preparation of Food:

1. Be aware of cost, and fix proper selling prices.
2. Control the cooking time of meat to reduce shrinkage.
3. Maintain a popularity index of dishes, and keep wastage to an absolute minimum.

Menu Planning and Costing

The most usual cause of failure to achieve targets is inadequate menu planning and costing. The following chart shows losses typically incurred in the cooking of meat.

Items:	Six Ribs of Beef
Weight:	188½ lb
Price per pound:	£1.60
Total value:	£301.60

Butchering Test

	Weight lb	oz	Unit Price	Cost	Ratio of Total Weight
Bone	11	1			5.9
Scraps	10	8			5.6
End cuts	13	12	£0.80	£11.00	7.3
Short ribs	22	3	£0.84	£18.64	11.8
Ribs for roasting	130	12	£2.08	£271.96	69.3
Loss in butchery		4			0.1
	188	8		£301.60	100.0%

Cooking Test

	Weight lb	oz	Unit Cost	Product Cost	Ratio of Total Weight
Ribs for roasting	130	12	£2.08	£271.96	69.3%
Weight after roasting	104	0	£2.615	£271.96	55.2%

Costings

	Portion Size	No.	Cost	Percentage Required	Selling Price
Restaurant	8 oz	208	£1.30	60%	£3.25 + V.A.T.
Banquet	6 oz	277	£0.98	65%	£2.80 + V.A.T.

Each dish must be properly costed; the raw product, including garnishes, needs accurate valuing. Below are listed the components of a typical one.

Roast turkey with vegetables and potatoes

	per portion
Roast turkey (60p per lb) excluding bones	30p
Chipolata sausage (80p per lb)	10p
Boiled potatoes (12p per lb)	6p
Brussels sprouts (30p per lb)	10p
Cranberry sauce	5p
Bread sauce	5p
Sausage meat	5p
Gravy	3p
Stuffing	5p
Garnish etc.	10p
Rolls, butter, salt, pepper etc.	10p
Total Cost of Main Course:	**99p**

Once a 'raw' cost has been acquired, it is necessary to determine the gross profit to ensure that a client is achieving his target. If he is selling this meal at £1.50 plus V.A.T., and anticipates 40%, then he has underpriced it: he will achieve only 34%:–

$$\frac{1.50 - 0.99 \text{ (cost)}}{1.50} \times 100 = 34\%$$

The Stocktaker would have to advise him to set his selling price at £1.65 plus V.A.T., in order to achieve his target, the price being calculated as follows:–

$$\frac{0.99 \text{ (cost)} \times 100}{100 - 40} = £1.65 + \text{V.A.T. (required selling price)}$$

On the cost price of £0.99, then, to achieve each of the following gross profits, the selling price would be:–

40% gross profit	£1.65 plus V.A.T.
50% gross profit	£1.98 plus V.A.T.
60% gross profit	£2.47 plus V.A.T.
70% gross profit	£3.30 plus V.A.T.
80% gross profit	£4.95 plus V.A.T.

SHOPS AND RETAIL OUTLETS: VALUATION OF STOCK

Retail Stock

It is extremely rare for a Stocktaker to be asked to prepare an extended report on a shop or industrial outlet. It would be virtually impossible to do, unless the Stocktaker attended the site regularly and was extremely accurate both in his count and in his extracting of information. If such a situation did prevail, the Stocktaker would treat the outlet in exactly the same way as a bar, producing a surplus or deficit figure and any other information normally obtained in the liquor operation. Before agreeing to such a task, the Stocktaker should remember that there are a considerable number of lines in an average shop, with different sizes demanding different selling prices, and each brand probably having a different retail value.

In most cases, though, the Stocktaker would simply be asked to prepare a valuation, either for a change of ownership, or for year-end valuation purposes, or at the request of accountants. The Stocktaker will occasionally be working for both parties (at a change of ownership); if this is his role, he must be impartial as between the vendor and the purchaser. He should liaise with both parties, discuss the stock in general terms, ensure that the method of taking stock is acceptable, and discuss procedures for dealing with out-of-date merchandise or damaged goods.

In a normal-sized shop, it would be both difficult and time-consuming to list every item on the premises, and then extract cost prices from invoices and catalogues. Specific details would have to be written down for each line; and in some cases, the same product would be on sale from different manufacturers. In many instances, stock would have been lying for a considerable period of time, and finding current cost prices would almost be impossible; it would certainly be time-consuming, making the fee non-cost-effective to the client.

In view of the difficulties involved in pricing goods, the more normal way to take stock in shops or other retail outlets is to count the stock at selling price, deduct V.A.T. if applicable, and then reduce this figure by the profit margin which brings the value down to cost. Because different categories of items might have totally different margins, the Stocktaker should prepare his valuation under various headings. For instance, if he is working in a news-agent's, he might count and calculate the stock in the following manner, using these headings:–

A regular monthly stocktake being carried out (Crewe Toll Service Station, Edinburgh).

STATIONERY	CIGARETTES	TOBACCO	NEWSPAPERS	BOOKS	CARDS ETC.
12 × 18	126 × 1·30	12 × 1·20	53 × 30	12 × 3·95	102 × 32
7 × 26	296 × 1·54	4 × 2·12	104 × 28	8 × 2·45	203 × 90
1 × 12	208 × 1·46		27 × 32	17 × 2·95	110 × 46
102 × 80	380 × 72			11 × 1·99	230 × 73
	400 × 1·54				80 × 31
	349 × 1·53				1200 × 50
					1004 × 34
£85·70	£2346·89	£22·88	£53·66	£139·04	£1400·00

In the example, newspapers and books are not subject to V.A.T., so a straight 'cost of sale' percentage would be applied.

When one considers that cigarettes have a gross profit margin of around 8% and cards of around 50%, it will be obvious why it is important to categorise each section accurately and apply the correct margins. Final calculations would be as follows:–

Cigarettes (retail value)	£2,346.89
Less V.A.T.	£306.12
	£2,040.77
Which, multiplied by 92% (being the cost of sale) =	£1,877.51

which would be the cost value of that particular category of product.

If cards totalled £1,400 or, less V.A.T., £1,217.38, the total cost value would be £608.69. The same procedure would apply to the other items listed, and other categories.

Percentages do pose a problem, and they vary according to the size of premises, the type of shop, and the locality. There is no objection to the practice of discussing with clients the particular profit margins anticipated in each category, and experienced Stock-takers will do this on a fairly regular basis, for it enables them to keep up-to-date with any adjustments or variations which might occur. It quite often happens, though, that there is a dispute between purchaser and vendor as to the percentages applied. The Stocktaker must be in a position to arbitrate, and to do this properly, he will need to have a clear idea of what percentages are in normal use locally. Because of the variations throughout the country, it is not possible to set out guidelines in this book.

Some Stocktakers do like to discuss margins with the vendor, either at the changeover or before. It can be helpful to know the overall percentage the shop made during the two previous years' trading, and also the individual percentage mark-ups in any areas where the shop holds more than average stock. These figures can be compared with known mark-ups, and a note made for future reference. The Stocktaker should be aware that items such as tea, coffee, sugar, cereals etc. are sometimes regarded as 'loss leaders', in which case the profit margin can be very low. It is a useful exercise, where possible, to select invoices at random and to compare these with selling prices, so that accurate gross profits can be determined for each category.

If the Stocktaker is acting for both parties, he must be absolutely sure that the stock is of good quality and saleable. Dust does not necessarily mean that the stock is old; but if the Stocktaker notices an exceptional amount of one product, or (for example) damaged cigarette packages, he would obviously be wary of including them in his valuation. Stock which, in his opinion, could not be sold at normal retail value should be withdrawn, and the vendor given the opportunity to remove it from the premises. In some cases the two parties might agree to have it included at a reduced charge, in which case the purchaser would be able to sell it at discounted prices.

The term 'stock at valuation' does not necessarily mean 'at cost': the historic or actual cost does not usually come into the calculation, and is not the final factor. What matters is the price agreed between the two parties, using either one or two valuers working on the basis already explained. The 'cost of replacement' value has a bearing on the overall figures; but the Stocktaker must always bear in mind the possibility of overstocking. If, for instance, he finds 1,000 half-litre cans of paint, all in good condition and easy to value, he would take them at their true retail price; but if most of them were of the same colour (e.g. 800 cans of yellow), then they would be valued at less than cost, because the purchaser would obviously have 'dead' stock on his hands for a considerable length of time. A newsagent's with 1,000 birth cards, adjacent to a maternity hospital, would be likely to sell them within the comparatively near future; but if that same shop was next to a geriatric unit, then the Stocktaker would reduce the value of those cards. He must consider the value of the stock held on the premises, and relate it to turnover in order to determine whether this value is realistic. If the stock is likely to be static on the premises for a considerable length of time, he should probably give a discount on the stock or suggest that the vendor remove some of it.

Cards present a special problem, and can be very time-consuming to count. Unwrapped ones tend to get dirtied by people fingering them, and would accordingly be difficult to sell, so the Stocktaker should withdraw soiled or damaged cards from the racks. The prices are usually given on the back of each, but in some instances he may have to work from code numbers.

The stocks of grocery shops are much easier to count than are those of newsagents, but the Stocktaker has to be very conscious of the 'sell-by' dates, and anything beyond the date given would be excluded from his valuation, as would surplus stocks close to the date of expiry. Once again, the vendor would be given the opportunity to remove these from the premises. Damaged or rusty cans would also be excluded. The stock would be taken in the way already described, except that the Stocktaker would probably use the following headings:—

Grocery products, including pet foods (standard rated)
Grocery products (zero rated)
Fruit and vegetables
Chemist's sundries
Bakery goods
Frozen goods
Cleaning materials
etc.

Sweets in jars can be difficult, and the only way to be completely accurate is to empty the contents of each jar on to the scales and weigh them. Another way is to check the weight of an empty bottle and deduct that from all future weights; but the most common method is to gauge each jar in exactly the same way as one would with spirits. If a full bottle contains six pounds, the Stocktaker would convert this to quarters (i.e. twenty-four), and then estimate the number of quarter-pounds in the bottle and multiply that by the selling price. There is currently a 50p deposit on glass bottles only.

There is of course no limit to the number of headings that could be used, but if it were excessive, there would be little point in separating the products. The final Certificate of Valuation is normally prepared in exactly the same way as one for a bar, and as many headings as the Stocktaker wishes can be shown, but it is probably advisable to restrict it to main titles, perhaps combining some of the smaller categories for presentation on the final certificate. The following is an example:—

Certificate of Valuation

Society Stocktaking Services Ltd.

Premises . . . .

We certify that a fair valuation of stock on hand at the above premises cost value excluding V.A.T. after close of business on Friday 15th July 1988 would be Two thousand nine hundred and fifty three pounds and fifty seven pence made up as follows

Cigarettes	656.82
Groceries	500.08
Confectionery	439.27
Cigars/tobacco	291.55
Chemist's sundries	211.25
Cards	154.56
Books/magazines	125.06
Cleaning materials	116.10
Household goods	90.68
Stationery	72.86
Minerals	72.78
Crisps	66.91
Clothing	42.20
Tobacco sundries	38.46
Ice-cream	20.38
Sundries	28.21
Subtotal	£2,927.17
Deposits	26.40
Total	£2,953.57

Stocktaker's signature . . . .

Paper bags, wrapping paper, cartons for hot food, cling-film and any other similar goods, given away to customers in the course of trading, should be taken at cost and added to the total valuation.

In some instances, Stocktakers will split their final valuation into three categories only: standard rated stock, zero rated stock, and book debts.

The last category applies particularly to newsagents' shops, where money is outstanding for newspaper or magazine accounts. These debts are likely to be paid to the purchaser, and should therefore be included in the valuation.

Occasionally, a purchaser or vendor will instruct the Stocktaker to do no more than count the stock and use an overall gross profit to bring the valuation down to cost. This is not an acceptable practice and should be discouraged, because the wide variability of profit margins would make it possible for the vendor to manipulate the end figure quite considerably by increasing stockholdings of specific products prior to the date of sale. If it had been agreed that the final calculations would be based on a 25% gross profit, and more than half the stock related to cards, then the final valuation could deviate from the correct amount by as much as 15%.

Stocktakers valuing stock in retail outlets, using the method described above, must equip themselves with a general knowledge of standard retail prices, because in some instances vendors will increase these just before the date of sale so as to boost the valuation.

Wholesale Stock

Wholesale stock held in garages or warehouses is seldom marked with a retail price, so would have to be listed and then valued at cost. It is quite common practice for a Stocktaker to be asked to check the count off against the client's own computer sheets or records, and these would obviously be priced; in such instances, it would be necessary only to take a physical count of the stock and check any discrepancies. The clients themselves would normally work out the valuation.

If the Stocktaker is preparing a valuation of spare parts in a garage, he must be careful to list all the parts and their code numbers accurately, as many items are produced by a variety of manufacturers, and cost prices do tend to vary. In addition, substantial discounts are available on list prices, and these would have to be taken into account in the valuation.

SHOPS AND V.A.T.

Generally speaking, it can be assumed that most food purchases either for one's own consumption or for resale are zero rated, but there are exceptions, and it is the way in which the food is used that determines whether or not V.A.T. will be attributed to that particular product.

Specific items which are subject to standard rate V.A.T. are ice-cream, confectionery, chocolate biscuits, alcoholic drinks, soft drinks, crisps, salted or roasted nuts, and pet food.

Ice-creams and Lollies

These items, including the wafers and cones sold with ice-cream, would be standard rated, as would ice-cream powders and mixes, lolly syrup, and frozen yoghurt on sticks.

Exception: frozen yoghurt which is thawed completely before being eaten.

Chocolates and Confectionery

The following would all be subject to the standard rate of tax: bars of chocolate, liqueur chocolates, any chocolate containing nuts or fruit, chocolate biscuits, boiled sweets, chewing gum, chewy cereal bars, compressed fruit bars, sweetened popcorn, marrons glacés, crystallised ginger, glacé or crystallised fruit.

Exceptions: ginger in syrup or dusted ginger, chocolate spread, liquid chocolate icing, chocolate chips, strands of vermicelli, toffee apples, edible cake decorations, Indian or Pakistani delicacies.

Chocolate Biscuits and Cakes

Standard rate V.A.T. applies to all biscuits coated in chocolate (either wholly or partly covered or decorated), petits fours, slimmer's meals in biscuit form with chocolate coating, marshmallows and fondant products without a biscuit base, also inedible cake decorations.

Exceptions: cakes (including sponge), pastries, éclairs, meringues, and biscuits with chocolate-flavoured coating.

Crisps and Nuts

All crisps, potato sticks and puffs, potato flour products, and savoury puffed cereals such as sweetened popcorn are standard rated for V.A.T., and so are all salted and roasted shelled nuts, and toasted coconut.

Exceptions: savoury biscuits, pork scratchings, non-salted nuts (e.g. Chinese).

Mixtures and Assortments

Mixtures and assortments containing both standard rated and zero rated items are treated as 'mixed supplies', and the following rules apply:–

Assorted Biscuits
If the weight of standard rated goods does not exceed 15% of net weight, the assortment is zero rated.

Fruit and Nut Mixtures
If the weight of standard rated goods does not exceed 25% of net weight, the mixture is zero rated.

As the kitchen can be a busy operation, it is important to consider the most suitable time to count the stock (Francesco's Restaurant, Rose Street, Edinburgh).

It is imperative that a methodical counting procedure be followed, in order that no bottles are overlooked (the Glencairn Hotel, Royal Circus, Edinburgh).

Petits Fours
If the net weight of the chocolate biscuits and sweets does not exceed
15% of net weight, the total is zero rated.

Alcoholic Drinks

All beers, ciders, wine, spirits and liqueurs, including home-made
and fermented communion wine, are standard rated.
    Exceptions: fruit preserved in alcohol, unfermented fruit juice
intended for sacramental use, Angostura Bitters.

Soft Drinks

V.A.T. is applied at standard rate to all carbonated drinks, fruit
cordials and squashes; mineral, table and spa water; alcohol-free
beers, fruit and vegetable juices; ginger, glucose, honey and barley-
water drinks; syrups, crystals and powders for making drinks;
flavourings for milk shakes; and laxatives.
    Exceptions: lemon juice for culinary purposes; cocoa and drink-
ing chocolate; coffee and coffee/chicory mixtures; all preparations
and extracts of yeast, meat, and egg; flavoured milk.

Edible Products not Classified as Food

The following are standard rated: medicines and medical preparations, appetite-suppressants and slimmer's laxatives, dietary supple-
ments, elixirs and tonics, malt extract, and capsules containing
vitamins, iron, calcium, yeast, garlic, ginseng etc.; synthetic food
flavourings, seasonings and colourings, bicarbonate of soda, emul-
sifiers, stabilisers, bread improvers and pie glazes, essential oils; salt
for water-softening and dish-washing purposes.
    Exceptions: baking powder, cooking oil, culinary herbs and
spices either natural or dried, whole, ground or milled; saccharin,
artificial sweeteners; cream of tartar, gravy thickenings, salt for
culinary use.

STOCKTAKING: SUMMARY OF GUIDELINES FOR STOCKTAKERS

1. Dress should be smart. First impressions are important.
2. Be methodical. Count clearly, from top to bottom and from left to right, and do not move from one end of the bar to the other merely because a similar bottle has been sighted.
3. Always use the same method for measuring part-used bottles.
4. Measures, glasses and selling prices should all be checked at regular intervals.
5. While working, the Stocktaker must have full authority over the bar. No transaction must take place without his knowledge.
6. Stocktaking cannot be completed effectively unless the Stocktaker is allowed to concentrate and carry on with his work without distraction.
7. Fraternization with bar staff is to be discouraged. The Stocktaker should be impartial, but should also remember that he is working for the proprietor in an official capacity.
8. Be totally security-conscious, and never divulge clients' confidential information.
9. A responsible person from the hotel or bar should always be encouraged to attend while stock is being taken. He will have knowledge of the whereabouts of stock which will prevent any being missed.
10. All bookwork must be carefully examined, and where practicable, cross-checked. Random inspections of duplicate pages of requisition books etc. are advisable.
11. Verify all figures given, and report any anomalies to the client as soon as possible.
12. Give prompt results; make sure they are properly checked, and be prepared to discuss them in depth with the client.

SECTION III
THE PRODUCT RANGE

CHAPTER 9

BEER AND BREWING;
SPIRITS, FORTIFIED WINES AND
LIQUEURS

There are about 150 breweries in Britain, most of which produce beer naturally. Methods vary from one part of the country to another; but basically, all beer is produced by extracting the natural goodness from barley, and adding hops and then yeast to create, by fermentation, an alcoholic drink.

Ingredients

Traditional beer is brewed from the following materials.

Barley: This is converted into malt, which gives the beer its body and alcohol content. Barley is not only the easiest cereal to grow, it is also the most suitable for the brewer, because the grain sprouts quickly when steeped in water during the malting process. It also has a high starch and relatively low nitrogen content, allowing the brewer to extract as much sugar as he wants. Barley is grown throughout the country, but the farmer must ensure that he selects the correct variety (the Brewers' Society will assist him with this); his success will also depend on the weather (ideally, dry conditions in the spring and moderate rainfalls later on). In normal circumstances, brewers will purchase only the highest quality of barley, in effect not more than one quarter of all that is produced.

Harvesting generally takes place during the late summer, and reaped barley is taken to the maltings, where immersion in large tanks of water causes it to germinate. The moistened grains are then transferred by conveyer to the germination area, where they are allowed to continue growing for another five to eight days, until shoots appear from the hard husk. The purpose of this process is to break down the cells of the barley, allowing the starch content to be converted into soluble sugars; it generally occurs in a large hall, where the grain lies about six inches deep and is constantly turned over with a shovel, or (nowadays) with some mechanical implement.

Once he considers it to be in perfect condition, the maltster will transfer the grain to a kiln, where it will be heated up to 60°C, to prevent further growth. The moisture content will begin to drop,

181

and simultaneously the temperature will be raised gradually to 110°C (or less, depending upon the type of malt required: the lower the temperature, the paler the beer, and *vice versa*). When the process has been completed, this finished product will be stored in silos ready for transfer to the brewery malt store.

Hops: Hops help to keep beer free from infection. They also impart the bitterness and aroma, the special flavours associated with individual beers. They are generally grown in the south of England; only the female plants are used in brewing, so the male hops (other than those retained for future fertilisation) have to be disposed of.

Hops are perennial, and emerge each spring from the root stumps of the previous year's plants. Because the hops need to climb, hop gardens are characterised by a system of poles, wires, strings etc., reaching to a height of twenty feet in some places. Insects, fungi and viruses create enormous problems, and constant vigilance is necessary to ensure a good crop.

Harvesting is at the end of the summer and, once picked, the hops are quickly taken away from the heat and humidity of the autumn air. As soon as they have been separated from the leaves and stems, the cones are taken into a building called an oast-house, where they are spread in a kiln to a depth of up to two feet, on an open batten floor covered with large horse-hair cloths. The heat is steadily increased for three hours and then maintained for six, by which time the hops are dry and ready to be spread on the floor of a cooling house, where they remain for several hours before being packed into large sacks called pockets.

Some hops are reduced to a fine powder and then compressed into small pellets before being sent to the brewery, but most are used straight from the pocket.

Water: The availability of good water very often determines the situation of a brewery. In the strongest beers water represents 10% of the total content, and in the weaker ones, up to 30%; so any impurities in the water could be detrimental to the final product. Burton on Trent made its name as a brewing centre because the gypsum content of the local well water helped to produce a first-rate clear beer, and London because the high degree of temporary hardness found in the waters of its shallow wells was similarly beneficial.

Throughout the world, brewers have tried to imitate the gypsum content of the Burton water. The process is known as 'Burtonisation', and is now accepted as an ideal way of combining the purity and consistency of water from public supplies with the special content which occurs naturally from the gravel beds above the Trent valley.

Yeast: Developed by germination in contact with saccharine liquids, yeast is made up of millions of individual microscopic organisms which develop considerable biochemical activity in reaction with sugar-rich liquids such as wort. Yeast is extremely temperamental, and is often the sole cause of 'bad brews'.

The Brewing Process

Initial Stages: Brewing generally starts in the early morning with the transfer of malt from the store to the hoppers at the top of the brewhouse, where it is sieved and screened to ensure the removal of any foreign objects. It is subsequently fed into a mill where it is ground into a grist ready to be mixed with hot liquor (the brewer's term for water heated up to about 77°C).

The grist and liquor meet in the mash tun, which is filled almost to the top. It is then allowed to stand for several hours, so that the malt is eventually able to dissolve into the liquor. An even temperature must be maintained throughout this process, and if the liquid cools, hot liquor is immediately pumped in through a slatted false bottom.

The liquid is run off through taps at the base of the vessel, leaving behind hot malt grains. In a procedure called sparging, hot water is sprayed over the bed of the mash, and this is continued until almost clear water emerges. Great care is needed here, because too little sparging leaves behind valuable sugars, whereas too much affects the taste of the beer. Most breweries today are automated, so the risk of human error is considerably reduced.

Wort, which is the name given to the sweet liquid which has just emerged from the mash tun, is then boiled in a copper with the hops; these are taken direct from the pocket, and sometimes different varieties are blended to produce the required flavour. The higher the proportion of hops, the more bitter the beer will be; but boiling beyond the prescribed time (one to two hours) will have the opposite effect, so the brewer must be very precise with his timings.

Boiling not only kills the bacteria in the wort, it also stops the action of enzymes which break down the starch in the malt during mashing. Sometimes sugar is added to the mix, to complement the natural sugars extracted from the malt. Once boiled, the contents of the copper are emptied into a hop back which has a false bottom. Here the hops settle on a slatted base, which acts as a filter as the wort seeps through. Since it is still boiling, the wort must now pass through compact cooling units on its way to the fermenting vessels.

Fermentation: Once in the fermentation hall, the wort is mixed with yeast, which generally comes in drums; the entire contents of the fermenting vessel are thoroughly mixed to ensure consistency. Because the brewer has to pay duty on the strength of the wort prior to fermentation, it is at this stage that the Excise Officer will take a sample.

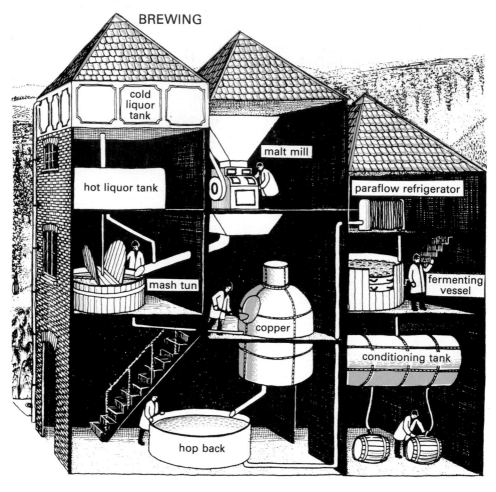

BREWING

cold liquor tank

malt mill

hot liquor tank

paraflow refrigerator

mash tun

fermenting vessel

copper

conditioning tank

hop back

Nine to twelve hours after the yeast and wort have been mixed together, the former will be multiplying rapidly, and within twenty-four hours a thick cream of yeast will have been blown up by the millions of bubbles of carbon dioxide gas which are given off as the yeast converts the sugars in the wort into alcohol. The yeast is continually skimmed off the surface, pressed, and stored at low temperature for future use.

After five days, the rate of fermentation decreases. Since the sugars are used up, the yeast still suspended in the brew begins to drop slowly to the base of the vessel. This process is speeded up by a coolant passed through a series of coils inside the fermentor. At this stage, the beer is referred to as 'green'. If a conical fermentor is used (a tall cylinder with a conical base), the process of fermentation is reduced to about two days.

Conditioning and Racking: Before being delivered to clients, the beer is conditioned. The bubbles of carbon dioxide created by ongoing fermentation contain substances which affect the flavour of unmatured beer, but in the conditioning tank most of the yeast can be eradicated by the addition of finings, a natural additive made from the bladders of certain fish. Priming sugar or caramel can be added at this stage, either to sweeten or to darken the beer, and once the sampler is satisfied that the quality is right, he will authorise the filling of containers in the racking plant. Before use, each container is washed, steamed and inspected. A new bung is hammered into the flat end of the cask, and after filling, the shive hole on the curve side is bunged; the beer is then ready for delivery.

Quite often, beer is racked prior to delivery; this means that finings are added to the container, to prevent continuing fermentation and to enable the beer to be used immediately on delivery. Non-racked beer takes up to twenty-four hours to settle, and cannot be disturbed while 'on tap'.

Bottled, Bright, and Keg Beers: The contents of bottled beers are prepared in exactly the same manner, except that, in most instances, the beer is subject to filtration, pasteurisation and pressurisation, all of which sterilise the beer and change its flavour significantly. Some beers, though, are still bottled in their natural condition; but most of these are so dark that the sediment cannot be seen.

Bright beer is the name given to beer which has gone through a system of filtration; it is stored in large tanks and chilled, so that most of the yeast sinks to the bottom, before being passed through a filter which removes any remaining solid particles. Some breweries filter their beer only partially, so that a little secondary fermentation still occurs.

Keg beer, sometimes known as unnatural beer, is pasteurised. Once filtered, it is brought to a temperature of 65°C for a few seconds, so that any remaining yeast is killed off. The beer is completely sterile, but its taste is different from that of natural beer: it is flat and lifeless, so needs an injection of gas to put some vitality into it. This process, normally carried out at the brewery, involves the pressurisation of the kegs with carbon dioxide gas; as a result, the beer tends to become fizzy and loses some of its character, since so many natural flavours have been removed during processing.

The Strength of Beer

The strength of beer can be measured in two ways, by its original gravity or by the proportion of alcohol.

Original Gravity: This is a measure of the amount of fermentable material added to water to make beer. The density of water is rated at 1,000 degrees, so that a beer brewed at 1,042 degrees will have 42 parts of fermentable material to every 1,000 parts of water, and so on. The measurement is taken before the wort begins to ferment, so gives an indication only of the body of the beer, not necessarily of its strength when served to the customer. Excise duty is, however, based on this figure, so it is a realistic one to use when assessing beer. The average bitter in this country is brewed at between 1,035 and 1,040 degrees, but the range is from 1,030 up to 1,100 (which would be extremely strong).

The Proportion of Alcohol: This is usually based on volume, and ranges from 2% to 10%, the most common strengths being from 3% to 4%. In low-alcohol and non-alcoholic beers, the strength can be 1% or less.

BEER AND THE PUB

Storage

Casks can be set either in the cellar or in the bar, but in the case of natural beer, the contents must be allowed to settle for up to two days so that yeast and hops can sink to the bottom. The cask is generally laid on its side on a gantry, and chocks are used to steady it. A tap is hammered into the bung on the flat end of the cask ready for future dispensing, and a soft spile is placed in the core of the shive at the top of the cask so as to allow carbon dioxide, produced by continuing fermentation, to escape. Hard spiles control the beer more rigidly, and prevent it from going flat. Since air is drawn in through the spile to replace the liquid drawn off, the cask needs to be emptied fairly quickly, before the contents deteriorate; and this is why brewers supply containers of different sizes.

Beer should always be stored at 14°C: temperature differences either way will affect the quality. Natural beer should never be moved once it is in use, because the yeast and hops would rise again to the surface and cause cloudy or sedimented beer.

Dispensing

Pumps are either manually or electrically operated. Manual pumps operate on a straightforward suction basis, and each time the handle is pulled, an amount of beer is dispensed through the font. With electrically operated pumps, the beer is pulled up to the bar, the amount being controlled either by a meter which regulates the flow (usually in half-pints) and ensures an exact measure, or on a free-flow basis which allows the barman to pull any amount of beer he wishes. In Scotland, the usual method is to push the beer up by converting water-main pressure into air pressure; but whichever of these three systems is used, the flavours and characteristics of natural beer are retained.

Keg beers are pressurised in the cellar: the container is coupled to a cylinder of carbon dioxide, which keeps air away from the beer and, displacing the liquid drawn off, forces the beer out under pressure.

Draught Beer – Legal Requirements

Two types of capacity serving measure may legally be used. With the brim measure glass, the level of the nominal capacity is denoted by the brim of the glass; the regulations governing the manufacture of pint brim measure glasses permit a maximum error of 34 millilitres (about 1.2 fluid ounces), in excess only. With the line measure glass, the line denoting one pint must be not less than 10 mm from the brim; and in this case, the regulations permit a maximum error in the placing of the line of plus or minus 17 millilitres (0.6 fluid ounces).

Whether or not beer is served with a head depends upon various factors – the type of beer, the equipment used to dispense it, and individual consumer preferences. Some customers prefer their beer to be served without a head, while others regard the head as essential. Because of these divergent demands, the courts have upheld that the head is part of the measure, provided that it is reasonable in the light of what the customer was to be taken as ordering.

When beer with a head is dispensed into a brim measure glass, the head must reach the brim or above it, to ensure that the quantity of beer dispensed, liquid and head, is at least a pint (or half-pint). As the head collapses, the small proportion of liquid it contains will fall into the rest of the beer, and the gas will disperse into the atmosphere. When the head has completely collapsed, the amount of liquid may be less than one pint. The law requires that when beer is served in a brim measure glass, and the liquid level of the beer does not at the time of service meet the customer's requirements, he can ask for a top-up. But if, after settling, the volume of the beer decreases slightly to below the line, then the licensee is not at fault.

When dispensed from a free-flow system into a line measure glass, the beer (liquor and head) must be sufficient to ensure that, after the head has completely collapsed, the liquid in the glass remains level with the line defining the measure.

Cellar Management

The cellar is often the heart of any liquor operation, and the final condition of its beers will depend upon the way in which they are prepared and handled in that cellar.

There are eight principal factors which determine the quality of beer served in a pub or hotel.

Cleanliness: A cellar must be scrupulously clean at all times. Dirt means dirty air, which can affect casks, beers and utensils. Spilled beer should be wiped up immediately, and none should be left standing about in buckets or containers. Products other than beer should not be stored in the cellar as anything with a pungent smell, such as paint, paraffin or disinfectant, will be detrimental to the beer, and should be kept well away. Dogs and other pets should never be allowed in that area.

Walls and Ceilings: These should be frequently cleaned, lime-washed or painted. In older cellars, this should be done at least once a year, as mould grows quickly in damp conditions, not only increasing the risk of air-borne infection to the beer but also giving rise to unpleasant smells. Where walls are damp, they can be sterilised by regular spraying with a weak solution of bleach; care must be taken, though, not to spray casks or utensils.

Floors: Where possible, good drainage should be available in all cellars; but if it is not, floors should be dried once they have been mopped or hosed down. The addition of ordinary washing powder to the water will help to maintain the cleanliness of both floors and ceilings.

Drainage: Drains and gulleys must always be kept clean and fresh, to prevent unpleasant smells and air contamination. If the cellar is not connected to the main drainage and a sump is installed, this must be thoroughly cleaned out at least once a week. The water inside must never be allowed to become stagnant, and it may well be necessary to scrape these drains if deposits build up on the surfaces.

Ventilation: Inadequate ventilation is the frequent cause of dampness and mould, so all cellars should have a throughput of air if at all possible. Air shafts and bricks must be kept clean and free from rubbish. On the other hand, draughts are harmful because cold air blowing directly on to a cask may cause a 'chill haze'. If the beer is not under top pressure it is replaced, as it is drawn off, by a similar volume of air entering through the spile hole. If this air is not fresh and clean, bacteria and mould spores will settle in the beer, producing noxious tastes.

In winter, some reduction in ventilation may be necessary to prevent severe temperature fluctuations; whereas in summer, the cellar flaps or windows should be opened early in the morning before the day warms up. Wall-mounted fan blowers with thermostatic controls provide the most suitable form of ventilation, but their thermostats should never be tampered with, so that an even temperature is maintained. Every cellar should have a thermometer placed, ideally, about three feet above the casks, and hung from the ceiling (away from the light) so that it reflects the temperature of the air rather than that of the wall.

Where the cellar's temperature is automatically controlled, it is advisable for the cellar door to be left open occasionally for a short time, to allow free passage of air.

Temperature Control: Most complaints concerning draught beer arise because the beer has been stored in a cellar whose temperature has not been properly controlled. Violent fluctuations are very detrimental, and must always be avoided.

Most brewers advise a static cellar temperature of between 55° and 58°F (12.8°–14.4°C). Others prefer the beers to be kept in conditions of between 56° and 60°F (13.3°–15.6°C). A 'chill haze' is likely to develop if temperatures drop below 54°F (12.2°C); and in the case of sedimented beer not under top pressure, low temperatures may cause loss of condition, while high temperatures can over-condition the ale and cause fobbing. This tends to happen more often in part-full kegs.

Lighting: There must be adequate lighting in the cellar, so that routine work can be attended to and dirt can be kept under control.

Stillages: Solid stillages of brick, concrete or stone must be kept thoroughly clean and as dry as possible, so that casks will not slip when tilted. Metal stillages (which are preferable to wood) must be kept clear of the wall, to allow adequate space for cleaning; and to prevent movement, they should be firmly fixed to the floor.

Cellar Safety

Gas cylinders not in use should be laid flat on the floor and chocked, to reduce the risk of personal injury.

Cylinders in use must be secured in proper brackets, to minimise strain on the dispensing equipment and to prevent liquid CO_2 from getting into the system. Failure to observe this could result in carbon dioxide leaking, or in the bursting of the red rubber tubing.

SPIRITS

The Distilling Process

Spirit is produced by the distillation of a fermented liquor – a liquor which can be made from any ingredient containing sugar, and capable of fermenting and producing alcohol. Two principal methods are used for distilling. The first is the pot still method, which is the original distilling procedure and the one used for better-quality spirits; it is slower and more costly than any other method, but the end result does retain the flavours and odours of the fermented liquor.

Many of these pot stills are made of copper. They are bowl-shaped with a spout extending from the top which is connected to a coiled copper pipe; this is enclosed in a water tank, so that vapours passing through the pipe condense and the end product runs out as spirit.

Alcohol boils at a lower temperature than water, and will therefore vaporise and be driven upward towards the spout. For more effective temperature control, the still is heated from underneath, generally by steam, and this process is designed in such a way that the vapour condenses back into liquid (now spirit) once it reaches the coiled pipe. If water or impurities (feints) remain, these will be removed by the spirit's being distilled a second time.

A great deal of skill is needed throughout the entire process to ensure that basic and essential flavourings are retained, so that the spirit keeps its taste and bouquet.

Once all the unwanted impurities have been removed, the spirit is poured into oak casks where it can breathe. By law, it must remain here for a minimum of three years, and although a certain amount of evaporation will take place, the longer the spirits produced by the pot still method are allowed to mature, the better will be their quality.

The second method is the patent or continuous still. The alcohol is continuously and rapidly distilled from the fermented liquor, and though it comes out at a high alcoholic strength its taste is milder, since most of its flavours have been lost during the process.

Whisky

It is worth noting here that 'whisky' refers to the spirit distilled in Scotland, whereas 'whiskey' is produced in Ireland. There are two principal types of Scotch whisky, malt and grain.

Malt Whiskies: These are generally categorised by the four main areas of their production – Highland Malts, Lowland Malts, Campbeltown Malts and Islay Malts. All have their own distinct characteristics; each area has a considerable number of distilleries, and each of these produces whisky with its own individual flavour and bouquet.

At every distillery, however, the basic process is the same: the grain is soaked before being spread on heated floors, where it is allowed to begin germinating. As a result, its starch will be converted into sugar, which in turn (throughout the fermentation stage) will be converted by yeast into alcohol. At the appropriate time, the grain will be dried in kilns heated by peat fires; and it is here that the distinctive personal flavour of each brand is acquired. The now

MALT WHISKY-POT STILL

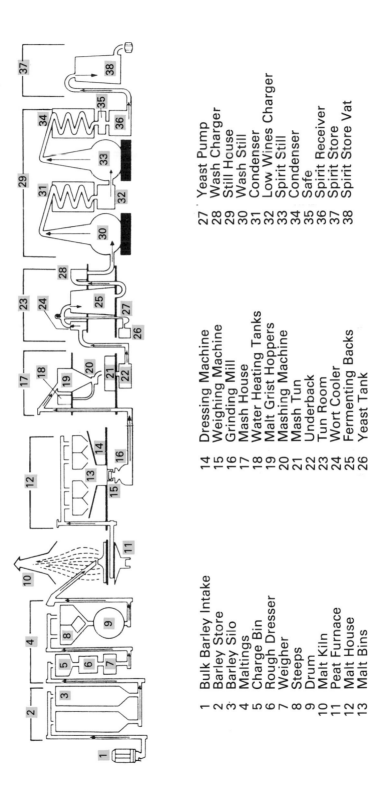

1 Bulk Barley Intake
2 Barley Store
3 Barley Silo
4 Maltings
5 Charge Bin
6 Rough Dresser
7 Weigher
8 Steeps
9 Drum
10 Malt Kiln
11 Peat Furnace
12 Malt House
13 Malt Bins

14 Dressing Machine
15 Weighing Machine
16 Grinding Mill
17 Mash House
18 Water Heating Tanks
19 Malt Grist Hoppers
20 Mashing Machine
21 Mash Tun
22 Underback
23 Tun Room
24 Wort Cooler
25 Fermenting Backs
26 Yeast Tank

27 Yeast Pump
28 Wash Charger
29 Still House
30 Wash Still
31 Condenser
32 Low Wines Charger
33 Spirit Still
34 Condenser
35 Safe
36 Spirit Receiver
37 Spirit Store
38 Spirit Store Vat

malted barley is crushed and mixed with hot water, so that all sugar is removed. The malt is drained, cooled and transferred to the mash tun, where it is allowed to ferment for about forty-eight hours. So as to ensure the removal of all impurities and the correct alcoholic strength, this procedure is generally carried out twice.

The whisky (now malt whisky) is stored in casks; it is from these that the spirit generally takes it colour, but if necessary caramel can be added. The age shown on each bottle indicates how many years the whisky has lain.

The strength of whisky in the cask is around 65% by volume (originally 115° proof), so distilled water must be added to bring it to whatever the required strength is.

Blended Whisky: A blended whisky is a combination of several malts and of whiskies produced by the patent still method. The final product is generally of a milder flavour; and because no distiller will declare his mix of ingredients, Scotch whisky is very difficult to imitate.

Not all malt whiskies are marketed by their distillers as individual brands; most are dispatched to the principal independent bottlers and become constituents of blended whisky, but some are combined as vatted malts.

Vatted Malts: There is no such thing as a bad malt; all are excellent, but some of the individualities and flavours have intimidated potential consumers, and this (given the differences between the regions) is understandable. Islay malts are noted for their peatiness, Lowland ones for their softness, and Highland malts for their smoky, smooth flavour with definite undertones of sherry.

Vatted malts are the result of a marriage between different single malt whiskies, from two to six in number. Since whisky is affected by outside factors such as climate and date of distillation, vatted malts tend to be more consistent. The best known is Strathcarron.

Age of Whisky: There is no fixed relationship between the age and strength of whisky; 40% alcohol by volume is generally the lowest strength, but there is a wide range above that, up to about 57% for a ten-year-old Macallan. 43% and 46% are readily available.

Age can vary from five to twenty-five years; older whisky is available, but now a rarity. Age and alcohol content do vary for different markets; Macallan Whisky, for example, is bottled at ten, eighteen and twenty-five years for the U.K. market, at ten, twelve, eighteen and twenty-five years for general export, and at seven years for the Italian market.

Not all whiskies carry an age on the label. Glenfiddich used to have a minimum age of ten years, but because of demand (– it is one of the top three export malts –) this was reduced to eight; there is now no minimum age at all.

Brandy

The official definition of brandy reads as follows:–

'Brandy is the distillation of wine made from the fermented juice of freshly gathered grapes'.

Cognac is usually recognised as being the superior type; it comes from seven particular districts, and is classified according to its type and its quality.

Grande Champagne – Grande Champagne Cognac
Petite Champagne – Fine Champagne Cognac (for the term Fine Champagne to be used, at least 50% of the grapes used must come from the Grande Champagne District)
Borderies – Fine Cognac
Fins-Bois – Fine Cognac
Bons-Bois – Cognac
Bois Ordinaires – Cognac
Bois Communs ('dit à Terroir') – Cognac

Grapes are gathered around October and distilled by the pot still method. To ensure complete removal of all impurities, two distillations are generally carried out. Most of the spirit from the Cognac District is sold to shippers who will mature and blend it according to their own requirements.

The spirit is stored in wooden casks, usually oak. The alcohol content reduces, and the golden colour develops from the wood of the casks. A superior-quality brandy will mature for up to sixty years, but an average one will take only a small proportion of that time.

Most brandy consists of a blend of different years and types. Prior to bottling, additional colouring will be added if necessary and the alcoholic strength will be reduced to the required level, through the addition of distilled water.

There is no legal obligation to show the age of brandy, but the following guides are currently in use:–

Symbol	Approximate Age
*	3 years and over
**	4 years and over
***	5 years and over
V.O. (Very Old)	5–10 years approximately
V.S.O. (Very Special or Superior Old)	10–15 years approximately
V.S.O.P. (Very Special or Superior Old Pale)	15–20 years approximately
V.V.S.P.P. or X.O. (Extra Old)	20 years and over

Armagnac is another well-known brandy; it comes from the Department of Gers, in the south-west of France. Grape brandy is a
cheaper variety, and is blended from pot still and patent still spirits.
Care must be taken to ensure that grape brandies are not confused
with good cognacs, which similarly bear 'V.S.O.P.' or 'Napoleon' on
their labels. Marc is made from the distilled residue of grapes which
have been pressed for wine-making; it can make a potent spirit,
but some types are capable of developing and maturing with age
into good-quality brandies.

Gin

Gin is generally made from rye and maize (or corn), sometimes from
malted barley. It is a cheap drink to produce, but sells at a high price
because of taxes and duties.

London Gin (which includes Gordon's, Gilbey's, Booth's and
Beefeater) is flavoured with juniper – the name 'gin' is derived from
the French word for 'juniper', 'genièvre' – and the other herbs
which give the different brands their distinctive flavours. No aging
process is necessary.

Genever Gin (often referred to in England as 'Geneva' Gin) is a
true Dutch speciality. It is a malt spirit, produced by fermentation
and a triple-pot-still distillation of barley, maize and rye. It is
rectified with juniper berries and other herbs. The Oude (or old)
Genever has a high malt spirit content, and Jonge (or young) a
lighter flavour.

Plymouth Gin is half-way, in flavour, between London and Dutch
gins.

Vodka

Both Russia and Poland claim to have invented vodka, which
probably originated as a herb-flavoured distilled spirit. (Because of
its increasing popularity in recent years, several countries have tried
to imitate it, and each has produced its own distinctive flavour.)
Before current scientific means of production were developed, the
spirit contained unpleasant oils which were detrimental to the
flavour, and herbs, roots, leaves, seeds and fruits were infused into it
to improve the taste. Present-day Russian vodka is known as the
'Petrovskaya' style of vodka, because it is made to a formula
approved by Peter the Great. In 1895, the production of vodka in
Russia became a state monopoly; today, under strict supervision,
highly purified alcohol is added to the mellow water used in its
production, and then filtered through quartz, sand and birch coal,
with the result that its taste and character are unequalled.

The imported vodka market is dominated by Stolichnaya (Russia)
and Wyborowa (Poland). Each has a subtle flavour, is mellowed, and

should be drunk neat and ice-cold out of small glasses. Flavoured vodkas are popular in Eastern Europe, and the Russian Zubrovka is available in Britain; its flavour and pale green colour are due to the infusion of certain grasses.

Most of the vodka drunk in this country is a colourless, clear and flavourless spirit with no aroma. Its base is usually cane spirit which, after a high degree of rectification, is passed through activated charcoal filters to remove any lingering flavour. It is used extensively in mixed drinks.

Rum

Rum is distilled from fermented sugar-cane juice, or, more commonly, from the molasses which remain after the extraction of sugar from cane. Irrespective of the base, it is divided into two groups, light and heavy (or dark).

Light Rum originally came from Puerto Rico and Cuba, and a fermented version can still be produced in under a day. Other Caribbean countries are now producing this type of rum.

Dark Rum has a fermentation period of up to twelve days; the best generally comes from Jamaica or Martinique. Barbados Rum is medium-light in colour, and the taste is soft rather than harsh. The best-known types of Barbados Rum come from the Mount Gay distilleries.

FORTIFIED WINES

This is the name given to wines which during their production have been 'fortified' by the addition of alcohol (usually brandy). The effect of this addition is to stop the natural fermentation before all the sugar has been converted into alcohol, and the result is that most of these wines are sweet and accordingly regarded (– with the exception of sherry –) as dessert wines. Their strength is usually between 16% and 20% alcohol by volume, but can go up to 24% or even more. The most common fortified wines are ports (see page 207) and sherries, but there are others too.

Sherry

The principal types of sherry are as follows:–

Manzanilla: Very pale straw-coloured sherry with a salty tang. This is occasionally made into the Amontillado or Oloroso types of sherry.

Fino: Very dry, and pale in colour. Best served chilled. It should be drunk quickly, as it rapidly loses its freshness.

Amontillado: True Amontillado is aged Fino Sherry which has gained a slightly nutty flavour from the wood. In commercial production, Amontillados are generally sweetened to produce a medium sherry.

Oloroso: Rich in flavour, but dry and made without development of the 'flor' (see below).

Palo Cortado: This has the character of a light Oloroso and a true Amontillado, delicately flavoured. The 'flor' is not allowed to develop, and the end result is a rich and soft sherry.

Rich Dessert Oloroso: A dark and heavy sherry, matured for greater richness.

Amoroso: Produced in the same style as Oloroso, but with a sweet finish.

Cream Sherry: An amber style of sweet sherry made from aged Oloroso.

Pale Cream: A popular style of sherry made by sweetening pale Finos.

Brown Sherry: A British term, rarely used now, for a style of dark sweet sherry.

Once picked, the grapes are pressed into large square wooden boxes called 'lagars'. Calcium sulphate is sprinkled on the top, and this gives the wine the special characteristic of sherry. The final product or 'must' is sent to warehouses or 'bodegas' for fermentation, after which it will be put into fresh casks where a secondary fermentation takes place. The wine will then be strengthened by the addition of spirit, so that is becomes a fortified wine.

A yeast-like growth will appear on top of the wine; it is called 'flor' or *Mycoderma Vini*. This will help to develop the wine, and where it grows well the product will develop into a dry or light sherry. Where for any reason it does not develop, the result will be an Oloroso or sweeter sherry.

Sherry is blended by being passed through a 'solera', and for each brand that a shipper wishes to have he will need a separate solera. This consists of a series of inverted casks which are never moved and through which the wine passes. It picks up the individual flavour of each of the casks, which are maintained at a static level: as more fluids are introduced into the system, each cask is topped up from the one above it. Sherry produced in this manner will be labelled and dated, showing the date when the solera was first established.

Other Fortified Wines
Madeira:

Sercial	Dry and slightly nutty.
Verdelho	Golden in colour, medium with a dry finish.
Bual	Darker and medium-rich – very mellow.

| Malmsey | The darkest Madeira – very complex and long-lasting. |
| Rainwater | A blend of wines – pale golden and easy to drink. |

Muscat de Beaume de Venise: French sweet wine produced from the Muscat grape, grown in the Rhône Valley. There are other French Muscats available.

Setubal: Portuguese Muscat, usually aged in barrels for twenty years and hence an excellent wine. Younger ones are also available.

Malaga: From Southern Spain, varying from dry to very sweet.

Marsala: Made in Sicily from a variety of grapes. The younger it is, the sweeter; but it can come in a very dry form.

Liqueur Muscats: Mostly from Australia, and generally marketed under a trader's name such as 'Brown Bros. Liqueur Muscat', or a brand name such as 'Show Tokay'.

Commandaria: From Cyprus; the best is sold as '100 years old', and is extremely sweet.

Prosek: A dessert wine from the Dalmatia district of Yugoslavia. It is very rare and difficult to find.

Worcester: A South African dessert wine from the Breede and Hex River Valleys, near the town of Paarl.

The following wines are not strictly fortified, but are worth mentioning in this section.

Tokay/Tokaji: From Hungary; this is an excellent dessert wine, especially Tokay Aszu and Tokay Aszu Eszencia, the latter being of the highest quality commercially available.

Mead: This is an English wine blended with honey, and produced primarily at Lindisfarne and Moniack.

Vermouth and Apéritifs

The best-quality vermouths, and the most popular, come from France and Italy.

French Vermouth is dry and light in colour. It is fortified with brandy, and infused with various herbs and flavourings. Like sherry, the wine has its fermentation stopped by the addition of brandy, and it is then allowed to mature for up to two years in casks which are left uncovered and exposed to the weather. After this, the various wines are blended in the required proportions, according to the style or type of vermouth being produced; and to this mixture is added a wine which has been mixed with various herbs and flavourings. The identities of these are the closely-guarded secrets of the producers, but they usually include coriander seed, camomile, angelica, gentian, or wormwood. To achieve a thorough mix, the vermouth is often put into a large vat which has mechanical paddles, so that constant movement is maintained until the wine is bottled.

The standard Italian Vermouths are as follows:–

Dry – this has no colouring and no additional sugar.

Bianco – this has no artificial colouring, but is sweetened, and carries a distinctive flavour of its own.

Sweet – this is a heavier and much darker coloured wine, which has had both caramel and sugar added.

Apéritifs such as Dubonnet, St. Raphael and Lillet are produced from both basic and Mistelle wines, and are flavoured according to the maker's requirements.

LIQUEURS

The word liqueur, or cordial as it is known in the United States, covers a multitude of different beverages. 'Liqueur' comes from the Latin *liquefacere*, which means to melt or dissolve; so the word refers to the way in which flavours are blended with a spirit base to make a complex drink. 'Cordial' derives from the Latin *cor*, meaning heart: many of the early herbal recipes were intended as stimulants for the heart.

Some recipes date back hundreds of years, and have even been discovered in ancient Egyptian tombs. The oldest known commercial wine, Commandaria, is fortified into a liqueur by a distillation of wine from the bottom of a previous vat, in the same way as ports and sherries are fortified by brandy.

Liqueurs are spirits which have been sweetened, flavoured and often coloured. The types and styles of liqueur will depend very much upon the fruits, herbs and spices used, and on the type of spirit used as the base.

Liqueurs can be categorised as follows:–

Eau de Vie

Complete fruits are made into brandies, which are usually bottled very young, as aging detracts from the delicate flavours. They are traditionally served very cold.

Fruit Liqueurs

Fruit concentrates are added to a spirit base. Brandy is the base of many popular fruit liqueurs and is never aged, as the re-distilling needed to make the liqueur would destroy all the complexities acquired by aging in wood.

Herbal Liqueurs

These include most of the old monastic recipes, which are usually based on a neutral spirit, although some of the more modern recipes are based on more distinctive ones such as Scotch whisky or Irish whiskey.

Liqueurs can be produced from almost any fruit, vegetable, herb, root or spice, but are largely dominated by oranges and stone fruits. Most Mediterranean countries produce liqueurs based on figs, but virtually none are exported. The pineapple is a fruit that seems to have been almost totally ignored in most old recipes.

Descriptive List of Liqueurs

The table on the following pages lists the principal liqueurs, with their country of origin and main flavouring.

Name	Country or area of origin	Principal ingredients
Abricotine	France	Apricots
Advocaat	Holland	Egg yolk – Brandy
Aiguebelle	France	Herbs
Akvavit/Aquavit	Scandinavia	Caraway – Potatoes
Almendrado	Mexico	Almonds – Tequila
Amaretto	Italy	Apricots (the whole apricot is used: the kernel gives it the almondy flavour)
Angelica/Angelique	Basque Region	Angelica
Anis	Spain	Aniseed
Anisette	France	Aniseed
Applejack	America	Apples
Apple of Paradise	Cuba	Apples
Apricot Brandy	Various	Apricots – Brandy
Arrack	East Indies	Rice – Palm juice
Ashanti Gold	Denmark	Chocolate
Aurum	Italy	Oranges
Bagaceiro	Portugal	Grape residue
Bahia	Brazil	Coffee
Barack Palinka	Hungary	Apricots
Barenfang/Barenjager	Prussia	Honey
Batida di Coco	Brazil	Coconuts
Battleaxe	Italy	Rum
Bénédictine B & B	France	Half D.O.M. – Half Brandy
Bénédictine D.O.M.	France	Herbs

Name	Country or area of origin	Principal ingredients
Ben Shalom	Israel	Jaffa oranges
Bessenjenever	Holland	Blackcurrants – Gin
Bezique		Citrus flavouring – Bacardi
Blackberry Brandy	Britain	Blackberries – Brandy
Bronte	Britain	Honey – Herbs
Cacao mit Nuss	Germany	Chocolate – Hazelnuts
Calisay	Spain	Bark – Quinine – Brandy
Calvados	France	Cider
Calypso	Britain	Bananas – Rum – Cream
Can-y-Delyn	Wales	Herbs
Capricornia	Australia	Tropical fruits
Carlsberg	Czechoslovakia	Herbs – Thermal waters
Carmeline	France	Herbs
Cascarilla	S. America	Bark – Spices – Brandy
Cayo Verde	America	Limes
Centerbe	Italy	100 herbs
Cera Sella	Italy	Cherries
Chartreuse (Green or Yellow)	France	Herbs
Cheri Suisse	Switzerland	Cherries – Chocolate
Cherry Blossom Liqueur	Japan	Cherry blossoms
Cherry Brandy	Various	Cherries – Brandy
Cherry Whisky	Britain	Cherries – Whisky
China China	France	Spices
Chocolate Mint	Britain	Chocolate – Mint
Chokalu	Mexico	Chocolate
Citroenjenever	Holland	Lemons – Gin
Clanrana	Scotland	Herbs
Coco-Ribe		Coconuts
Cocuy	Venezuela	Sisal roots
Cointreau	France	Oranges
Cordial Médoc	France	Wine – Brandy

Creme de . . . – signifies at least 35% sugar

Creme d'Amandes	France	Almonds
Creme d'Ananas	France	Pineapples

Name	Country or area of origin	Principal ingredients
Creme de Bananes	France	Bananas
Creme de Cacao	France	Chocolate – Vanilla
Creme de Café	France	Coffee
Creme de Cassis	France	Blackcurrants
Creme de Fraises	France	Strawberries (strawberry-coloured, not to be confused with Eau de Vie)
Creme de Framboises	France	Raspberries (raspberry-coloured, not to be confused with Eau de Vie)
Creme de Kirsch	France	Cherries (cherry-coloured, not to be confused with Eau de Vie)
Creme de Mandarine	France	Tangerines
Creme de Menthe	Various	Peppermint
Creme de Moka/Mocca	France	Coffee
Creme de Noisette	France	Hazelnuts
Creme de Noix	France	Walnuts
Creme de Noyau (Pink or White)	France	Almonds
Creme de Pecco	Holland	Tea
Creme de Prunelle (Green)	France, Holland	Sloes
Creme de Roses	France	Oil of roses – Vanilla
Creme de Thé	France	Tea
Creme de Vanille (Red)	France	Vanilla
Creme de Violettes	France	Violets
Creme Yvette	America	Parma Violets
Cuarenta y Tres	Spain	Herbs
C.L.O.C. (Cumin Liquidum Optimum Castelli = 'the best caraway in the castle')	Denmark	Caraway – Kummel
Cumberland Club	Australia	
Cumquat	Corfu	Cumquat oranges

Name	Country or area of origin	Principal ingredients
Curaçao (Orange, White, Red, Blue, Brown and Green)	Holland	Oranges – Brandy
Cynar	Italy	Artichokes
Dewmiel	Scotland	Herbs
Domuz	Portugal	Nuts
Dopio Cedro	Italy	Lemons
Drambuie	Scotland	Whisky – Honey – Herbs

Eau de Vie – dry colourless spirit distilled from fruits

E.d.V. d'Abricot	Alsace	Apricots
E.d.V. d'Alsace	Alsace	Mixed fruits
E.d.V. de Baie de Hous	Alsace	Holly berries
E.d.V. de Cerises	Alsace	Cherries
E.d.V. de Cidre	Normandy	Cider (version of Calvados)
E.d.V. de Figures	Mediterranean Countries	Figs
E.d.V. de Framboises	Alsace	Raspberries
E.d.V. de Kirsch	Alsace	Black cherries
E.d.V. de Mirabelles	Alsace	Golden plums
E.d.V. de Mure	Alsace	Blackberries
E.d.V. de Myrtille	Alsace	Bilberries
E.d.V. de Poires	Alsace	Pears
E.d.V. de Pommes	Alsace	Apples
E.d.V. de Quetsch	Alsace	Purple plums
Edelweiss		Mountain plants
Elexir d'Anvers (Yellow)	France	Herbs (similar to Chartreuse)
Elexir d'Armorique	Normandy	Herbs
Elexir de China	Italy	Aniseed
Elexir de Monbazillac	France	Herbs
Elexir de Mondorf	Luxembourg	Herbs
Elexir de Spa	Belgium	Herbs
Elexir Végétal	France	Highly concentrated essence of Green Chartreuse
Escarchado	Portugal	Aniseed
Escorial Grun	Germany	Spices
Ettaler	Germany	Herbs
Filfar	Cyprus	Curaçao

Name	Country or area of origin	Principal ingredients
Fiore d'Alpe	Italy	Flowers – Herbs; a twig is placed inside the bottle on which the sugar forms into crystals
Fleur des Alpes	France	As above
Forbidden Fruit	America	Oranges – Shaddocks – Grapefruit
Fraise de Bois	France	Wild strawberries
Galliano	Italy	Herbs
Genepy	Italy	Herbs – Crystal Liqueur
Ginger Liqueur	England	Ginger
Glayva	Scotland	Whisky – Herbs
Glen Mist	Britain	Whisky – Whiskey – Honey
Golden Heart	Holland	Herbs – Gold flakes
Goldwasser	Germany	Coriander – Gold leaf
Gorny Doubnyak	Russia	Ginger – Roots – Acorns – Oak shavings
Grand Cumberland	Australia	Passion-fruit
Grand Gruyère	Switzerland	Herbs
Grand Marnier	France	Oranges – Brandy
Grappa	Italy	Grape residue
Grappa alla Rutta	Italy	Grappa – Grass – Herbs
Grignan	Rhône	Herbs
Half om Half	Holland	Half Curaçao – Half Orange Bitters
Himbeergeist	Germany	Raspberries
Irish Cream	Ireland	Chocolate – Cream – Whiskey
Irish Mist	Ireland	Whiskey – Herbs
Irish Velvet	Ireland	Coffee – Honey – Whiskey
Izarra (Green or Yellow)	Basque Region	Armagnac – Herbs
Jägermeister	Germany	Herbs
Jarzebiak	Poland	Rowanberries – Vodka
Jerzynowka	Poland	Blackberries
Kahlua	Mexico	Coffee

Name	Country or area of origin	Principal ingredients
Karpi	Finland	Cranberries
Kibowi	Holland	Kiwi-fruit
Kirsch	Alsace	Cherry juice
Kitro	Greece	Citrus fruits
Kitron	Greece	Lemon leaves
Kontiki		
Koum Kouat – see Cumquat		
Kummel	Holland	Caraway – Grain spirit
Lakka	Finland	Cloudberries
La tintaine	France	Herbs
Latte de Suocera (= 'mother-in-law milk')	Italy	Herbs
L'eau Clairette	France	Lemon – Rose petals – Herbs
Lindisfarne Liqueur	England	Honey – Whisky
Liqueur des Moines	France	Aromatic plants – Cognac
Liqueur d'Or	France	Orange and lemon rind – Gold flakes
Liquore Villacidro	Sardinia	
Malibu	Britain	Coconuts – White Rum
Mallorquin	Majorca	Oranges
Mandarine	France	Tangerines
Maraschino	Dalmatia	Marasca cherry
Marc de * (* – Bourgogne, Champagne, Gewurztraminer, Meursault etc.)	France	Grape residue
Marnique	Australia	Oranges – Brandy (version of Grand Marnier)
Marillenbrand	Austria	Apricots
Mastic/Masticha	Greece	Liquorice
Mentuccia – see Centerbe		
Mersin	Turkey	Triple Sec
Mescal	Mexico	Mescalin – Cactus
Mesimarja	Finland	Arctic Brambles
Midori	Japan	Melons
Millefiori	Italy	1,000 flowers
Misty		Yoghurt
Monte Aguila	Jamaica	Rum – Cloves etc.

Name	Country or area of origin	Principal ingredients
Mozart	Germany	Chocolate nougat
Mus	Turkey	Bananas
Nocino	Italy	Various nuts
Obstwasser	Germany	Mixed fruits
Okelehao	Hawaii	Root of the Ti plant
Old Vienna	Vienna	Coffee – Brandy
Ouzo	Greece	Aniseed
Oxygenee	America	Aniseed
Oyjen	Spain	Aniseed – Liquorice etc. (sweeter version of Absinthe)
Paradis	Italy	Herbs – Crystal Liqueur
Parfait Amour	France	Vanilla – Violets
Pasha	Turkey	Coffee
Pêche	France	Peaches
Pelinkovac	Yugoslavia	Herbs – Red Wine
Persico	Holland	Almonds
Pimento Dram	Jamaica	Rum – Pepper essence
Pimpeltjens	Holland	Oranges – Herbs
Pisco	Latin America	Grape residue
Pomeranzen	Germany	Curaçao
Ponche Soto	Spain	Sherry
Portakal	Turkey	Citrus fruits
Prunelle	France	Plums – Brandy
Quetsch	France	Prunes
Rabinowka	Russia	Rowanberries
Raspail	France	Aromatic herbs
Rock & Rye	America	Citrus fruits – Rye
Royal * Chocolate (* – Mint, Banana, Cherry, Ginger, Orange or Nut)	France	Chocolate
Sabra	Israel	Bitter oranges – Chocolate
St. Hallvard	Norway	Potato spirit – Herbs
Sake	Japan	Rice – Sake (rice wine)
Sambuca	Italy	Aniseed
Sapin	Spain	Plants – Spices
Sechsamter Tropfen	Germany	Herbs
Senancole	France	Herbs
Seve	France	Oranges – Herbs

Name	Country or area of origin	Principal ingredients
Seve Patricia	France	Oranges – Herbs – Brandy
Silverwasser	Germany	Aniseed – Silver leaf
Slivovitz	Hungary	Plums
Sloe Gin	England	Sloes – Sweet gin
Sorbes	France	Rowanberries
Soumuvrain	Finland	Cloudberries
Southern Comfort	America	Bourbon – Peaches
Stonsdorfer	Germany	Herbs
Strega	Italy	Oranges – Herbs
Subrouska (Zubrovka)	Poland (Russia)	Vodka – Bison Grass
Suze à la Gentiane	France	Gentian root
Swedish Punch	Sweden	Rum – Spices
Tapio	Finland	Herbs – Juniper
Tea Breeze	France	Tea
Tequila	Mexico	Agave pineapples (cactus)
Tia Maria	Jamaica	Rum – Coffee
Tornado	Holland	Pineapples
Trappistine	France	Herbs
Tres Castillos	Puerto Rico	Aniseed
Tresterschnapps	Germany	Grape residue
Triple Sec	Holland	Oranges – Brandy
Van der Hum	S. Africa	Tangerines – Cape brandy
Vandermint	Holland	Mint – Chocolate
Verveine du Velay (Green or Yellow)	France	Herbs
Veuve Champion	France	Apricot and peach kernels
Vielle Cure	Gironde	Armagnac – Cognac – Roots – Aromatic plants
Zolotaya Osen	Caucasus	Damsons – Apples – Quinces
Zwetschgenwasser	Germany	Plums

CHAPTER 10
WINES

Port is available in a wide variety of types, but all true ports come from a small area in Portugal known as the Douro Valley. This region stretches from Peso da Regua in the west to the Spanish border, near Freixo de Espada-a-Cinta, in the east. Ruby port, the most common type, is the one sold in nearly all bars; but there are several other varieties, which are listed below.

White Port	– made from white grapes, and rather dry; mostly drunk as an apéritif.
Ruby Port	– aged briefly in wood, and rougher than tawny.
Tawny Port	– aged in wood, but bottled, by modern techniques, without a sediment.
Crusted Port	– good-quality port made from a blend of different lesser vintages, and bottled with sediment so that it improves with age.
Late Bottled (L.B.)	– similar to vintage, but kept in wood for twice as long so that it ages more quickly with a lighter style.
Vintage Port	– the wine of one single exceptional year, aged in oak casks and bottled early for laying down to mature. The wine will bear the shipper's name and the year of production, e.g. Warre's '63. The details appear on the bottle label, or on the wax or plastic cap over the cork.

Even though it is fortified, a great vintage port is undoubtedly to be placed amongst the world's best wines. Other ports of near-vintage standards are only moderate by comparison.

For a first-class vintage port to be produced, the wine may require fifteen to twenty years in the bottle, and will need to be treated at all times with total respect. The making of the wine will not be completed until after its bottling, when the sediment will cause a crust to form in the bottle. If the bottle is moved without due care, the crust will break and mix with the wine, making decanting and filtering essential before serving.

The notable years for the production of vintage port have been as follows:–

1927 – 30 shippers declared.
A great classic vintage, the number of wines shipped being the largest in any recorded year.
1931 – Not generally declared, but producing some good wines.
1934 – 12 shippers declared.
A well-balanced vintage.
1935 – 15 shippers declared.
A very successful, high-quality vintage.
1944 – Not properly declared, but a good-quality vintage.
1945 – 22 shippers declared.
One of the classic concentrated vintages.
1947 – 11 shippers declared.
1950 – 13 shippers declared.
Not a good year.
1955 – 26 shippers declared.
The most highly regarded vintage of its period.
1960 – 24 shippers declared.
A good, well-balanced, long-lived vintage.
1963 – 25 shippers declared.
A classic vintage.
1966 – 20 shippers declared.
The best are excellent, others only fair.
1967 – 5 shippers declared.
Cockburn's and Martinez produced the best.
1970 – 23 shippers declared.
A great classic, long-lived year, for drinking from 1987 to 1995 – and beyond, for the best.
1975 – 17 shippers declared.
Very varied, but producing stylish wines ready for drinking from 1986 to 1992, with Fonseca probably the best.

Of all the ports, the following will generally fetch the highest prices, and are listed according to their value: Taylor's, Warre's, Croft, Fonseca, Cockburn's, Dow's and Graham's. The presence of a whitewash mark on the bottle is not detrimental: the mark is placed there by the shipper to indicate the position in which the bottle is to be stored, with the mark uppermost so that the crust forms on the opposite side and future handlers will be aware of its position.

From the Douro Valley, the port is transferred to one of the lodges in the Vila Nova de Gaia (one of the suburbs of Oporto), to age a little before its bottling and distribution. It is here that all the famous names are to be found – Barros, Croft, Cockburn, Calem, Dow, Delaforce, Fonseca, Ferreira, Gonzalez Byass, Graham, Hunt

Roope, Kopke, Martinez, Mackenzie, Noval, Niepoort, Sandeman, Taylor, Warre, Wiese & Krohn, etc.

The production of vintage port from these 'quintas' is subject to stringent controls, and the vineyards are classified and awarded points according to their productivity, the age of the vines, the distance between the vines, the vine variety, and the degree of care with which the vineyard is maintained, together with soil conditions and altitude. According to this system of assessment, which is managed by the Portuguese Port Wine Institute, the points awarded for these and other features are totalled to provide a basis for the yield per 'quinta' or estate. The best score, 1,200 points or more, allows production of 600 litres per 1,000 vines; the lowest, going down to 400 points, entitles the estate to only 260 litres per 1,000 vines.

The price is determined by the quantity produced and the quality of that production, and also, to a lesser extent, by what market forces will allow. It is, therefore, not profitable to allow more than three vintages to be declared in any one decade. The decision as to whether or not a vintage should be declared is left entirely to the individual, and this may lead to one or two shippers bottling a 'vintage' in a year that is considered below top quality by others. Some years are considered vintage by all shippers; those of the 1960s – 1960, 1963, and 1966 – are all good examples, the '63 being particularly fine. '77 is of good quality, but still needs a little more time to develop; '75, by comparison, is a little thinner and needs drinking fast. The '70 will continue to improve, and is only just ready for consumption; of the more recent vintages, '80 and '82 should be good in another ten or twelve years. Of the older vintages, the best are:–

1890 – 24 shippers declared.
        A great classic vintage.
1900 – 22 shippers declared.
        The first of four great classic years prior to World War I.
1904 – 25 shippers declared.
        A light vintage.
1908 – 26 shippers declared.
        A dark and full-bodied vintage.
1912 – 25 shippers declared.
        A good rich vintage, the finest this century.
1917 – 15 shippers declared.
        Another light year.
1920 – 23 shippers declared.
        Good, ripe, robust vintage.
1922 – 18 shippers declared.

WINES — TYPES AND PRODUCTION

Soil and Climate

Different wines vary considerably, as does the same wine from year
to year. The extent of this variation is governed by two major
factors, the soil and the climate in which the vines are grown.

The soil imparts its own flavour, and can be pebbly as in
Châteauneuf, chalky as in Champagne, or full of limestone as in
Chablis. Two varieties of grape grown in different soils will retain
their own separate identities, but both will gain a characteristic of
each soil which experts can distinguish.

The climate, together with the method of planting and the skill
with which the vineyard is maintained, will determine the yield and
quality of the wine. Temperamental vines need a good rainfall in
their ripening stages, followed by a dry period, if a full-flavoured
grape is to be produced. The balance between grape sugar and
acidity determines whether the fruit will develop other subtle
flavours; and the slower the ripening, the better the balance. Rain at
the wrong time, either too early or too late, can ruin an entire crop.

The Harvest

In the Western Hemisphere this normally occurs during the
autumn, when the majority of grapes are picked either by hand or
by machine, and subsequently brought in for sorting.

Fermentation

This is the name given to the natural process which converts grape
juice into wine. In the winery, the grapes are sorted, de-stemmed
and crushed in a machine called an egrappoi. Because of the
presence of natural yeasts on the grape skin, this process changes
the sugar in the grape into alcohol. If it is allowed to occur
uncontrolled, the alcohol level would rise to 15% of volume before
the yeast died, so that all wine would be naturally dry. To prevent
this, fermentation is rigidly controlled, by the addition of sulphur,
which anaesthetises the yeast, or by the addition of alcohol to
increase the percentage, or, occasionally, by filtration. By adopting
one of these methods, the producers are able at an early stage to
determine the style of the wine which will result.

Types of Wine

White Wine: Though white wine is occasionally produced from
black grapes, it is more usual for white to be used. Once the stalks
have been removed, the grapes are fed into a press (of which there
are several varieties, the most common being the horizontal or

basket); this is used to extract the 'must' (fresh juice), which falls into a trough and is then pumped into a vat for its first fermentation.

Sweet White Wine: The liquid is removed from the vat before the fermentation process is complete, while there is still some sugar in the juice. The fermentation is controlled by the addition of sulphur, or by filtering, as too much sulphur will cause the wine to irritate the back of the throat or, in worse cases, to develop a smell of bad eggs.

Champagne and Sparkling Wine: Again, the liquid is removed from the vat before fermentation is complete. The process is allowed to reach its final stage in a bottle, when it develops the secondary by-product of fermentation, the carbon dioxide gas which creates the natural fizz. The grape juice remains in the capped bottle over a period of years, and is regularly turned and angled so that the sediment is collected in the neck. This is eventually frozen, in a process called de-gorgement, and later removed. As a result of these procedures, a little liquid is lost and what is left is very dry. To compensate for this, a mixture of wine and sugar is added before the final corking and caging.

Champagne is classed as 'brut' when less than 2% of sugar is added; 'extra dry' when 1.5–2.5% is added; 'sec' when 2–4% is added; and 'demi-sec' when 4–6% is added.

Dry White Wine: The wine is fully fermented, so that all the sugar is converted into alcohol. The governing regulations for each appellation require it to conform to stipulated minimum alcohol levels, which may be 10.5 or 11%.

Rosé Wine: Rosé wines are made from red or black grapes whose skins have been allowed to impart a little colour and flavour by being left in contact with the 'must', before the latter is filtered. The colour of the wine thus depends on how long the skins have remained with the 'must'.

Red Wine: The quality of red wine is determined by whether or not the skins, stalks and pips have been left in the juice. These impart flavour, and also a natural ingredient called tannin, which is also found in tea; it not only gives young wines their 'teeth-cleaning' sharpness, but is also responsible for giving wine its ability to mature for years, and for providing the 'backbone' found in many varieties.

Where wines are of a lighter style, the standard practice is to separate the wine and the skins after a few days, and to finish the fermentation separately.

In Spain, California and Australia, fermentation occurs at high temperatures; as this has the effect of extracting too much tannin and colour from the skins, a method called cold fermentation is used to counteract it. The vat is temperature-controlled, a procedure which preserves all the aromas and flavours in white wine, but is slightly detrimental to red. Another method, used principally in the

Beaujolais region, is that of whole-berry fermentation, or 'maceration carbonique'. The juice actually ferments inside the uncrushed grapes within the vat, but the weight of those on top starts the normal fermentation process in those crushed at the bottom, producing a perfumed, sweet aroma.

Most wines have a tendency to secondary fermentation, once the wine is racked off its lees or barrel bottoms. (In some areas such as Muscadet, wines are bottled straight from the lees, and this creates a yeasty flavour.) This secondary or malolactic fermentation is the action of bacteria on the malic (apple) acid, and converts it to lactic (milk) acid. This softens the sharpness of wine in countries or areas of high acidity, and where the acidity is low, the secondary fermentation is controlled by a raised level of sulphur dioxide.

Good red wines will ferment within ten days at temperatures of around 75°F (24°C), but where cold fermentation has occurred, this will take as long as four to six weeks and sometimes even longer, in temperatures of around 60°F (15.5°C).

Bottling and Maturation

To ensure a brilliant and clear wine, the product should be strained or filtered before bottling; but as this tends to extract some of the flavour, the traditional method is to use egg whites as a fining agent.

Before the wine is served, its maturation must be considered. Simple wines made for drinking early will lose colour and freshness if left to age, whereas wines made for aging are too harsh to drink early and need time to develop, either in the bottle or, preferably, in oak casks prior to bottling. This maturing adds to the wine flavours and tannins which, in time, are effective as softening agents. As a wine becomes older, its colour changes from bright ruby or purple to an amber brown. One can, therefore, discern a little about a wine simply by looking at it; and this is how professional tasters can identify the age and type of a wine even before they have sampled it.

Bottle Sizes

There is a large variety of bottle sizes, the most usual being 70, 73 and 75 cl; but as from January 1989, all wines bottled in the E.E.C. must conform to a standard size of 75 cl. This could result in an increase in cost prices, particularly for wines from countries like Germany which traditionally have used 70 cl bottles. This legislation does not affect spirits.

LABEL LORE

Sample wine labels

FRANCE

name of wine-producing property

contents by volume

château owner's name

producer's address

bottled at the château

area of production

country of origin

appellation contrôlée

vintage

LABEL LORE

FRANCE

area of production

vintage appears
here or on neck
label

individual
vineyard
within the
appellation

appellation
contrôlée

producer's name
and address

contents by
volume

% alcohol by
volume

bottled on
the domain
or estate

Châteauneuf-du-Pape

75 cl

13,9 % vol.

Domaine du

Vieux Télégraphe

APPELLATION CHATEAUNEUF-DU-PAPE CONTROLÉE

MIS EN BOUTEILLE AU DOMAINE

GAEC H. BRUNIER ET FILS, PROPRIETAIRES-RECOLTANTS
ROUTE DE CHATEAUNEUF-DU-PAPE 84370 BEDARRIDES FRANCE

SPAIN

LABEL LORE

% alcohol by volume

12.7 Alc.

bottling details— this is bottled by the producer at the bodega

seal of original Rioja

name of the town where the bodega is located

contents by volume

country of origin

PRODUCT OF SPAIN

75 cl.

MARQUÈS DE MURRIETA

Bottled by BODEGAS MARQUÉS DE MURRIETA - YGAY

Vinos de Rioja

YGAY

(LOGROÑO)

MARCA REGISTRADA

EMBOTELLADOR Nº 53 LO

R.S.I. 30.2.209/LO

COSECHA 1981

vintage

producer's name. Rioja wines are known by the bodega/producer rather than the vineyard

name of estate

LABEL LORE

GERMANY

· RHEINPFALZ ·

QUALITÄTSWEIN
MIT PRÄDIKAT

A. P. Nr.
5 106 026 15 84

1983er

DEIDESHEIMER HERRGOTTSACKER

RIESLING SPÄTLESE

Erzeugerabfüllung aus dem Weingut

JOSEF BIFFAR 6705 DEIDESHEIM A. D. WEINSTRASSE
Produce of Germany

70 cl e

3329

REGION—this is one of
11 designated regions
for quality wines

quality
control
number
**

vintage

vineyard site
or grosslage

type of wine
i.e. late
gathered

e denotes that
the bottling
is to E.E.C. accepted
standards

contents by
volume

QmP: quality
wines with a
particular
distinction

village name
with suffix
-er

type of vine
used

name of
producer

**
5 number of control centre where wine was tested
106 number of the location in which the wine was bottled
026 registered number of the bottler
15 sequential number in the year of application from the bottler, unique to this bottling
84 year of application for the A.P. number

LABEL LORE

AUSTRALIA

name of estate

blend of grape
varieties used,
typical of New
World wines

name and address of
producer/bottler

Stanley

STANLEY WINE COMPANY

Private Reserve

1982

WATERVALE COONAWARRA

SHIRAZ-

CABERNET SAUVIGNON

A blend of 60% Shiraz grapes from Watervale in
South Australia's Clare Valley and 40% Cabernet
Sauvignon grapes from Coonawarra. The wine
was matured in oak for 6 months before bottling.
It has developed into an excellent dry red style
with elegant Cabernet Sauvignon bouquet and
a soft Shiraz finish. Excellent cellaring potential.

VINTAGED BY THE STANLEY WINE CO PTY LTD
7 DOMINIC STREET CLARE SOUTH AUSTRALIA

PRODUCT OF AUSTRALIA   750 ml

12.0% ALC/VOL

vintage

wine-making
region

production details
not often found on
the front label

% alcohol by
volume

country of origin

contents by
volume

AUSTRALIA

LABEL LORE

company's name

estate's name

vintage

contents by volume

importer's name and address

grape variety used
or principal type
and not necessarily
100% of type stated

% alcohol by
volume

name and address of
producer/bottler

M^cWILLIAM'S

HANWOOD

CABERNET SAUVIGNON

1984

11.5% ALC./VOL.   75 cl.
PRODUCED & BOTTLED IN AUSTRALIA BY
McWILLIAM'S WINES PTY. LTD.   SYDNEY   AUSTRALIA

IMPORTED BY ANGLO AUSTRALIAN WINE CO.
CROWTHORNE   BERKS

France

Champagne: This is produced within a specific area whose chief towns are Épernay, Reims and Ay. All Champagne houses produce a luxury brand, of which Dom Pérignon is probably the best example; others are Perrier-Jouet La Belle Époque and Bollinger R.D. As the result of a recent decision in the European Court of Justice, the official producers of Champagne have won the exclusive right to use the term 'méthode champenoise', and as from 1994 no other company will be able to display these words on its label.

Bordeaux: These wines come from many areas – Médoc, including Saint-Estèphe, Pauillac, Saint-Julien, Margaux, Cantenac and Labarde; Saint-Émilion, Pomerol; Graves; Sauternes, including Barsac; Entre-deux-mers; and Côtes de Bourg. All these wines contain varying proportions of different types of grapes; the prices, too, vary considerably.

Burgundy: Côte de Nuits: This area includes Fixin, Gevrey-Chambertin, Morey-Saint-Denis, Chambolle-Musigny and Vosne-Romanée; the latter has the distinction of possessing the greatest vineyards on earth, belonging to the estates of the Domaine de la Romanée-Conti (which also owns La Tâche, major parts of Richebourg, Echézeaux and La Romanée Saint-Vivant, as well as France's smallest Appelation Contrôllée, the two-acre Grand Cru of La Romanée).

Côte de Beaune: Within this area are Aloxe-Corton, Savigny-lès-Beaune, Pommard, Volnay, and Chassagne-Montrachet, sources of some of the best white wines, such as Montrachet, Bâtard Montrachet, Corton-Charlemagne and Meursault.

Côte Chalonnaise: Geographically, this region continues from the Côte de Nuits and Côte de Beaune districts. They are sometimes referred to, collectively, as the Côte d'Or; and although, because of similar cultivation and vinification techniques, the wines produced are almost identical in style, the price does vary considerably. The principal areas are Mercurey and Givry, both producing red wine almost exclusively, and Rully and Montagny, from where the fine whites come.

La Mâconnais: This area stretches to the Beaujolais borders. White wines are very similar to the northern Burgundies, but the reds have their own distinctive personality, and are very different from their counterparts. The principal wines from this area are Pouilly-Fuissé, Pouilly-Vinzelles, Pouilly-Loché, Mâcon-Prissé, Mâcon Villages and Mâcon Rouge. Saint-Véran, too, which used to be sold as Beaujolais Blanc, comes from here, as do two newcomers which both have good potential futures, Clos du Chapitre from Vire and Quintaine-Clessé from Quintaine.

Beaujolais: This district stretches from Saint-Amour in the north to the Côte de Brouilly in the south, and includes all nine Grand Cru districts – Brouilly, Chénas, Chiroubles, Côte de Brouilly, Fleurie, Juliénas, Morgon, Moulin-à-Vent and Saint-Amour. George Duboeuf, who has done more for the reputation of the area than anyone else, is currently trying to establish a tenth Cru, to be known as Beaujolais-Régnié.

Wines from 'Côte de Brouilly' may not be called 'Brouilly', and *vice versa*. There are considerable differences between Grand Cru wines: Morgon, for instance, generally lasts longer, and after ten years can taste like a good Burgundy; Juliénas has more body; Saint-Amour is lighter in style; while Brouilly is even richer. Their one common factor is their derivation from the same variety of grape, the Gamay, which gives them the characteristic grapey/fruity nose and purple colour when young. This is perhaps best appreciated in Beaujolais Nouveau, which is released on the stroke of midnight on the third Wednesday of each November.

The areas producing the ordinary Beaujolais, Beaujolais-Supérieur and Beaujolais-Villages lie in the southernmost part of the district.

Chablis: This region, to the north of the Côte d'Or, is now dedicated to the production of clear, perfumed and lively light white wine, and its name has now become synonymous with this.

Rhône: Wines from this area include Côtes du Rhône, Crozes Hermitage and Hermitage (both red and white), Côte Rôtie and Châteauneuf-du-Pape (including the heavy white).

Alsace: In this region, the wine produced (although by French methods) is German in style; and throughout the whole area, in fact, the German influence is present both in language and in food. Most of the wine produced, though, is white, and has a higher degree of alcohol and more body than are usual in Germany. The wines are not only highly spiced and racy, but also aromatic and long-lived; as in Germany, the wine-growers refer on the label to the grape variety used, the most popular being Riesling and Gewurtztraminer, and this may be followed by the bottler's name, e.g. Hugel.

Loire: Loire wines are very diverse, from the Muscadets around Nantes through the sparkling wines of Saumur to the light reds of Chinon and Bourgueil, from the rosé wines of Anjou to the sophisticated whites of Pouilly-Fumé and Sancerre. Saumur's sparkling wines are of a fine quality, with such familiar names as Gratien et Meyer and Ackermann being the most popular. (Ackermann-Laurance was the first 'méthode champenoise' house of the Loire.)

Midi and Provence: Principally from the south originate some very nice house wines, such as Hérault, Fitou, Minervois and Corbières.

Other Areas: The term Vin de Pays is given to country wines; V.D.Q.S. stands for Vin Délimité de Qualité Supérieure, and A.C. for Appelation Contrôlée, referring to the best-quality wines from specific areas.

Germany

The main wine-producing areas are Nahe, Rheinhessen, Rheingau, Rheinpfalz and Mosel-Saar-Ruwer. Green (occasionally, blue) bottles are generally used for Mosel, and brown (occasionally, black) for all the other wines.

German wines take their name from the village of origin, with -er added as suffix; this is followed by the vineyard, the grape variety, and finally the style, e.g. Hocheimer Domdechaney Riesling Spätlese.

Tafelwein: This is made from wine imported from E.E.C. countries and blended in Germany, whereas Deutscher Tafelwein comes entirely from German vineyards.

Landwein: Each of these is a superior Deutscher Tafelwein from one of fifteen specific districts.

Q.b.A. (Qualitätswein bestimmtes Anbaugebiet):   These cover a good section of middle-quality wines. In Germany, 95% of all wines reach this quality category, whereas in Italy 87% and in France 64% of wines are classed as Table Wines rather than Quality Wines.

Q.m.P. (Qualitätswein mit Prädikat):   These quality wines of distinction, made from grapes with sufficient natural sugar to eliminate the need for additives, are classified as follows according to sweetness, time of harvesting, and selection of individual grapes:–
    Kabinett: This is first-quality wine with no added sugar.
    Spätlese: The grapes used cannot be picked earlier than seven days after the start of the main harvest. This type is the one most profitable for the producer, and is also the one most popular with the consumer.
    Auslese: This is produced from selected grapes, not necessarily late-picked but in many cases those attacked by Noble Rot or Edelfäule (*Botrytis Cinerea*).
    Beerenauslese: This is made from overripe grapes attacked by Edelfäule; it is very sweet, but low in alcohol (5.5%) because the remainder of the sugar stays in the wine unfermented.
    Trockenbeerenauslese: The grapes from which this is produced are the most heavily infected and shrivelled, and therefore the sweetest. They are hand-picked, either off the vine or in the press house. This wine is only harvested in very fine vintages, and as it is very expensive to produce, its price is prohibitive for the ordinary

consumer. (On average, this Trockenbeerenauslese costs eight times as much as the ordinary Auslese.) In 1971, the 7½-acre vineyard of Graacher Himmelreich produced only 214 bottles.

Eiswein: This is quality-controlled, and should not be confused with Austrian Eiswein, which is of a poorer standard. The grapes are naturally frozen at the time of pressing; the water remains in the form of ice crystals and concentrates the grape acids and sugar. The process seldom occurs before the third week of November. Although Eiswein is made from ripe grapes, it can be produced in lesser years when Beerenauslese and Trockenbeerenauslese are not available.

Spain

The main wine-producing areas in Spain are Rioja, including Rioja Alta, Rioja Alavesa, and Rioja Baja, and Catalonia, which includes the modernised vineyards of Miguel Torres, producing some of the finest wines in the country.

Riojas do not vary as much as some of the red wines from Burgundy and Bordeaux. This is partly because of the more consistent climate, and partly because of the blending of wine from better vintages in poorer years. It is aged in oak casks for as long as is necessary to develop the classic oaky or vanilla flavour which marks a good Rioja, though in recent years there has been a tendency to lessen the oaky flavour in white Riojas.

Italy

Italy is not only the world's biggest producer of wine: it also has the largest consumption figure per head of population, approximately 100 bottles per annum. A large area of the country produces mediocre house wines for local consumption.

The principal wine-producing areas are:–

Piemonte	– producing Barolo, Barbera, Barberesco and Asti Spumante.
North-East	– producing Lambrusco (white and red), Merlot del Pavia etc.
Veneto	– producing Valpolicella, Soave and Bardolino.
Tuscany	– centred on Florence in central Italy, and producing the famous Chianti.
Umbria	– producing Orvieto and Rubesco di Torgiano.
Sicily	– producing Marsala, used extensively in cooking.

The wine laws are not as strict as in France, but there are certain gradings:–

First Grade
Vino Tipico   This is a new category for wines of stated and
                            proven origin.

Second Grade
V.Q.P.R.D.   – This is used in conjunction with D.O.C. for
                            quality wines from restricted areas, in accord-
                            ance with E.E.C. rules.

Third Grade
D.O.C.   – Denominazione di Origine Controllata. This is
                            the principal category, and is governed by a
                            body which stipulates specific grapes and
                            methods of production. It also limits yields and
                            ensures proper aging of the wines.

Top Grade
D.O.C.G.   – The new top rank, awarded to approved top
                            wines from best-quality zones, which must carry
                            a government seal for which the producer takes
                            full responsibility.

Where 'classico' appears against the name of a wine, it indicates that
it is produced from a vineyard in the centre of an area.

U.S.A.

The predominant wine-producing area in the U.S.A. is along the
central coast of California. Appropriate grape varieties, combined
with brand names and new technology, are the key to its success;
and in this area the principal wine-producing regions are Santa
Barbara, Santa Cruz, Monterey and San Luis. Amador, famous for
Zinfandel, lies in the Sierra Foothills; and the Napa Valley, north of
San Francisco, is well established as a top-quality area. Sonoma here
has several well-known wineries, such as Clos du Bois, Preston's and
Iron Horse.

In the Napa Valley, the more popular wineries are Trefethen,
Joseph Phelps, Rutherford Hill, Frog's Leap, Heitz Cellar, Stag's
Leap, Opus One, and the famous Robert Mondavi Winery. In the
central coastal area, wines worthy of note come from the Firestone
and Edna Valley Vineyards.

Wine is produced in a number of other states. The best (after
California) are Washington and Oregon, in the Pacific North-West
(e.g. Château St Michelle Vineyard). In New York and the Eastern
States, good wine is produced at the Great Western and Heron Hill
Vineyards.

Australia and New Zealand

Wines produced in this part of the world tend to come either from New South Wales or from Southern Australia. In the former, the principal vineyards are the Rosemount Estate, Tyrrell's and McWilliam's; the entire area is divided between the Upper Hunter Valley and the Lower Hunter Valley, but there is very little difference between the two. In Southern Australia, the important areas are Barossa Valley, Clare Valley, the Southern Vales and Coonawarra, where the big names are the Hill-Smith Estate, Pewsey Vale, and Hardy's and Wynn's Coonawarra Estates. The style of these wines, both in description and in type of label, is very similar to that of California. A small quantity of wine is also produced in Tasmania.

Labels on Australian wines are becoming less and less informative, and at the same time consumers are becoming more sophisticated. The information supplied is usually sketchy, although there is sometimes a label on the reverse which gives bottling details. Prizes won in shows carry great weight, and provide a useful guide in a country which has no established grades.

In New Zealand white wines dominate the scene, a large proportion of them deriving from Müller-Thurgau grapes. The big wine-producing estates here are Cook's, Hawkes Bay, Hunter's, McWilliam's, Montana, Penfold's and Te Mata.

South Africa

The best wine comes from the state co-operative, KWV (Kooperatieve Wijnbouwers Vereniging), e.g. Roodeberg and Chenin Blanc; another good estate in the Cape area is Meerlust.

South America

Wines from South America are constantly improving, and production from that continent is now one in every seven bottles of the world's wines. Argentina ranks number five in the world's production table, but we hear little of these wines because of the insatiable appetite of the country's own people. Miguel Torres, who makes wine in Spain, has produced the cold-fermented variety here by using Riesling, Sauvignon, Chardonnay and Semillon grapes.

United Kingdom

The term 'British wine' is of little importance, because it refers to wine concentrates or bulk wine bottled or adulterated in this country. 'English wine' is produced by dedicated people who are trying to create a market and a reputation. For climatic reasons most of the vineyards are in the south, the best-known being Pulham,

Lamberhurst, Hambledon, Adgestone and the Carr Taylor vineyards. There are also a few in South Wales, notably at Pembroke and outside Aberavon.

Most of these vineyards employ modern growing techniques which, along with updated bottling and production plants, ensure a high-quality product. The system appears to be successful, because these wines do well (compared with market leaders) in tasting sessions all over the world. The grapes used are mostly Müller-Thurgau, Seyval Blanc, Ruländer and the new crossed vine from Germany, the Reichensteiner.

Austria

Most of the Austrian wine industry is concentrated in the Burgen-land area, around Vienna, Gumpoldskirchen and Styria. A flourishing wine industry existed until the scandal of the mid 1980s, when diethylene glycol (anti-freeze) was discovered in certain wines. However, new legislation should ensure that nothing comparable ever happens again.

Other Wine-producing Countries

These include:–

Lebanon	Château Musar
Portugal	Mateus Rosé, Vinho Verde and the Dão Wines
Hungary	Tokay
Yugoslavia	Lutomer Riesling
Greece	Retsina
Bulgaria	Cabernet, Chardonnay and Merlot

THE WINE LIST

The principal purpose of a wine list is to let the customer know what wines are available on the premises, and what each will cost. It should be comprehensive, practical and appealing, so as to encourage sales.

Most wine lists follow a similar pattern in their format, but more fun pubs, country inns etc. are now being developed which want to provide a small but effective wine list, mainly to increase turnover and to offer further facilities to their clients.

If a Stocktaker is asked to prepare a wine list for a client, he will be expected to produce something which is original, compatible with the client's wishes, and at the same time likely to be popular with the people frequenting the premises. He will prepare his draft along the lines of Example 1 on pages 226–8, so that the client can project its eventual profitability.

More formal wine lists generally run in the following order, and contain items under each of these headings:–

Champagne
Sparkling Wines
Red Bordeaux (Claret)
White Bordeaux
Red Burgundy
White Burgundy
Rhône
Alsace and Loire Wines
German Wines (Hocks, Mosel)
Italian
Spanish
Others (including Yugoslavian, Californian, Australian, English etc.)

EXAMPLE 1

Bin No.	Wine	Cost Price	Retail Price	% Profit

CHAMPAGNE
1 Lanson Black Label N.V. Pineappley, Chardonnay flavour. Soft, creamy fruit.
2 Moët & Chandon N.V. Delicate style, yet characterful, and the most popular brand of this distinguished drink.

SPARKLING WINES
3 Lafayette Brut or Demi-Sec. A good clean, fresh wine in the brut, or a sweet fruity wine in the demi-sec.

RED BORDEAUX
4 Château la Tour Pradots 1983/4 A.C. Bordeaux. A classic Bourdeaux wine with bags of raspberry fruit flavour.
5 Médoc N.V. A.C. Médoc. A soft young wine with lots of bite, round and well made.

Example 1 – (continued)

Bin No.	Wine	Cost Price	Retail Price	% Profit

6   Château Croix de Pez 1982 A.C. Saint-Estèphe. If you like Claret, this is for you; an earthy wine, well-balanced, with a blackcurranty flavour.

WHITE BORDEAUX

7   Bordeaux Blanc N.V. A.C. A soft, simple and clean-tasting example of this mouth-filling wine.

RED BURGUNDY

8   Beaujolais N.V. A.C. A light attractive wine with a good Gamay character.

9   Fleurie 1985 A.C. Rich fruit with wild raspberry overtones. To get the best from this wine, try it lightly chilled.

WHITE BURGUNDY

10   Saint-Véran 1985 A.C. A crisp, clean dry wine of real character – excellent value at half the price of its famous neighbour Pouilly-Fuissé.

RHÔNE

11   Côtes du Rhône N.V. A.C. An easy, light, fruity wine with a hint of wild plums.

12   Châteauneuf-du-Pape N.V. Rich, soft, ripe, mellow, fruity wine with a good body, but not too heavy.

LOIRE/ALSACE

13   Muscadet de Sèvre et Maine 1985. A young fresh wine, almost tangy, and one of the most refreshing wines.

14   Gewurztraminer 1983 A.C. A racy, spicy, highly aromatic wine – a must with rich food.

Example 1 – (continued)

Bin No. Wine	Cost Price	Retail Price	% Profit

GERMAN

15 Bereich Bernkastel Riesling 1984 Q.b.A. A light medium wine, crisp and fruity, a lovely drink on its own.

16 Bereich Nierstein 1985 Q.b.A. A straightforward, clean, honeyed wine, well-balanced and grapey.

ITALIAN

17 Lambrusco N.V. D.O.C. A light, fresh, lively, slightly sparkling fun wine, to be drunk any time, any place.

NON-ALCOHOLIC WINES

18 Masson Light N.V. For those occasions when you want a drink without the alcohol, this pleasant, slightly sparkling wine from the House of Paul Masson is a good choice.

WINES FOR THAT SPECIAL OCCASION

19 Chablis 1er Cru 'Montmains' 1984 A.C. Good oaky, Chardonnay nose with a delicate floral crispness. A luscious wine.

20 Gevrey Chambertin 1983. A deep round classic example of this meaty red wine.

HOUSE WINES

21 House White. A light, fruity, crisp wine, with a hint of honey and wild flowers.

22 House Red. A soft, mellow, young, ripe wine, suitable for drinking on its own or with meat or cheese.

Example 2 is a wine list of a different style, aimed at the middle market, but suitable only for a limited range of types of venue.

EXAMPLE 2

Dry White
83 Muscadet de Sèvre et Maine A.C.:
   Pale colour, slightly green and with a very pleasant crisp flavour (Loire).
83 Mouton Cadet Blanc A.C. Rothschild:
   Pale colour, dry sharp flavour, ideal as an apéritif (Médoc).
Soave:
   Light and pale in colour, fresh and smoothly dry (Verona).
Chablis:
   Crisp, light, dry and delicious (Burgundy area).

Medium White – Hock
84 Liebfraumilch Q.b.A.:
   Light yellow/green colour, fruity flavour, with an association of apples and pears.
84 Niersteiner Gutes Domtal:
   Made from Riesling grapes, and potentially a really noble drink.
83 Oppenheimer Krotenbrunnen Kabinett:
   A quality wine, medium-dry, light and elegant.
82/83 Hanns Christof Kabinett:
   'Kabinett' indicates a stage up in the hierarchy of German wines – very good indeed.
83/84 Liebfraumilch Blue Nun Q.b.A.:
   What is there to add about this most popular of wines?

Medium White – Mosel-Saar-Ruwer
84 Bereich Bernkastel Q.b.A.:
   A famous Mosel wine.
84 Piesporter Michelsberg Q.b.A.:
   Lightly coloured. This is a fruity medium-dry wine, with a pleasant flinty finish.
82/83 Bernkasteler Kurfürstlay Spätlese Q.m.P.:
   A good-quality wine, conveying the expected fresh Mosel characteristics.
83 Graacher Himmelreich Riesling:
   Graach, hardly more than a hamlet in size, is capable of producing this excellent wine, which is one of the finest Rieslings of the Mosel.

Sweet White
83 Tiger Milk:
   A Hungarian wine; it has a pleasant sweet taste and a long-lasting rich flavour.

La Flora Blanche:
  A fine-quality sweet dessert wine, which has a rich nose enhanced in tasting.

Rosé
Mateus Rosé:
  Ever-popular rosé wine from northern Portugal. Pleasant dry flavour, and a slight bubble.
Cabernet d'Anjou A.C., Rosé:
  One of the top French pink wines, fruity and fresh.

Red Wines
81 Château Monbousquet, Saint-Émilion:
  One of the wines from this really fine region of red wine production, fruity and rich with a heady aroma.
79 Château Haut Marbuzet, Saint-Estèphe:
  From the Haut-Médoc, full-bodied.

Red Burgundy
84 Beaujolais A.C. La Ruffière:
  A light red wine which is often described as having a pinkish tint, light and refreshing.
82 Côte de Beaune Villages A.C.:
  A pleasantly robust red wine, particularly suitable for drinking with cheese.
78 Nuits-Saint-Georges A.C.:
  Excellent red wine, made in the area of the same name on the Côte de Nuits. A great Burgundy.

Others
Rioja Campo Viejo Reserva, Red:
  A Spanish wine with a distinctive woody nose, full-bodied.
Chianti:
  Probably the most famous of Italian red wines – a bright ruby colour, very full-bodied with long-lasting flavour.
Lambrusco Frizzante:
  A medium-coloured red wine with a slight sparkle. Described as one of the few sweet red wines of the world.

Sparkling Wine and Champagne
Saumur Vin Mousseux, Demi-Sec:
  A medium-sweet sparkling wine produced in France. Ideal for any celebration.
Schloss Rheingarten, Hallgarten:
  A German sparkling wine.
Moët & Chandon, Première Cuvée:
  A well-known French Champagne, for that special occasion.

Bollinger:
   An excellent example of a classic Champagne.
Valmonte Demi-Sec:
   A medium-sparkling wine with a crisp freshness.

It is of course possible to put together an informal wine list by condensing some of the headings shown in Example 1 (page 226), or by listing wines from dry, through medium, to sweet for the white wines, and from light, through medium, to full-bodied for the reds, not forgetting rosé wines. In many instances there is a brief description of each wine which acts as a guide to the consumer. It is evident that this does help promote the sale of wines, but it is not necessarily appropriate to every type of venue. For example, in a five-star hotel or restaurant with a wine butler, and a huge variety of wines available, a list of this type would be quite out of context.

The wine list has to complement the establishment; it has to cater for the uninitiated as well as for the connoisseur, so it must always have both popular wines which are familiar and also some carefully selected wines from around the world. Because of the increasing price of some of the more famous French wines, hoteliers and restaurateurs are tending to introduce more from California, New Zealand and Australia.

The most significant item on any wine list is the house wine. This is likely to sell in large quantities, so it is important for it to be good and generally acceptable to the public. It is sometimes necessary to sacrifice profit for quality, and it is well worth the effort to do a little research in order to find the right one.

It is advantageous to add a disclaimer to all wine lists, giving management the right to offer wines of a different vintage should supplies of the one stated become exhausted. It should also be mentioned that all prices are inclusive of Value Added Tax; and that descriptions are intended only as a guide, and may not represent other people's views.

Whichever way a wine list is presented, it is desirable that as much information as possible should be provided, particularly as to the shipper, style of wine and vintage. However, if space is a problem, certain descriptions can be omitted; the type of operation, the situation and the price structure will determine how much information can be included.

Wine lists can in some instances be very extensive, possibly incorporating several hundred bins. More common is the type shown in Example 2, which is informal, has good descriptions, and is intended to appeal to the clients of middle-range establishments. Example 1 is more formal, and shows a small wine list in the process of being compiled, with all the preliminary workings but without certain details such as price. Once the content is agreed, the Stocktaker and the client will be able to decide on a final choice of wines, suppliers and selling prices.

Mark-ups on wine lists are much criticized, as being excessive; but the average is 50% on receipts, which is 100% on cost (see page 166). This can rise to as high as 60–65%, depending upon the type and nature of the extablishment. When a wine list is being priced, it should be looked at in total, and it might be necessary to reduce the anticipated gross profit on some wines but to load it on others. It is unusual for champagnes to sell on a full profit margin because of their high cost, but sometimes, to compensate, cheaper wines can be priced higher than projected. The overall gross profit should be maintained at the required level, but might fluctuate slightly according to the mix of sales during any one period.

One of the biggest concerns in the trade relates to the sale of wine by the glass, and the huge variability of the amount served. A voluntary code of practice was drawn up in 1984 by a working group of publicans and restaurateurs with help from the Department of Trade and Industry, and its recommendations were as follows:–

1. That no bar or restaurant should use both metric and Imperial measures;
2. That no bar or restaurant should sell wine in any more than two different measures, and that there should be at least 2 fluid ounces or 50 millilitres between the sizes;
3. That quantities should conform to the five Imperial or six metric glass sizes listed in the Weights and Measures Act, 1963 (see page 94);
4. That quantities and prices should be displayed on menus, price-boards and wine lists whenever possible.

CHAPTER 11
FOOD AND TOBACCO

FOOD

This section consists of lists showing the seasonal availability of various types of game, shellfish and fresh fish; a list describing cheeses of different national origins; illustrative diagrams of meat, fish and cheese; and lists showing the seasonal availability of various types of vegetables and fruit.

Game

Commodity	Season	Peak eating time
Blackcock	20 Aug.–10 Dec.	September–October
Capercaillie	12 Aug.–10 Dec.	September–October
Grouse	12 Aug.–10 Dec.	August–October
Guinea-fowl – Farmed	All year	February–April
Hare	1 Aug.–31 Mar.	October onwards
Leveret	August–February	October–December
Mallard/other wild duck	1 Sept.–28 Feb.	November–January
Partridge – Red-Legged	1 Sept.–31 Jan.	October–December
– Grey	1 Sept.–31 Jan.	October–December
Pheasant	1 Oct.–31 Jan.	November–January
Ptarmigan	September–April	September–October
Quail – Farmed	All year	
– Wild	September–February	September–October
Rabbit – Farmed/ Imported	All year	
– Wild	Early autumn – February	Winter
Snipe	12 Aug.–31 Jan.	November
Teal	1 Sept.–28 Feb.	November–December
Venison – Farmed/Frozen	All year	
– Wild:		
Doe (female)	Late June–January	August–September
Buck (male)	Late June–30 Sept.	August–September
Widgeon	1 Sept.–28 Feb.	November–December
Wild Boar	October–31 Jan.	October–December
Wild Goose (in this country, strictly illegal)	September–February	November–December
Woodcock	1 Oct.–31 Jan.	November–December
Wood-pigeon	No closed season	March–October

Shellfish

Commodity	Season	Peak eating time
Clams	All year	Autumn
Cockles	October–April	
Crabs	April–December	May–October
Crawfish	May–September	
Crayfish	All year	March–October
Lobsters	All year	April–August
Mussels	September–March	November–February
Oysters	September–April	September–April
Prawns	All year	All year
– Dublin Bay	All year	May–November
– Pacific (imported)	All year	
Scallops	September–March	October–December
Shrimps	February–October	Summer
Whelks	All year	September–February
Winkles	All year	October–May

Fresh Fish

Commodity	Season	Comments
Bass	May–July	
Bream – Freshwater	November–February	
– Sea	May–December	
Brill	January–April	
Carp	June–April	
Cod	October–April	
Conger Eel	March–October	
Dab	June–December	
Dogfish (huss, flake, rigg)	October–June	
Dover Sole	May–February	
Eel	All year	
Flounder (fluke)	September–February	(scarce December–January)
Grey Mullet	September–February	
Gurnard	July–April	
Haddock	November–January	
Hake	July–March	
Halibut	August–April	
Herring	July–February	(all year)
John Dory	January–April	
Lemon Sole	December–March	
Ling	December–March	
Mackerel	All year	
Megrim	August–March	
Mock Halibut	March–October	(all year)
Monkfish	All year	
Perch	June–March	(not readily available)

Fresh Fish – (continued)

Pike	September–March	(not readily available)
Pilchard	June–February	(not readily available fresh)
Plaice	January–March	
Redfish	All year	
Red Mullet	May–September	
Rockfish	September–February	
Saithe (coley)	February–April, August–October	
Salmon	May–July	
– Farmed	All year	
– Smoked	All year	
Sardine	June–February	
Scad (horse mackerel)	May	
Skate	October–April	
Smelt	July–March	
Sprat	October–March	
Squid	May–October	
Trout – Brown	April–August	
– Rainbow	All year	
– Sea (salmon trout)	April–July	
Turbot	May-July	
Whitebait	February–July	
Whiting	August–March	(all year)
Witch	August–April	

Cheeses

Name	Type	Comments
France		
Adondance	Semi-hard cheese	
Babybel	Semi-hard cheese	French-type Edam
Beaufort	Hard cheese	Like Gruyère
Beaumont	Semi-hard cheese, mild and creamy	
Bleu d'Auvergne	Blue cheese	
Bleu de Bresse	Blue cheese	
Boursault	Triple-cream soft cheese	
Boursin	Triple-cream soft cheese	Available with herbs and garlic
Brie	Soft cheese	
Camembert	Soft cheese	
Cantal	Semi-hard cheese	Oldest French cheese
Chevret	Soft goat's milk cheese	
Comté	Hard cheese	
Demi-sel	Fresh soft cheese	
Fourme d'Ambert	Blue cheese	French Stilton
Fromage Frais	Unripened rennet curd	

Cheeses – (continued)

Gournay	Soft cheese	Like Camembert
Livarot	Soft cheese	
Pont l'Evêque	Soft cheese	
Port-Salut	Semi-hard cheese	
Pyrénées	Semi-hard cheese	
Reblochon	Semi-hard cheese	
Roquefort	Ewe's milk cheese, blue-veined	
Saint Paulin	Semi-hard cheese	Similar to Port-Salut
Valençay	Goat's milk cheese, covered with wood ash; smooth and soft	

Germany

Backsteiner	Semi-hard cheese	
Bavaria Blue	Blue cheese	
Bergkäse	Hard pressed cheese	Similar to Emmental
Frühstückskäse	Soft cheese	Popular breakfast cheese
Limburger	Soft cheese	Originally from Belgium
Mecklenburger Magerkäse	Hard cheese, coloured with saffron	
Quark	Unripened curd cheese	
Speisequark	Skimmed mild curd mixed with fats	
Tilsiter	Semi-hard cheese, flavoured with caraway	

Italy

Asiago	Hard cheese	Sometimes made from ewe's milk
Bel Paese	Semi-hard cheese	
Bitto	Hard cheese	Made from cow's milk or any combination of milks including goat's and ewe's
Cacio a cavallo	Hard cheese	
Caprini	Curd cheese	Goat's milk cheese
Dolcelatte	Blue cheese	
Formaggelle	Soft fresh cheese	Ewe's, goat's or cow's milk cheese
Gorgonzola	Blue-veined cheese	
Grana Padano	Hard cheese	
Mozzarella	Soft cheese	Used on pizzas
Parmigiano (Parmesan)	Hard cheese	Mostly sold grated
Provolone	Hard cheese	
Ricotta	Whey cheese	Bland and soft; or ripened, salty and dry; or matured, dry and hard

Cheeses – (continued)

Stracchino	Soft cheese	Generic term for older cheeses made in winter when cows were brought down from the mountains

U.S.A.

American	Hard cheese	Also called American Cheddar
American Blue	Blue cheese	
Bakers	Fresh soft cheese	
Brick	Semi-hard cheese	Type of American Cheddar
Coon	Hard cheese	
Creole	Fresh curd cheese	
Gold'n'Rich	Semi-soft buttery cheese	
Monterey Jack	Semi-hard cheese	
Philadelphia	Cream cheese	Brand name for best-known cream cheese
Vermont	Hard cheese	Best American Cheddar

United Kingdom

Blue Cheshire	Blue cheese	
Blue Stilton	Blue hard cheese	
Blue Wensleydale	Blue hard cheese	
Bonchester	Unpasteurised soft cheese	Camembert type
Caboc	Soft white cheese	Scottish
Caerphilly	Semi-hard cheese	Welsh
Cambridge	Soft cheese	
Cheddar	Hard cheese	
Cheshire	Semi-hard cheese	
Cottage cheese	Low-fat granular cheese	
Crowdie	Unpressed cheese, sour-tasting	Scottish
Derby, Sage Derby	Semi-hard cheese	
Double Gloucester	Hard cheese	
Dunlop	Hard cheese	Scottish
Herefordshire	Semi-hard cheese	
Howgate	Fresh cream cheese, rolled in oats	Scottish
Lancashire	Semi-hard crumbly cheese	
Leicester	Hard cheese	
Lymeswold	Blue-veined cheese	
Satterleigh	Firm goat's milk cheese	
Swaledale	Semi-hard cheese	
Wensleydale	Semi-hard cheese	
White Stilton	Semi-hard white cheese	As this matures it will go 'blue', but not as strong as Blue Stilton

Cheeses – (continued)

Other countries

Asco	Ewe's milk cheese	Corsica
Auton	Goat's milk soft cheese	
Bryndza	Salty ewe's milk cheese	Hungary, Poland, Czechoslovakia
Bunder Alpkäse	Thick hard cheese	Switzerland
Cabrero	Semi-hard cheese	Spain
Castelo Branco	Ewe's milk semi-hard cheese	Portugal
Danablu	Semi-hard blue cheese	Scandinavia
Edam	Semi-hard cheese	Holland
Emmental	Hard cheese	Switzerland
Fetta/Feta	Ewe's milk cheese, either crumbly or hard	Italy, Greece
Gammelost	Semi-hard cheese	Scandinavia
Gjetost	Goat's milk whey cheese	
Gruyère	Hard cheese	Switzerland, France
Haloumi	Fibrous ewe's milk cheese	Greece
Hervé	Strong pungent soft cheese	Belgium
Kashkaval	Ewe's milk cheddar-type cheese	Bulgaria
Kwark	Soft curd cheese	Holland
Manchego	Ewe's milk cheese	Most famous Spanish cheese
Mesost	Whey cheese	Sweden
Mutschli	Semi-hard sweet-tasting cheese	Switzerland
Mycella	Blue-veined cheese	Scandinavia
Samsø	Semi-hard cheese	All-purpose Danish cheese
Sapsago	Hard cheese	Switzerland
Vacherin Fribourgeois	Semi-hard cheese	Oldest Swiss cheese

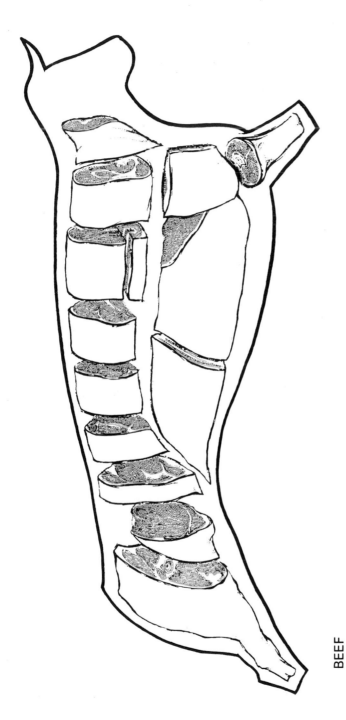

BEEF

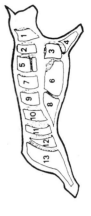

1 HEAD
2 & 3 CLOD & STICKING
4 SHIN
5 SHOULDER
6 BRISKET
7 MIDDLE RIBS

8 FLANK
9 RIBS
10 SIRLOIN
11 RUMP
12 BUTTOCK
13 LEG

BRISKET OF BEEF

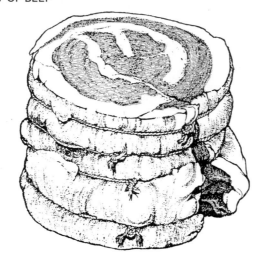

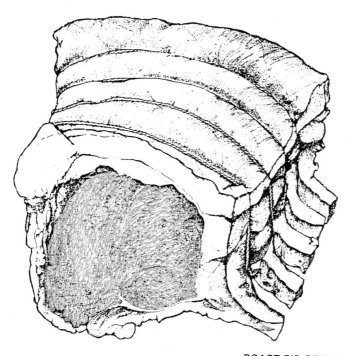

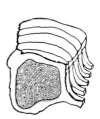

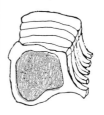

ROAST RIB OF BEEF

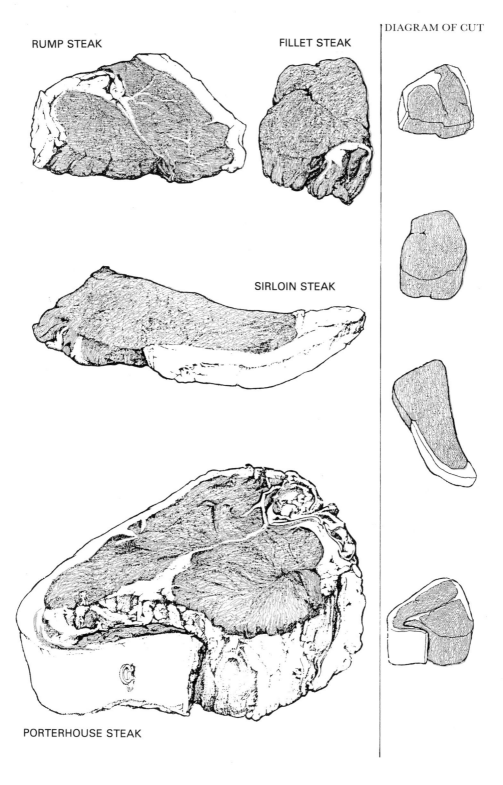

RUMP STEAK

FILLET STEAK

DIAGRAM OF CUT

SIRLOIN STEAK

PORTERHOUSE STEAK

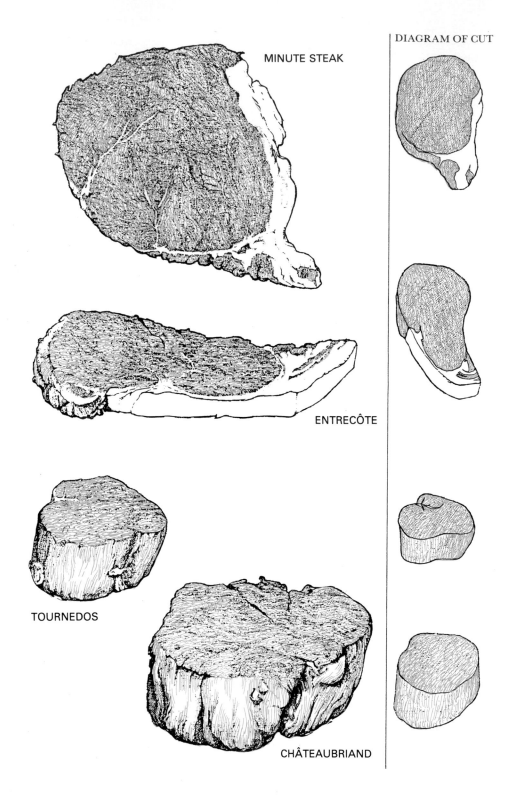

MINUTE STEAK

DIAGRAM OF CUT

ENTRECÔTE

TOURNEDOS

CHÂTEAUBRIAND

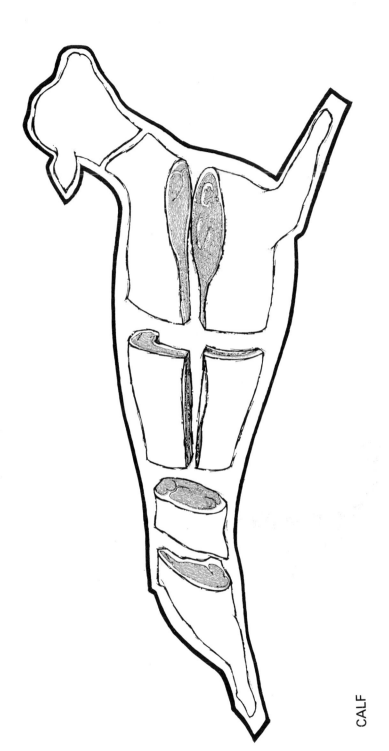

CALF

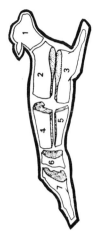

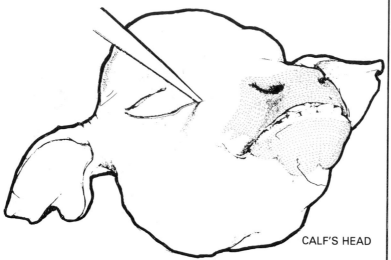

CALF'S HEAD

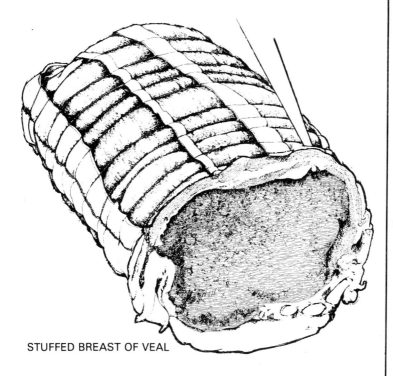

STUFFED BREAST OF VEAL

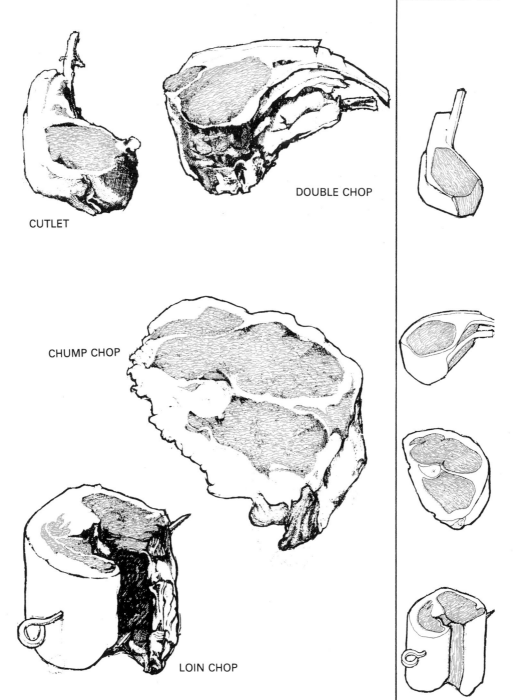

CUTLET

DOUBLE CHOP

DIAGRAM OF CUT

CHUMP CHOP

LOIN CHOP

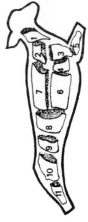

DIAGRAM OF CUT

1 HEAD
2 SHOULDER PIECE
3 SCRAG
4 MIDDLE NECK
5 SHOULDER
6 BREASTS

7 BEST END
8 LOIN
9 CHUMP
10 LEG
11 KNUCKLE LEG

LAMB OR MUTTON

CÔTE

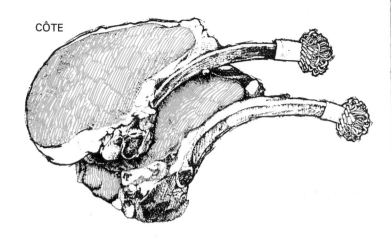

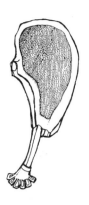

PAUPIETTE

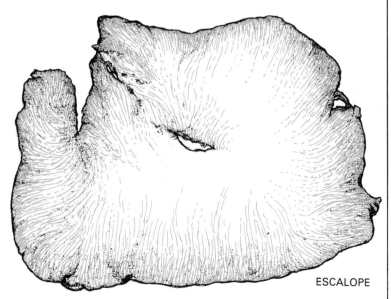

ESCALOPE

STUFFED LOIN OF LAMB OR MUTTON

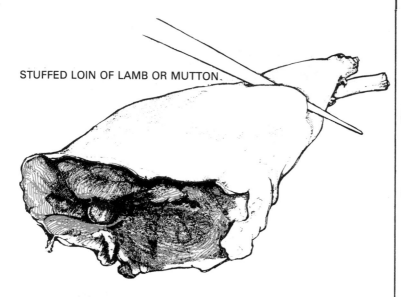

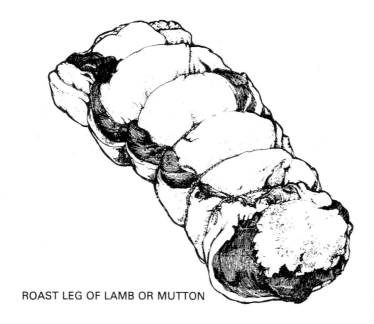

ROAST LEG OF LAMB OR MUTTON

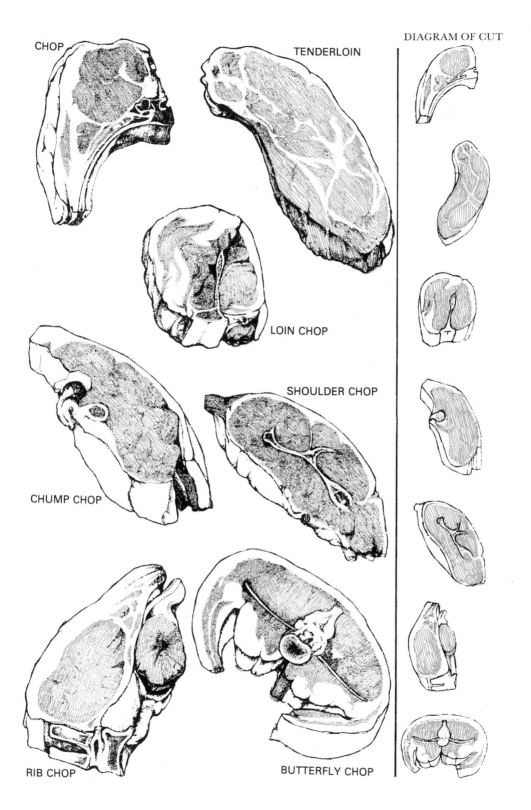

CHOP

TENDERLOIN

DIAGRAM OF CUT

LOIN CHOP

SHOULDER CHOP

CHUMP CHOP

RIB CHOP

BUTTERFLY CHOP

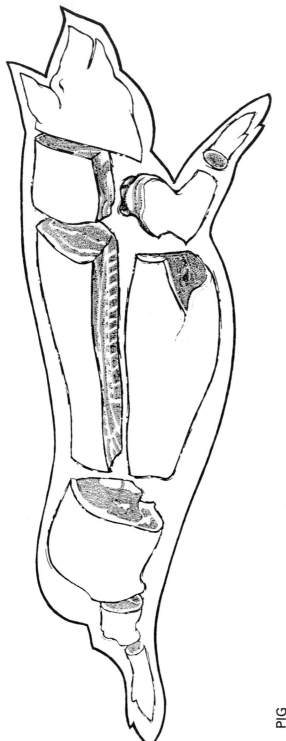

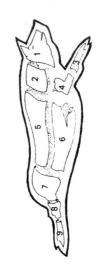

1 HEAD
2 NECK END
3 FORE END
4 FORE LOIN
5 BEST LOIN

6 BELLY
7 W LEG
8 K LEG
9 KNUCKLE

PIG

ENGLISH CHOP

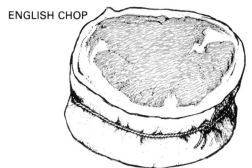

FRENCHED RIB CHOP

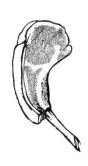

LEG STEAK

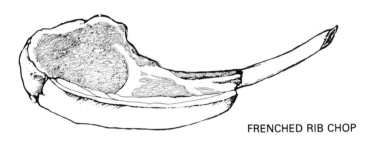

SARATOGA CHOP

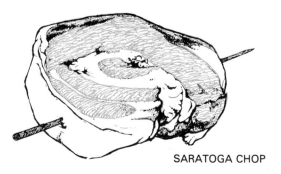

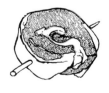

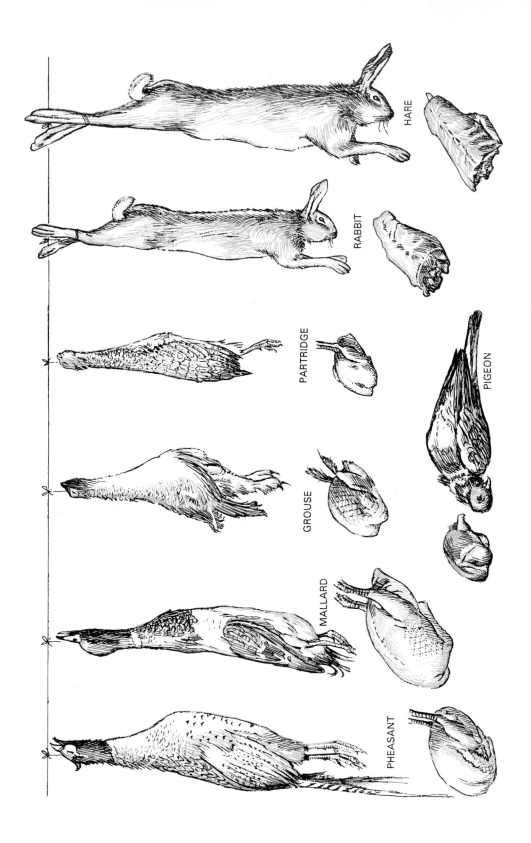

HARE

RABBIT

PARTRIDGE

PIGEON

GROUSE

MALLARD

PHEASANT

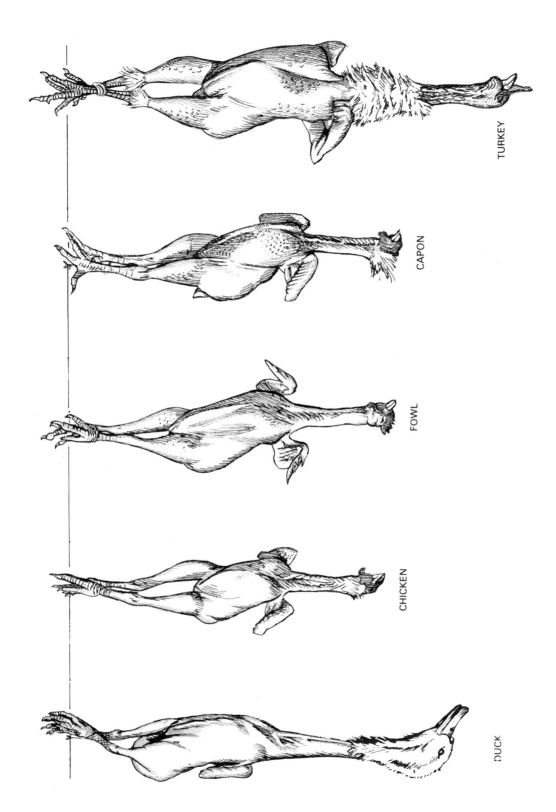

TURKEY

CAPON

FOWL

CHICKEN

DUCK

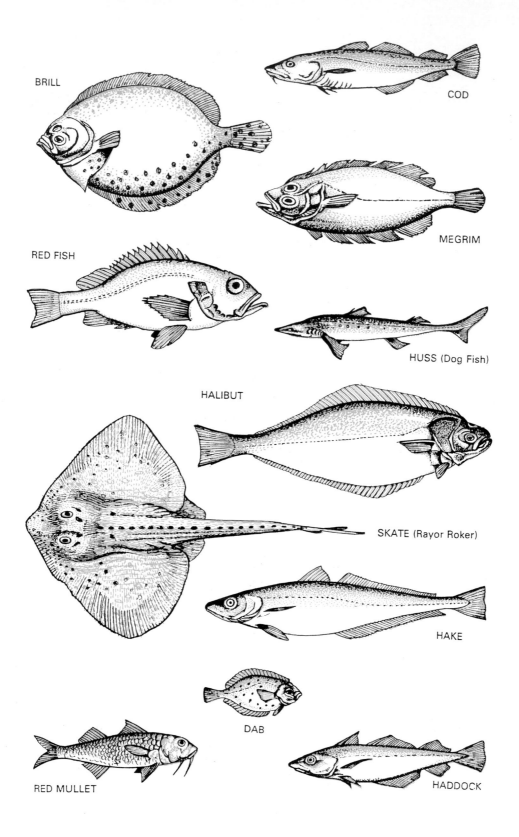

BRILL

COD

MEGRIM

RED FISH

HUSS (Dog Fish)

HALIBUT

SKATE (Rayor Roker)

HAKE

DAB

RED MULLET

HADDOCK

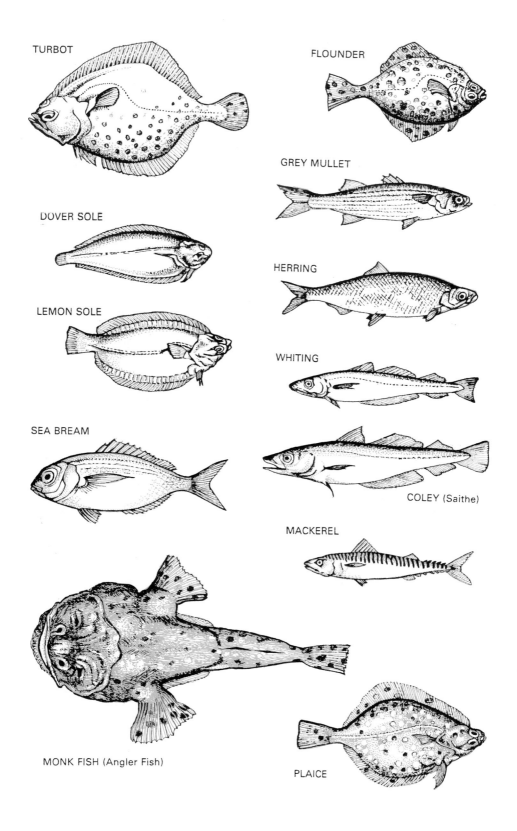

TURBOT

FLOUNDER

GREY MULLET

DOVER SOLE

HERRING

LEMON SOLE

WHITING

SEA BREAM

COLEY (Saithe)

MACKEREL

MONK FISH (Angler Fish)

PLAICE

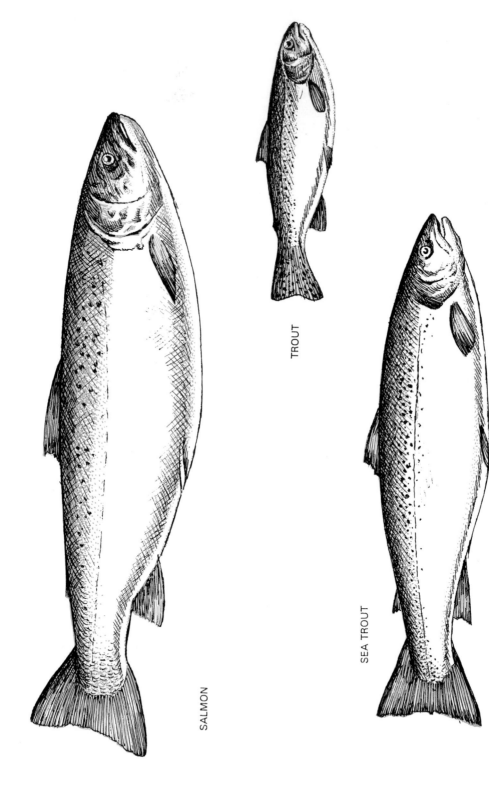

TROUT

SALMON

SEA TROUT

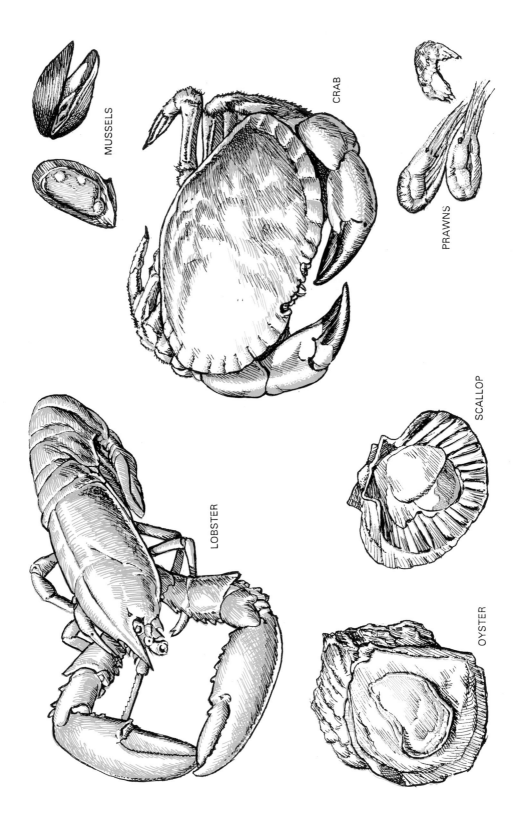

MUSSELS

CRAB

PRAWNS

LOBSTER

SCALLOP

OYSTER

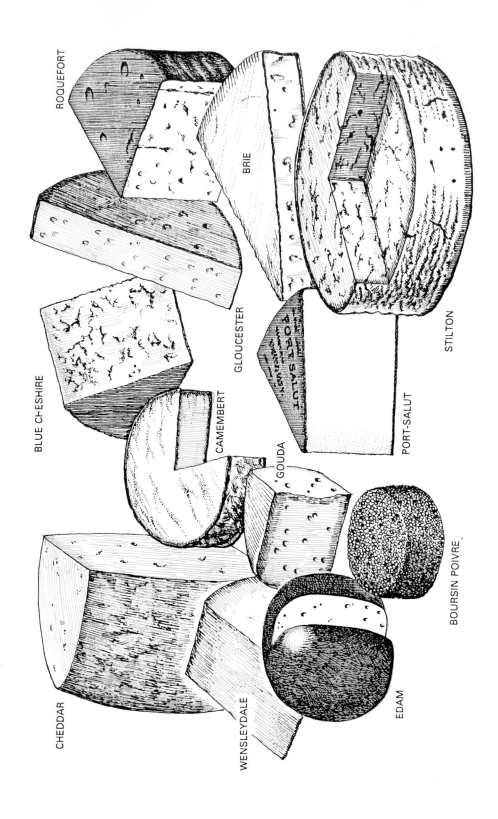

ROQUEFORT

BRIE

STILTON

GLOUCESTER

BLUE CHESHIRE

CAMEMBERT

GOUDA

PORT-SALUT

CHEDDAR

WENSLEYDALE

EDAM

BOURSIN POIVRE

Vegetables

Commodity	Season	Peak eating time
Asparagus	May–June	May
Aubergine (imported)	All year	
Avocado (imported)	All year	
Beetroot	All year	Autumn
Black Salsify	October–March	Winter
Broad Beans	April–September	August
Broccoli	Most of year	November–February
Brussels Sprouts	August–March	October–December
Calabrese	July–December	Autumn–winter
Carrots	All year	
Cauliflower	Most of year	July–August
Celeriac	October–March	Winter
Celery	Most of year	December
Chicory	Most of year	
Courgette	All year	
Cucumber	All year	Late summer
Endive	Late autumn–winter	November
French Beans (imported)	All year	
Garlic	All year	
Globe Artichoke (imported)	All year	Late summer
Horseradish	September–March	Winter
Jerusalem Artichoke	October–March	December
Kale	November–May	Winter
Kidney Beans	June–mid-November	July–November
Kohl Rabi (imported)	July–April	
Leeks	August–May	September–November
Lettuce – Cabbage	All year	Summer
– Cos	All year	Summer
– Webb	All year	Summer
Mange-tout (imported)	Most of year	
Marrow	July–October	September
Mushrooms – button, cup and flat	All year	September–October
Mustard and Cress	All year	
Okra (imported)	December–June	Spring
Onions	September–March	
Parsley	All year	Winter
Parsnips	September–April	Winter
Pea Beans	Early summer	
Peas	May–October	June–August
– Early Varieties	May	
Pickling Onions	July–October	July–September
Potatoes	All year	
Pumpkin (imported)	Summer–autumn	Autumn
Radishes	All year	
Red Cabbage	August–January	November–December
Red/Green (also orange/ yellow) Peppers (Pimentos) (imported)	All year	

Vegetables – (continued)

Runner Beans	Mid-July–end October	August–September
Salsify – Local	End October–May	Winter
– Imported	October–March	Winter
Savoy Cabbage	August–May	Winter
Sea Kale	August–March	Winter
Shallots	September–March	September
Spinach	All year	March–April
Spinach Beet	All year, but rare	
Spring Cabbage	April–May	Spring
Spring Greens	November–April	Spring
Spring Onions	Most of year	March–May
Swedes	September–May	Autumn
Sweet Corn (Corn-on-the-cob)	July–November	Summer
Sweet Potatoes (imported)	Winter	
Tomatoes	All year	September–October
Truffles (imported)	November–March	November–December
Turnips	August–March	Late summer
Watercress	All year	
White Cabbage	October–February	Winter
Winter Cabbage	August–March	Winter

Fruit

Commodity	Season	Peak eating time
Apples, Dessert –		
Early varieties: George Cave, Scarlet Pimpernel, Granny Smith etc.	Mid-July–September	Depends on variety
Later varieties: Pearmain, Cox's Orange Pippin, Crispin, Tydeman's Early	End September–April	
Apricots	May–August	
Bananas (imported)	All year	All year
Bilberries	July–August	August
Blackberries	July–October	End July–end September
Blackcurrants	July–August	July–August
Blueberries	July–September	End July–August
Cherries – Imported	April–August	May–July
– Morello	July–August	
– Others	Late June–July	June–July
Chinese Gooseberries (imported)	July–February	
Chinese Lanterns (Cape Gooseberries) (imported)	All year	

Fruit – (continued)

Clementines (imported)	November–February	Around Christmas
Crab Apples	September–October	September–October
Cranberries (imported)	October–February	November–January
Damsons	Late August–September	August–September
Dates (imported)	September–March	Winter
Figs – Fresh (imported)	August–December	September–November
Gooseberries	End April–early September	Mid-summer, depending on variety
Grapefruit (imported)	All year	All year
Grapes – Black and White (imported)	All year	
Greengages	August–September	August
Kumquats (imported)	All year, but often scarce	
Lemons (imported)	All year	All year
Limes (imported)	All year	All year
Loganberries	Early July–end August	August
Loquats (imported)	All year, but very scarce	
Lychees (imported)	December–February	December–January
Mandarins (imported)	October–March	Around Christmas
Mangos (imported)	January–September	Spring–early summer
Melons (imported)		
– Cantaloup		
– Charentais	All year	Depends on country
– Honeydew	All year	Depends on country
– Ogen	All year	Depends on country
– Watermelons	All year	May–September
Naartje (imported)	November–January	Around Christmas
Oranges (imported)		
– Seville	January–February	January–February
– Other varieties	All year	All year
Papayas (imported)	June–December	
Passion-fruit (imported)	Most of year	
Pawpaws (imported)	June–December	Autumn
Peaches	May–October	June–July
Pears – Conference	September–February	October–December
– Cooking	October–December	
– Imported	February–June	
– William	August–October	August
Persimmons (imported)	October–January	November–December
Pineapples (imported)	All year	All year
Plantains (imported)	All year, but often scarce	
Plums – Imported	January–March	
– Local	August–September	Depends on variety
Pomegranates (imported)	September–January	September–December
Quinces	October–November	October
Raspberries		
– First crop	July–August	July
– Second crop	August–September	September
Redcurrants	July–August	July–August
Rhubarb – Forced	Mid-December–mid-April	January–February
– Main crop	Mid-March–end June	May–June

Fruit – (continued)

Satsumas (imported)	October–February	Around Christmas
Strawberries		
– First crop	May–July	Mid-summer
– Second crop	Autumn	
Tangerines (imported)	October–March	December
Uglis (imported)	October–February, but often scarce	
White Currants	July–August	July–August

TOBACCO

Cigars

The Havana Cigar: The origin of the Havana cigar dates back to the days of Columbus: in 1492 two scouts from his expedition, who had just spent fourteen days reconnoitring eastern Cuba, reported that, amongst other things, the islanders 'drank smoke'. They had been near the River Caonao in the province of Oriente, where they had discovered the Tainos (a tribe of Aboriginal Indians), who had the strange habit of inhaling the fumes from a bowl of burning tobacco leaves directly through their nostrils, by means of a hollow reed. This form of smoking was referred to as 'tobago', and it is from this that the word 'tobacco' derives.

The Tainos also rolled the tobacco in palm leaves to form long cylinders, thus creating the cigar as we know it today. The explorers did not publicise their discovery, and it was not until the Peninsular Wars of the nineteenth century that the French and British soldiers rediscovered the early Havana cigar.

Tobacco is grown throughout the Caribbean and in many parts of both North and South America, but in Cuba a combination of rich soil, wind, humidity and climate have created ideal conditions. It is grown all over the island, but some areas produce better tobacco than others, just as some vine-growing areas produce better wine than others. The four principal regions are the Oriente province, the Remedios region of Las Ville, the Partados region south-west of Havana, and the Vuelta Abajo region in the westernmost province of the island, Pinar del Rio.

The seed is hand-reared in a nursery and planted in October, which generally marks the end of the rainy season. The leaves start maturing at the base and continue upwards as the plant grows. Picking commences in January with the bottommost leaf (called the 'sand leaf') and continues up as far as the leaves are mature. Normally only two to five leaves are picked off each plant, but by the end of March, when it will have reached full maturity and be almost six feet high, the pickers will have extracted another ten or twelve.

This rather laborious process ensures that the leaves are consistent, perfectly mature, and ready for curing.

The leaves are then removed to the 'casas de tobaco' (curing barns), where they are sewn together and hung on lines between the rafters or beams. This process takes several weeks, during which time the leaves lose most of their moisture. The atmosphere is rigidly controlled to prevent any changes in humidity or temperature, and by the end of the process the leaves have changed from green to golden brown.

Before being rolled, they are piled ready for fermentation, during which they are continually turned so as to ensure consistency.

The final cigar is made up of three main parts: the filler, the binder and the wrapper. The filler makes up almost three-quarters of the cigar, and is held together by the binder, which is a thicker leaf from the lower part of the plant and is chosen for its slow-burning qualities. The wrapper leaf, which generally comes from Vuelta Abajo, is grown under a muslin roof to protect it from direct sunlight.

After fermentation, the leaves are sprayed with water to make them pliable. The excess is shaken off, and after the best leaves have been selected, they are stripped of their stalks and taken to the 'trocederos' (cigar rollers) who, according to a custom which goes back to the middle of the nineteenth century, sit in huge rooms of up to 200 people, rolling cigars.

The Tools of the Cutter: These are as follows:–

1.   A cutting board (which must never be allowed to dry out).
2.   A very sharp broad blade which is curved, and is used for trimming and ensuring uniformity. It is called the 'chaveta'.
3.   A small guillotine, for trimming the cigar to the required length.
4.   A gauge made from wood, for checking the girth of the cigar.
5.   A small container of flavourless vegetable gum.

The process of rolling requires absolute precision. From two to four leaves of various sizes, selected for their aroma and flavour rather than for their beauty, are laid end to end. Before placing the filler in the binder and introducing it to the specially selected wrapper, the roller will ensure that the blend is consistent and that the leaves are distributed evenly throughout.

He will then lay the binder (with its filler) on the board, and place it at an angle of 45° across the wrapper, which is then wound round; but his skill must ensure that the overlap is the same the entire length of the cigar. He then gently rolls the wrapped portion with the flat side of the 'chaveta', to polish and stretch the wrapper so that it fits smoothly and evenly. The rounded end of a cigar is formed in one of two ways: either a hook is cut at the end of the wrapper leaf, which is flicked over and stuck down with a pinhead of the vegetable gum, or else a separate cap or disc of leaf is cut from excess wrapper, and stuck over the end with the same gum. Once guillotined and cut to the required length, the cigar is stored for a short period in a cedarwood cupboard, which helps to extract any excess moisture. After this stage, the cigar is ready to be sold.

In a good box of Havana cigars, all should be of the same colour and all should be wrapped the same way, either left-handed or right-handed. If there are variations, it normally indicates that someone has made up the box, which is, therefore, not of top quality.

Shapes and Sizes: Cigars vary considerably in shape and size; the following list describes the characteristics of the various grades.

Corona
A fairly straight cigar with a rounded top, approximately 5½ inches or 14 cm long.

Très Petit Corona
The same shape as a Corona but slightly smaller, approximately 4½ inches or 11.5 cm.

Lonsdale
Again the same shape as a Corona, but approximately 6½ inches or 16.5 cm.

Ideale
A slender, tapering cigar, measuring approximately 6½ inches or 16.5 cm.

Panatella
Open both ends (i.e. a cheroot type of cigar), approximately 5 inches or 12.5 cm.

The expression 'cigar-shaped' conjures up, in most people's minds, an image of something whose shape is well-defined; but in fact, a cigar can be of almost any shape at all.

In Cuba, the cigar rollers have produced around 950 different shapes, including the pressed cigar, which is square and very popular with the Swiss. This is achieved by rolling the cigar rather more loosely than usual, and placing it in a box along with others; by the time it is ready to be smoked, it will have acquired a uniform squareness. Another example is the Italian 'toscanelli' cigar, which is very dark and gnarled, and tapered at both ends; because it burns so slowly, the Italians cut it in the middle, and the result is two (slightly tapered, rather strong and pungent) cigars for the price of one.

Packaging: Cigars are graded according to their colour:–

1.   CCC Claro – light golden brown wrapper.
2.   CC   Colorado Claro – medium brown wrapper.
3.   C   Colorado – dark brown wrapper.
4.   CM   Colorado Maduro – very dark wrapper.
5.   M   Maduro – extra dark wrapper.

Havana cigars are normally packed in square cedarwood boxes which allow them to draw from one another and thus to continue to mature. Cigars packed in glass jars do not mature but remain fresh, moist and green.

Storage: Very often, the cigar is wrapped in a sheet of cedarwood and packed in an aluminium tube. This is a convenient way of carrying it safely, but the best way to store it is in a humidor, which can be used to lessen or increase the moisture in the cigar's environment. It is important for this humidor to be properly controlled, so that the cigars neither dry out completely nor become overmoistened. (In either case, they will begin to smell musty and will be beyond repair.) If not kept in a humidor, cigars should be stored in a well-ventilated area where no dampness exists, and where a constant temperature of about 15° to 18°C is maintained.

Despite their delicate nature, cigars will last for up to fifteen years if properly looked after; but if at any time they are brought into contact with strong odours (e.g. from food), which will readily penetrate their light cedarwood boxes, they will absorb the smell and deteriorate. Other enemies are dry heat, drastic variations in temperature, and damp. A lot of care is taken in the production of good cigars, and it is essential that they be looked after properly. If a cigar does not smell of tobacco, then it is useless and should be discarded.

Cigars can take up to several years to mature fully, and during this time they may 'sweat' slightly, causing a fine greyish powder to appear along their lengths. This powder, which can also be caused by changes in humidity, is known as 'bloom'. There is absolutely no harm in this – it is natural, and does not affect the cigar in any way. It is also quite easy to remove, preferably with a soft cloth or brush. Light yellow or green spots caused by the sun's action on drops of moisture, while the leaf was still in its growing stages, will also have no effect on the smoking quality of the cigar; but if the wrapping on the cigar is slightly green, it means that this particular product is still young and not fully conditioned.

The cigar is essentially a personal thing; but because of its value, the Stocktaker must be very conscious, especially at changeovers or valuations, of what he is counting. He must not include any cigars which are past their best; and he must ensure that those on premises where he works are stored correctly.

Cigarettes

Cigarettes are usually sold from vending machines. Where this is the case, the Stocktaker will have nothing to do with the operation: the machines will be rented, and the suppliers will pay the premises a small commission on any sales, at the same time remaining fully responsible for the equipment and its contents. Some hotels and pubs, however, actually own their cigarette machines, and in such instances the Stocktaker must account for all the stock they contain and any surplus held elsewhere (see page 94).

SECTION IV
APPENDICES

APPENDIX 1
COMPUTERS AND CALCULATORS; HYDROMETERS

COMPUTERS

Because so many varieties of computer are available, the Stocktaker considering the purchase of one should be very careful about what he is buying. He needs a computer which is easy to operate, and produces the style and scale of report which he requires. In most cases, printers are sold separately; he will need to make a decision about one of these, therefore, at the same time as he is choosing a computer. Generally speaking, the more expensive the equipment, the quicker it will be at producing a result; so the Stocktaker will need to establish at what level he wishes to operate his business. Relevant factors may be the speed of the computer, the speed of the printer, the print quality of the latter and, above all, the programs available for use with the computer: selection of the appropriate program(s) should perhaps even determine the choice of a computer.

For the computer and the printer – the hardware – will only do what they are programmed to do: it is the program which is the important factor. Programs are known as software; and packages made specially for the licensed trade Stocktaker are now available from a wide variety of sources. It is vitally important to select the correct program, the one which will enable the individual Stocktaker to produce for his clients the information that he wants to give them. An excess of information may discourage clients, but by using the computer judiciously, the Stocktaker should be able to offer comprehensive, useful results which are reasonably concise.

It may well be that the hardware (though not the software) will be suited to other uses, and the Stocktaker may be able to purchase programs for dealing with business such as his purchase ledger, sales ledger or P.A.Y.E. The potential is immense, and the amount of money spent on the purchase of this type of equipment must be balanced against the time saved by using it.

Listed below are some of the advantages of computerisation. Many of them refer to additional items which may be advantageous to management and which place no special demands on the Stock-taker, after the initial 'setting-up' of each outlet.

1. Printed working stock sheets, produced entirely by the computer, giving details of previous stock on hand, cost prices, retail prices, and units of measure.
2. Rapid production of extended figures.
3. Easy access to changing cost and retail prices.
4. Gross profit percentages produced for each commodity, for each group, and as an overall figure.
5. Stock on hand expressed in number of days holding – figures which can assist management in ordering and help to prevent overstocking.
6. Sales ratios produced for individual items or groups of commodities.
7. All V.A.T. calculations carried out automatically where required.
8. Production of gross profit, both estimated and retail.
9. Stock surplus or deficit calculated, with percentage of gain or loss.
10. Average weekly or daily takings produced.
11. Average daily sales calculated per item.
12. Sales at cost and retail recorded.
13. Listing of stock on hand at cost.
14. Deliveries at cost recorded.
15. Any given number of copies produced, according to client's requirements.

It may be that not all of these particular facilities are available from every program; but all can usually be incorporated, if the Stocktaker requires them, as can anything else not listed above which he feels would benefit his business.

CALCULATORS

Most calculators have several facilities available which can, if properly utilised, make the work of a Stocktaker much easier, particularly if he is producing results manually. Calculators vary, however, and the instructions for each should be read carefully. The formulae below are applicable only to certain machines, but most others are capable of achieving the same results, if the procedures are appropriately adapted.

To Divide by a Constant

If the cash price of a case of a dozen bottles is £300.00, each bottle will cost £25.00. If the Stocktaker has several calculations of this nature to perform, he can set his calculator to create a constant:–

a) Enter 300
b) Press divide
c) Enter 12
d) Press =

Then, simply by entering the cost price per case, the correct unit price will be displayed:–

$$
\begin{array}{ll}
 & (\pounds) \\
\text{e.g.} \quad 336 = & 28.00 \\
360 = & 30.00 \\
480 = & 40.00
\end{array}
$$

To Multiply by a Constant

If liqueurs all sell at the same price, say £33.60, there is no need for the entire calculation to be carried out with each item. There would be one principal calculation to perform: the master price of £33.60 must be entered, then either one × or, in some cases, two.

The price is now constant, and all the Stocktaker has to do is enter the total count:–

e.g. $1^2/$ Benedictine –   enter 1.2 =
       $6^5/$ Grand Marnier –   enter 6.5 =
       $7^8/$ Cointreau –   enter 7.8 =
       $4^3/$ Tia Maria –   enter 4.3 =

The answers will come up correctly after each entry:–

$$
\begin{array}{r}
(\pounds) \\
40.32 \\
218.40 \\
262.08 \\
144.48
\end{array}
$$

The same calculation can be used for producing sales mix ratios and sales comparison figures, and for calculating, both at the same time, cost and retail prices.

Sales Mix Ratios:

Beers	£10,390
Minerals	£4,260
Spirits	£9,611
Wines	£3,215
Sundries	£1,090
Total	£28,566

(a) Enter the first figure (10390)
(b) Press divide

(c) Enter the total sales figure (28566)
(d) Press %: displays 36.37

Next enter the second figure (4260) and press the % key. The correct percentage, 14.91, will appear.

By continuing use of the same method, sales ratios of 33.64, 11.25 and 3.82 will be produced for the three remaining items.

The total of the sales ratio column should equal 100.

Extending Cost and Retail Prices Simultaneously:

Sales –
Bottles of Whisky   123^2/
at cost value   £8.43
at retail value   £16.00

(a) Enter 123.2
(b) Press ×
(c) Enter the cost value (8.43)
(d) Press =: displays 1038.57 at cost
(e) Enter the retail value (16.00)
(f) Press =: displays 1971.20 at retail

Comparisons of Sales Trends:

	Last Stock Sales at Retail		Current Stock Sales at Retail
Beers	£8,700		£10,390
Minerals	£3,585		£4,260
Spirits	£6,014		£9,611
Wines	£2,700		£3,215
Sundries	£900		£1,090
Total	£21,899		£28,566
Income	£22,000	Income	£26,200
Surplus	£101	Deficit	£2,366

(a) Enter current income figure (26200)
(b) Press divide
(c) Enter previous income figure (22000)
(d) Press =: displays 1.19
(e) Press × (1.19 now acts as constant)
(f) Enter 8700 =:   displays   10353
            3585 =:   4266
            6014 =:   7156
            2700 =:   3213
             900 =:   1071

As can be seen, most of the sales for the period are compatible with those of the previous one, but spirits do show a relative increase in sales of £2,455 (£9,611–£7,156). The reasons for the deficit are clearly connected with this, and the Stocktaker should check thoroughly his purchase and extension figures within the spirits section. The same exercise can be applied to each particular item, until the exact problem is pinpointed.

The Memory

Most calculators have a memory, and this can be very useful during a valuation or similar exercise, for adding up figures which are displayed in turn. For example:–

	(£)	
$4^6/$	4.6×3.24	press memory
$8^7/$	8.7×11.29	press memory
$21^6/$	21.6×8.73	press memory
$15^1/$	15.1×9.05	press memory
$1^3/$	1.3×6.80	press memory

Press memory recall to acquire final figure: displays 447.19

The memory can be used for a variety of different calculations.

HYDROMETERS

Proof and Hydrometers

Proof is the term used for expressing the strength of spirits. Originally this assessment was made by burning off the spirit and measuring the volume of water left behind, but today there are much more sophisticated methods.

In 1802, a committee of enquiry was appointed to establish whether any reliable measurement of proof could be introduced. Various schemes were put forward, and eventually the one proposed by Bartholomew Sikes was adopted, defining proof in Britain as a mixture of 57.1% alcohol to 42.9% water. In the United States the system is somewhat different, and is based on proportions of 50% alcohol to 50% water.

Proof is specified as 100°, so any spirit sold at 70° is in fact 30° under proof. Exported blends still go to the United States at 75° on the Sikes scale, which corresponds to 86.8° proof on the American system.

On 1st January 1988, all the old methods were officially super-seded by a single universal system, which has been adopted by all countries subscribing to the International Organisation of Legal Metrology (O.I.M.L.). This system is the only one permitted within the E.E.C., and quantities are measured in hectolitres, litres and centilitres. Conversions are based on an equivalence of one gallon to 4.5609 litres.

The comparative table below shows the relationship between the old Sikes and new metric systems.

Sikes	O.I.M.L.
65.5	37.4
70	39.9
75	42.8
80	45.6
100	57.1
106	60.5
111	63.3
115	65.6
120	68.5

Whisky, gin and rum are generally 40% by volume on the O.I.M.L. scale, whereas vodka and bacardi are 37.5%.

Use of Hydrometers

A hydrometer is an instrument for measuring the relative density of a liquid. It is principally used in licensed trade stocktaking for checking on the adulteration of spirits, deliberate or accidental, by water or other liquids.

The Sikes instrument has been in use for over three centuries, but it was not until 1816 that it became legally acceptable, remaining so for 164 years. The instrument showed the strength of a spirit as under- or over-proof, proof being defined as 49.3% of alcohol by weight or 57.1% by volume at 60°F. In 1980, the U.K. joined other countries in adopting a straight percentage as the measure of alcoholic strength. The standard spirits, previously labelled 70° proof, were now marked 40% by volume.

The current spirit hydrometer is calibrated in density kg/m^3, and the table on page 290 shows the percentage of alcohol at a temperature range of 10–30°C.

In practice, the spirit sample is poured into a trial jar containing the hydrometer and a thermometer. It is left for a few minutes to achieve a uniform temperature, and then the thermometer is read while still immersed in the spirit (a magnifying glass can be useful). After the thermometer has been removed, the stem of the hydrometer should be briefly spun between thumb and finger to dislodge any air bubbles which might contribute to a false reading. When the hydrometer floats steadily, a reading is carefully taken from the stem and compared with the tables. Any meniscus (a slight curve where the level of the liquid touches the stem) should be ignored.

If only one test is to be made, the jar and instruments should be rinsed immediately in water (not too hot, and without detergent) and dried with a clean cloth; but if several different types of spirit are being dealt with, they should be tested in order of increasing strengths of flavour, i.e. starting with vodka or white gin and progressing to dark rum, the implements being drained but not necessarily rinsed between tests.

Strongly-coloured spirits such as rum or brandy will often give a reading two or three degrees below their true strengths, a phenomenon known as obscuration. In practice any small discrepancies should be viewed with tolerance, because Stocktakers, although they are using reasonably accurate equipment, are not working under laboratory conditions. Certain spirits such as liqueurs cannot be tested because of their high sugar content, but if in doubt, the Stocktaker should remove any suspect stock from the shelves and report his suspicions to his client.

Deliberate 'cutting' of spirits with water or mineral water will almost always show an alcohol level substantially below strength; and if such a condition is uncovered, a report should be made to a responsible person, together with advice to withdraw the offending spirit from sale immediately. In these circumstances, all open bottles of spirit should be checked by the Stocktaker, and written reports made. If he is working for a managed house, he should make a telephone call to head office immediately, backed by written reports. Since the consequences for staff can be quite serious, the Stocktaker must be sure of his facts; if he is at all doubtful, he should open a sealed bottle of the same brand and carry out a control test.

The old Sikes hydrometer, a beautiful but expensive instrument of gold-plated brass in its plush-lined polished hardwood case, with an assortment of weights, can still be of occasional use. If it is suspected that fortified wine has been tampered with, the new hydrometer is of little use, but the old instrument can give a comparison reading. Using a sealed bottle of the suspect brand, experiment with the weights until a reading can be obtained on the stem. Transfer this to the suspect bottle, and if the instrument floats to the surface or to a level substantially higher than in the first sample, dilution is proved.

Other types of hydrometer are made for use with such diverse liquids as beer, industrial spirits and perfumes; but these are mainly the province of the manufacturer and the Excise man. It should also be remembered that the spirit hydrometer can only provide a reading of alcohol strength where very little or no sugar is present.

Hydrometers used by brewers, and even home-wine-makers, calculate the amount of sugar converted to alcohol during fermentation by deducting the final gravity from the original gravity, which, when divided by 7.36, gives an approximate indication of alcohol by volume.

APPENDIX 2
TABLES AND CHARTS

MARK-UP TO YIELD GROSS PROFIT

10%	9.09%
15%	13.04%
20%	16.67%
25%	20.00%
33.3%	25.00%
40%	28.57%
45%	31.03%
50%	33.33%
60%	37.50%
75%	42.86%
100%	50.00%
150%	60.00%
200%	66.66%
250%	71.43%
300%	75.00%

GROSS PROFIT PERCENTAGE MULTIPLIER

Required %	Multiplier	Required %	Multiplier
2.5	1.18	39	1.886
3	1.184	40	1.917
4	1.198	41	1.949
5	1.211	42	1.983
6	1.223	43	2.018
7	1.237	44	2.054
7.5	1.243	45	2.091
8	1.25	46	2.13
9	1.264	47	2.17
10	1.278	48	2.212
11	1.292	49	2.255
12	1.307	50	2.30
13	1.322	51	2.347
14	1.337	52	2.396
15	1.353	53	2.447
16	1.369	54	2.50
17	1.386	55	2.556
18	1.403	56	2.614
19	1.42	57	2.675
20	1.438	58	2.738
21	1.456	59	2.805
22	1.474	60	2.873
23	1.493	61	2.948
24	1.513	62	3.027
25	1.533	63	3.108
26	1.554	64	3.195
27	1.575	65	3.286
28	1.597	66	3.382
29	1.62	67	3.485
30	1.643	68	3.594
31	1.667	69	3.71
32	1.691	70	3.834
33	1.717	75	4.60
34	1.743	80	5.75
35	1.769	85	7.67
36	1.797	90	11.50
37	1.825	95	23.00
38	1.855		

To achieve the gross profit percentage required, multiply the cost price of the item (excl. V.A.T.) by the multiplier to arrive at the retail price (incl. V.A.T. at 15%).

GROSS PROFIT PERCENTAGES

In the licensed trade, the Gross Profit is expressed as a percentage of the selling price and not as a percentage of the cost.

To calculate the Gross Profit percentage on selling, the following equation is used:–

$$\text{Gross Profit percentage} = \frac{\text{Gross Profit}}{\text{Selling price}} \times 100$$

$$= \frac{(\text{Selling price} - \text{cost price})}{\text{Selling price}} \times 100$$

e.g. $\dfrac{(8.00 - 3.20)}{8.00} \times 100 = \dfrac{4.80}{8.00} \times 100 = 60\%.$

To calculate the Gross Profit percentage on cost, the following equation is used:–

$$\text{Gross Profit percentage} = \frac{\text{Gross Profit}}{\text{Cost price}} \times 100$$

$$= \frac{(\text{Selling price} - \text{cost price})}{\text{Cost price}} \times 100$$

e.g. $\dfrac{(8.00 - 3.20)}{3.20} \times 100 = \dfrac{4.80}{3.20} \times 100 = 150\%.$

In both cases, the cost price and selling price should be exclusive of V.A.T.; if, however, V.A.T. is added to both cost and selling prices, then the result would be the same:–

i.e. Cost price   3.20 + 15% V.A.T. = 3.68
       Selling price   8.00 + 15% V.A.T. = 9.20
       Profit $(9.20 - 3.68) \div 9.20 \times 100 = 60\%$

It is not unknown for some Stocktakers to do all calculations including V.A.T. and then deduct the V.A.T. content on the reports.

VALUE ADDED TAX CONVERSIONS

Sample Figures

(a)   Cash Income £10,120.68 inclusive of V.A.T.
(b)   Selling Price £6.00 inclusive of V.A.T.

To deduct V.A.T. at 15% from V.A.T.-inclusive figures, in order to calculate gross profit percentages, proceed as follows:–

(i)   *Either*: divide the figure by 7.667 and deduct, i.e.:–
       (a)   £10,120.68 ÷ 7.667 = £1,320.03 V.A.T. content.
             Therefore £10,120.68 less £1,320.03 = £8,800.65,
             i.e. the V.A.T.-exclusive figure.
       (b)   £6.00 ÷ 7.667 = £0.78 V.A.T. content. Therefore £6.00
             less £0.78 = £5.22, i.e. the V.A.T.-exclusive figure.
(ii)   *Or*: divide the figure by 1.15 to arrive automatically at the
       V.A.T.-exclusive figure, i.e.:–
       (a)   £10,120.68 ÷ 1.15 = £8,800.59, i.e. the V.A.T.-exclusive
             figure.
       (b)   £6.00 ÷ 1.15 = £5.22, i.e. the V.A.T.-exclusive figure.

To add V.A.T. at 15% to V.A.T.-exclusive figures, in order to calculate V.A.T.-inclusive figures, proceed as follows:–

(i)   *Either*: divide the figure by 6.667 and add, i.e.:–
       (a)   £8,800.59 ÷ 6.667 = £1,320.02 V.A.T. content.
             Therefore £8,800.59 plus £1,320.02 = £10,120.61,
             i.e. the V.A.T.-inclusive figure.
(ii)   *Or*:   multiply the figure by 1.15 to arrive automatically at the
       V.A.T.-inclusive figure, i.e.:–
       (a)   £8,800.59 × 1.15 = £10,120.68, i.e. the V.A.T.-inclusive
             figure.

WINE AND CHAMPAGNE BOTTLE SIZES

Quarter bottle	18¾	cl	
Half bottle	37½	cl	
Bottle	75	cl	
Magnum	2	bottles or	1½ lt
Jeroboam	4	bottles or	3 lt
Rehoboam	6	bottles or	4½ lt
Methuselah	8	bottles or	6 lt
Salmanazar	12	bottles or	9 lt
Balthazar	16	bottles or	12 lt
Nebuchadnezzar	20	bottles or	15 lt

In addition, the following sizes are produced in Bordeaux only:–

Jeroboam (Triple Magnum)	6	bottles or 4½ lt	
Imperiale	8½	bottles or 6½ lt	

MAXIMUM YIELDS FOR SPIRITS, LIQUEURS AND WINES

Litres	*Tots per container* at 5 out (fl oz)	at 6 out	at 4 out
22.72 (5 gals. Imp.)	800.00	960.38	640.00
20.00	704.00	845.14	563.20
5.00	176.00	211.28	140.80
4.545 (gal. Imp.)	160.00	192.08	128.00
3.784 (gal. U.S.)	133.20	159.90	106.56
2.272	80.00	96.04	64.00
2.00	70.40	84.51	56.32
1.50	52.80	63.39	42.24
1.136	40.00	48.02	32.00
1.00	35.20	42.20	28.16
.946 (qt U.S.)	33.30	39.98	26.64
.757	26.65	31.99	21.32
.75	26.40	31.69	21.12
.738	26.00	31.21	20.08
.71	24.99	30.00	19.99
.70	24.64	29.58	19.71
.696	24.50	29.41	19.60
.682	24.00	28.81	19.20
.653	23.00	27.61	18.40
.568	20.00	24.01	16.00
.50	17.60	21.13	14.08
.483	17.00	20.41	13.60
.142	5.00	6.00	4.00
.085	2.99	3.59	2.39
.071	2.50	3.00	2.00
.035 (4 out)	1.25	1.50	1.00
.028 (5 out)	1.00	1.20	—
.024 (6 out)	.833	1.00	—

THE ¼, ⅕, ⅙ OPTIC

There are many tables available which give anticipated yields from different sizes of bottle via different sizes of optic. In the absence of tables, however, the Stocktaker can (provided that he remembers what each measure relates to) carry out his own calculations to obtain anticipated yields, using the figures and formulae given below.

1 gill = ¼ Imperial pint = 5 fluid ounces.

To obtain Imperial measures for each size of optic, the formula is as follows:–

¼ gill = 5 fl oz ÷ 4 = 1.25 fl oz
⅕ gill = 5 fl oz ÷ 5 = 1.00 fl oz
⅙ gill = 5 fl oz ÷ 6 = 0.833 fl oz

The Imperial capacity of the bottle would then be divided by the number of fluid ounces relating to the optic in use to produce the yield achievable.

The same procedure would apply to metric equivalents, as shown below:–

1 gill = 5 fluid ounces = 142 millilitres or
14.2 centilitres.

Therefore:–

¼ gill = 14.2 cl ÷ 4 = 3.55 cl
⅕ gill = 14.2 cl ÷ 5 = 2.84 cl
⅙ gill = 14.2 cl ÷ 6 = 2.36 cl

The metric capacity of the bottle would then be divided by the number of centilitres relating to the optic in use to produce the yield achievable.

METRIC/IMPERIAL CONVERSION TABLES

Length

centimetres (cm)	cm or inches	inches (in)
2.54	1	0.394
5.08	2	0.787
7.62	3	1.181
10.16	4	1.575
12.70	5	1.969
15.24	6	2.362
17.78	7	2.756
20.32	8	3.150
22.86	9	3.543
25.40	10	3.937
50.80	20	7.874
76.20	30	11.811
101.60	40	15.748
127.00	50	19.685

kilometres (km)	km or miles	miles
1.609	1	0.621
3.219	2	1.243
4.828	3	1.864
6.437	4	2.485
8.047	5	3.107
9.656	6	3.728
11.265	7	4.350
12.875	8	4.971
14.484	9	5.592
16.093	10	6.214
32.187	20	12.427
48.280	30	18.641
64.374	40	24.855
80.467	50	31.069

Mass (weight)

kilograms (kg)	kg or lb	pounds (lb)
0.454	1	2.205
0.907	2	4.409
1.361	3	6.614
1.814	4	8.819
2.268	5	11.023
2.722	6	13.228
3.175	7	15.432
3.629	8	17.637
4.082	9	19.842
4.536	10	22.046
9.072	20	44.092
13.608	30	66.139
18.144	40	88.185
22.680	50	110.231

tonnes (t)	t or UK tons	UK tons
1.016	1	0.984
2.032	2	1.968
3.048	3	2.953
4.064	4	3.937
5.080	5	4.921
6.096	6	5.905
7.112	7	6.889
8.128	8	7.874
9.144	9	8.858
10.161	10	9.842
20.321	20	19.684
30.481	30	29.526
40.642	40	39.368
50.802	50	49.210

Area   ## Volume

hectares (ha)	ha or acres	acres	litres	litres or UK gallons	UK gallons
0.405	1	2.471	4.546	1	0.220
0.809	2	4.942	9.092	2	0.440
1.214	3	7.413	13.638	3	0.660
1.619	4	9.884	18.184	4	0.880
2.023	5	12.355	22.730	5	1.100
2.428	6	14.826	27.276	6	1.320
2.833	7	17.297	31.822	7	1.540
3.237	8	19.769	36.368	8	1.760
3.642	9	22.240	40.914	9	1.980
4.047	10	24.711	45.460	10	2.200
8.094	20	49.421	90.919	20	4.399
12.140	30	74.132	136.379	30	6.599
16.187	40	98.842	181.839	40	8.799
20.234	50	123.553	227.298	50	10.998

BARRELAGE AND GALLONAGE CONVERSIONS

Barrelage

To convert quantities in smaller containers to equivalent quantities in 36-gallon barrels:–

Gallons of draught beer and cider: divide by 36.

Dozen quantities of bottled beer and cider: divide according to table below.

Size of container	Conversion divisor
4 litre	3.409
3 litre	4.546
2 litre	6.818
1½ litre	9.092
flagon	12
litre	13.638
pint	24
550 ml	24.796
500 ml	27.276
15½ fl oz/large can	30.968
440 ml	30.995
375 ml	36.368
355 ml	38.417
330 ml	41.327
½ pint	48
275 ml	49.592
250 ml	54.552
nip (Gold Label etc.)	75.766
125 ml	109.103

e.g. $2^{7}/_{12}$ dozen 2 litre bottled beers in terms of 36-gallon barrels:–

$2^{7}/_{12} \div 6.818 = 0.38$ barrels.

Gallonage

To convert canisters, 'bag in box' packs, and draught cordials to gallons:–

Size of container	*Conversion divisor*
20 litre	0.227
18.75 litre	0.242
18 litre	0.253
10 litre	0.455
5 litre	0.909
2 gallon	0.50
4 gallon	0.25

e.g. $2\frac{1}{10}$ 18.75 litre canisters in terms of gallons:–

$2\frac{1}{10} \div 0.242 = 8.67$ gallons.

To convert dozen quantities of bottled and canned minerals to gallons:–

Size of container	*Conversion divisor*
3 litre	0.126
2 litre	0.189
$1\frac{1}{2}$ litre	0.253
1.22 litre	0.311
flagon	0.333
litre	0.379
850 ml	0.446
750 ml	0.505
26 fl oz	0.513
570 ml	0.665
$\frac{1}{2}$ litre	0.758
$15\frac{1}{2}$ fl oz/large can	0.860
440 ml	0.861
330 ml	1.148
$\frac{1}{2}$ pint	1.333
$\frac{1}{4}$ litre/250 ml	1.515
200 ml	1.894
7 fl oz/split	1.905
150 ml	2.526
125 ml	3.031
4 fl oz/baby	3.333
Pony, Cherry 'B', Moussec, Babycham	3.788

e.g. $3\frac{8}{12}$ dozen 850 ml bottled minerals in terms of gallons:–

$3\frac{8}{12} \div 0.446 = 8.22$ gallons.

POSTMIX CONTAINERS, 'BAG IN BOX' TYPE (AVERAGE) – METRIC
SCALE

Weight in kg	Litres of syrup
0.63	Empty
1.9	1
3.1	2
4.4	3
5.6	4
6.9	5
8.2	6
9.5	7
10.7	8
11.9	9
13.2	10
14.5	11
15.7	12
17.0	13
18.2	14
19.5	15
20.8	16
22.0	17
23.3	18
24.5	19
25.8	20

This table is not applicable to every supplier and every dilution
factor; so although it may be used as a guide, additional reference
should always be made to the details provided for the product
concerned.

POSTMIX TANKS — IMPERIAL SCALE

Weight in lbs	Pints/gallons of syrup	
10	Empty	
11¼	1 pint	
12½	2 pints	
13¾	3 ,,	
15¼	4 ,,	
16½	5 ,,	
17¾	6 ,,	
19	7 ,,	
20½	8 ,,	(1 gallon)
21¾	9 ,,	
23	10 ,,	
24¼	11 ,,	
25½	12 ,,	
26¾	13 ,,	
28	14 ,,	
29½	15 ,,	
31	16 ,,	(2 gallons)
32¼	17 ,,	
33½	18 ,,	
34¾	19 ,,	
36¼	20 ,,	
37½	21 ,,	
38¾	22 ,,	
40	23 ,,	
41½	24 ,,	(3 gallons)
42¾	25 ,,	
44	26 ,,	
45½	27 ,,	
46¾	28 ,,	
48¼	29 ,,	
49½	30 ,,	
50¾	31 ,,	
52	Full	

ALCOHOLIC STRENGTH BY VOLUME OF A MIXTURE OF WATER AND ETHANOL AT VARIOUS TEMPERATURES EXPRESSED IN DEGREES CELSIUS, AS INDICATED BY AN ALCOHOL HYDROMETER CALIBRATED IN DENSITY KG/M³

DENSITY kg/m³	10	11	12	13	14	15	16	17	18	19	20	21	22	23	24	25	26	27	28	29	30	DENSITY kg/m³
											TEMPERATURE °CELSIUS											
940	48.6	48.2	47.8	47.4	47.1	46.7	46.3	45.9	45.5	45.1	44.7	44.4	44.0	43.6	43.2	42.8	42.4	42.0	41.6	41.2	40.8	940
941	48.0	47.6	47.3	46.9	46.5	46.1	45.7	45.3	45.0	44.6	44.2	43.8	43.4	43.0	42.6	42.2	41.8	41.4	41.0	40.6	40.2	941
942	47.5	47.1	46.7	46.3	45.9	45.6	45.2	44.8	44.4	44.0	43.6	43.2	42.8	42.4	42.0	41.6	41.3	40.9	40.5	40.1	39.7	942
943	46.9	46.5	46.1	45.8	45.4	45.0	44.6	44.2	43.8	43.4	43.0	42.6	42.2	41.9	41.5	41.1	40.7	40.3	39.9	39.5	39.1	943
944	46.3	46.0	45.6	45.2	44.8	44.4	44.0	43.6	43.2	42.8	42.4	42.1	41.7	41.3	40.9	40.5	40.1	39.7	39.3	38.9	38.5	944
945	45.8	45.4	45.0	44.6	44.2	43.8	43.4	43.0	42.6	42.3	41.9	41.5	41.1	40.7	40.3	39.9	39.5	39.1	38.7	38.3	37.9	945
946	45.2	44.8	44.4	44.0	43.6	43.2	42.8	42.4	42.0	41.7	41.3	40.9	40.5	40.1	39.7	39.3	38.9	38.5	38.1	37.7	37.3	946
947	44.6	44.2	43.8	43.4	43.0	42.6	42.2	41.8	41.4	41.0	40.6	40.2	39.8	39.4	39.0	38.6	38.2	37.8	37.4	37.0	36.6	947
948	44.0	43.6	43.2	42.8	42.4	42.0	41.6	41.2	40.8	40.4	40.0	39.6	39.2	38.8	38.4	38.0	37.6	37.2	36.8	36.4	36.0	948
949	43.4	43.0	42.6	42.2	41.8	41.4	41.0	40.6	40.2	39.8	39.4	39.0	38.6	38.2	37.8	37.4	37.0	36.6	36.2	35.8	35.4	949
950	42.8	42.4	42.0	41.6	41.2	40.8	40.4	40.0	39.6	39.2	38.8	38.4	38.0	37.6	37.1	36.7	36.3	35.9	35.5	35.1	34.7	950
951	42.1	41.7	41.3	40.9	40.5	40.1	39.7	39.3	38.9	38.5	38.1	37.7	37.3	36.9	36.5	36.1	35.7	35.3	34.9	34.5	34.1	951
952	41.5	41.1	40.7	40.3	39.9	39.5	39.1	38.7	38.3	37.9	37.5	37.1	36.6	36.2	35.8	35.4	35.0	34.6	34.2	33.8	33.4	952
953	40.9	40.4	40.0	39.6	39.2	38.8	38.4	38.0	37.6	37.2	36.8	36.4	36.0	35.6	35.2	34.8	34.4	33.9	33.5	33.1	32.7	953
954	40.2	39.8	39.4	39.0	38.6	38.1	37.7	37.3	36.9	36.5	36.1	35.7	35.3	34.9	34.5	34.1	33.7	33.3	32.9	32.4	32.0	954
955	39.5	39.1	38.7	38.3	37.9	37.5	37.0	36.6	36.2	35.8	35.4	35.0	34.6	34.2	33.8	33.4	33.0	32.6	32.2	31.8	31.3	955
956	38.8	38.4	38.0	37.6	37.2	36.8	36.3	35.9	35.5	35.1	34.7	34.3	33.9	33.5	33.1	32.7	32.3	31.9	31.5	31.1	30.6	956
957	38.1	37.7	37.3	36.9	36.4	36.0	35.6	35.2	34.8	34.4	34.0	33.6	33.2	32.8	32.4	32.0	31.5	31.1	30.7	30.3	29.9	957
958	37.4	37.0	36.5	36.1	35.7	35.3	34.9	34.5	34.1	33.7	33.3	32.8	32.4	32.0	31.6	31.2	30.8	30.4	30.0	29.6	29.2	958
959	36.6	36.2	35.8	35.4	35.0	34.6	34.1	33.7	33.3	32.9	32.5	32.1	31.7	31.3	30.9	30.5	30.1	29.7	29.3	28.9	28.5	959
960	35.9	35.4	35.0	34.6	34.2	33.8	33.4	33.0	32.6	32.1	31.7	31.3	30.9	30.5	30.1	29.7	29.3	28.9	28.5	28.1	27.7	960

Hydrometer and tables are available from Peter Stevenson Ltd, Edinburgh.

IMPORTED BEERS

		Alcohol by Vol.
AMERICA	DIXIE BEER, brewed and bottled in New Orleans, full-flavoured, ideal with Creole/Cajun cuisine	4.5%
	NEW ORLEANS BEST, light Louisiana beer	4.07%
	ROLLING ROCK, from Pittsburgh	
	MICHELOB, from the world's largest brewer	
	SCHLITZ, from Milwaukee, Wisconsin	
	COORS, from Colorado	4.3%
	NEW AMSTERDAM, the Beer of New York, brewed and bottled by Old New York Brewing Co.	4.8%
TEXAS/MEXICO	EL PASO LIGHT, the beer of the border	3.6%
AUSTRALIA	BIG BARREL, brewed and canned by Coopers, Adelaide	
	TOOHEYS, brewed in Australia	
	COOPERS ADELAIDE LAGER, still independent	4.4%
	COOPERS SPARKLING ALE, reputedly one of the world's finest beers, bottle-conditioned	5.3%
	CASTLEMAINE, Australian brewed	
AUSTRIA	GOLDFASSL VIENNA LAGER, brewed by Ottakringer, Vienna	
BELGIUM	CHIMAY ROUGE, Trappist Beer	6%
	CHIMAY BLEU, strong and will mature in bottle	9%
	CHIMAY GRANDE RESERVE, élite bottle-conditioned	9%
	MORT SUBITE GEUZE, famous 'sudden death' wheat beer – 'from Biere to Bier'	
	CRUZE PREMIUM, brewed in Belgium	
BRAZIL	BRAHMA PILS	4.5%
CANADA	YUKON GOLD, brewed and bottled at the Old Fort, Prince George, scene of the Klondike Gold Rush	5%
	IRONHORSE MALT LIQUOR, from the Old Fort, British Columbia	5.7%
	MOLSON, brewed and bottled in Canada	5%
	LABATT BLUE, brewed in UK	
	MOOSEHEAD, brewed in UK	
CHINA	SHANGHAI, Premium Chinese brewed Lager beer	5.15%
	TSINGTAO, brewed from Laoshan spring water, perhaps the most famous Chinese beer	
CYPRUS	KEO, brewed and bottled in Cyprus	
CZECHOSLOVAKIA	BUDWEISER BUDOVAR, the original	5%
	PILSNER URQUELL, the true 'pilsner'	5%
DENMARK	CARLSBERG ELEPHANT, strong beer brewed in Denmark	7%

ENGLAND	CORNISH REAL STEAM LAGER, natural extra strong	
	CORNISH REAL STEAM BITTER, natural extra strong	
FRANCE	EXPORT ADELSHOFFEN, biere blonde from Strasbourg, typical French lager	
	RHEINGOLD, the strong lager beer from Strasbourg	
	ADELSCOTT, unique whisky flavour from peat-smoked malt	6.4%
	JENLAIN, BIERE DE GARDE	
	OBERNAI MINI FUT	
	PELICAN	6%
	KRONENBOURG 1664, from Alsace	5.2%
GERMANY	PATRIZIER EXPORT GOLD, brewed and bottled in Bavaria	4.3%
	PATRIZIER PREMIUM PILS, brewed under German laws of purity	4%
	BECKS BIER, Bremen	5%
	BERLINER WEISSE, serve with fruit flavours	3%
	EKU 28, reputedly the strongest beer in the world	
	FURSTENBURG EXPORT	5%
	ST. BERNHARD BRAU	
	CAESARUM	
HOLLAND	GROLSCH	
	HOBEC	
HONDURAS	PORT ROYAL, Draft Pilsner	4.7%
INDIA	GOLDEN EAGLE INDIAN LAGER, brewed and bottled in Bombay	4.5%
INDONESIA	BIR BINTANG, brewed and bottled in Jakarta. A favourite beer on magical Bali	
IRELAND	GEORGE KILLIANS RED ALE, originally in Enniscorthy, now brewed under licence in France	
ISRAEL	MACCABEE, brewed and bottled in Netanya	
ITALY	PERONI NASTRO AZZURO	
JAPAN	KIRIN	
	ASAHI DRAFT, 'Beer of the Rising Sun'	
	SUNTORY DRAFT	
	SAPPORO DRAFT BEER	
KENYA	TUSKER PREMIUM, brewed and bottled in Nairobi	4.9%
MEXICO	BOHEMIA, from Cerveceria Cuauhtemoc, Monterey	
	DOS EQUIS, from Cerveceria Moctezuma	
	SOL, from Cerveceria Moctezuma	
N. ZEALAND	STEINLAGER, brewed and bottled in Wellington	5%
NORWAY	FREYDENLUND, from Oslo	
POLAND	TATRA ZWIEC	
PORTUGAL	SAGRES EUROPA	
RUSSIA	ZHIGULI, the Beer of Russia, brewed and bottled in Moscow	4.3%
SCOTLAND	OLD JOCK, Broughton Brewery, Biggar	
SINGAPORE	TIGER BEER, from Malayan Breweries	5%

S. AFRICA	LION LAGER, Ohlsson's Cape Brewery	4.7%
	CASTLE LAGER	4.7%
SPAIN	SAN MIGUEL ESPECIAL	
SWEDEN	PRIPPS EXPORT (Category 111), Sweden's biggest brewer	5.6%
SWITZERLAND	DEMON BEER, the most alcoholic pale beer in the world	12%
THAILAND	THAI AMARIT, brewed and bottled in Bangkok	5.9%
TURKEY	EFES PILSNER	
YUGOSLAVIA	PIVO NIKSIC	
LOW ALCOHOL BEERS	ALSATOR LOW ALCOHOL LAGER, from Strasbourg, full flavour	0.8%
	CLAUSTHALER, from Germany	0.5%
	WEIZENTHALER	0.5%

N.B. – These beers are generally available from Continental Beer Distributors, London.

GLASSWARE

OPERA SHERRY

HAMLET LIQUEUR

ELGIN SCHOONER

CELEBRATION ROCKS

HASTINGS WINE

CONTINENTAL

GALA WINE

CELEBRATION HIBALL

OLD FASHIONED

HILTON PILS GOBLET

CROWN WORTHINGTON

SAVOY GOBLET

RIALTO SHERRY

TULIP BEER

BREWSER TANKARD

GALA OLD FASHIONED

GALA OLD FASHIONED

CROWN VIKING

BURGUNDY   PARIS WINE   TULIP   CLUB GOBLET   STRATFORD

FLUTE   AGINCOURT   CROWN VIKING   OLD FASHIONED   HIBALL

COPITA   SOAVE GOBLET   FINE RIM BRANDY   WELLINGTON   PILSNER

TUDOR TANKARD   PANELLED CROWN TANKARD   NONIC   SAXONY

CONSUMPTION BY PERSONS UNDER 18

Under the provisions of The Licensing Act 1964, IT IS AN OFFENCE for any person under 18 to buy, attempt to buy, or consume alcoholic liquor in this bar.

Maximum Penalty £400

IT IS ALSO AN OFFENCE for anyone to buy, or attempt to buy, alcoholic liquor for consumption by a person under 18.

Maximum Penalty £400

Section 169 (2)(3)

WEIGHTS AND MEASURES ACT 1985
Unless Supplied Pre-packed

GIN RUM VODKA WHISKY

Are offered for sale or served in these premises in quantities of

ONE-SIXTH OF A GILL
OR MULTIPLES THEREOF

DRINKING-UP-TIME

Under the provisions of The Licensing Act 1964, a period of 10 minutes is allowed at the end of the morning and evening periods of Permitted Hours, for the consumption of alcoholic liquors purchased during such hours. IT IS AN OFFENCE for customers to consume alcoholic liquor after this 10 minute period.

Maximum Penalty £400

Section 155(3)

APPENDIX 3
GLOSSARY

Baby	4 fl oz/113 ml bottle, generally used for fruit juices or mixers.
Balance Sheet	A statement of the financial position of a business and its assets at a given time.
Barrelage	The volume of draught, bottled or canned beer sales during a given period, converted into casks, i.e. 36-gallon units.
Bin Cards	Part of a cellar control system (see entry): each item has a bin card which shows purchases, stock held, and the bars to which any has been dispensed.
Bond	The place where liquor is held until duty is paid.
Broker (Valuer)	A person employed by a brewery, or independently, as the middleman at a tenancy change.
Business Done	Income from both cash and credit sales.
Cask Beer	Traditional or real ale.
Cellar Control System	A system controlling the movement of cellar stock, i.e. goods received in a central cellar and then dispensed to the various bars.
Cheap Sale Allowance	An allowance given for stock sold at less than the normal retail value.
Composite Figures	Barrelage (see entry) including bottled beers converted into 36-gallon units.
Consumption	The value of sales, either at cost or at retail.
Corkage	A charge made by hotels or restaurants for handling liquor brought into the premises by clients for their own consumption.
Corked	Term applied to badly-stored wine which has been contaminated by air penetrating the cork, making the wine undrinkable.
Cost Price	The price charged by the brewery or wholesaler to the tenant or proprietor.

297

Credit Note	A document, often printed in red, showing any refund for returned or sub-standard goods.
Deficit (Shortage)	The amount by which actual sales (or takings) fall short of estimated or computed sales.
Delivery Note	The document which accompanies a delivery, and is signed by the receiver of the goods; it shows the quantity and size of the items, but is usually unpriced.
Deposit	1. The element of a purchase price representing the value of a returnable container. 2. Money paid in advance for a function or other booking, to show good faith or to provide confirmation. 3. Sediment or residue left in a bottle or barrel.
Dipstick/Dip-rod	A graduated, four-sided rule used for measuring the contents of casks and other containers.
Drawings	1. Money taken from the business for the proprietor's personal use. 2. The actual money received, often referred to as income, revenue or takings.
Float	A sum of money held on the premises, used to maintain an adequate level of change and sufficient cash to make any petty cash payments.
Free-flow System	Unmetered dispensing of beer, the flow continuing until the tap is turned off.
Free House	Licensed premises which are not brewery-owned; the proprietor is usually free to purchase his goods from any supplier he chooses.
Glassware	General term for glasses and other articles used in a bar.
Goods Received	Deliveries received during a given period, details of which are often summarised in a Goods Received Book.
Gross Profit	The profit on the sale of commodities, without overheads or wages being taken into account.

Hardware	1. General term for the non-consumable items assessed at a changeover or valuation. 2. Computers and related equipment, excluding programs.
Imprest System	An arrangement whereby petty cash and wages are paid out and a cheque is received to reimburse the total, usually on a weekly basis.
Income (Revenue, Takings)	The actual money received by the business.
Input V.A.T.	V.A.T. (see entry) recoverable on purchases.
Invoice	The bill of sale which is sent shortly after a delivery, showing quantity, cost price, V.A.T. total, and details of any containers delivered or returned.
Keg Beer	Pressurised or lager-type beer.
Managed House	Usually, licensed premises which are brewery-owned, a manager being appointed to run the business.
Measured Pulls	Metered dispensing of beer, the flow being programmed to stop automatically at a set measure (quarter-pint, half-pint or pint).
Net Profit	The final profit on the sale of commodities, after overheads and wages have been taken into account.
Obscuration	The effect on a hydrometer reading of the presence of sugar in certain spirits (such as rum), for which a tolerance must be made.
Output V.A.T.	V.A.T. (see entry) payable on sales.
Overage	See *Surplus*.
Overstocking	The holding of excess stock, either as a whole or in the case of an individual commodity.
Par Stock	A recommended level of stock to be held in any one area, up to which requisitions will generally be made.
Petty Cash	Money paid out for cash purchases (generally small amounts), usually analysed in a Petty Cash Book.
Portion Control	Regulation of the amount of food allocated per portion.

Promotion	An occasion on which a licensee or an independent body charges a cheaper price than usual for a product, in order to promote sales of it.
Purchaser	The (incoming) person buying the business.
Requisition	A document passed from a bar to the cellar, requesting additional stock.
Revenue	See *Income*.
Selling Price	The price charged to customers for any particular item, often referred to as the retail price.
Shortage	See *Deficit*.
Software	Computer programs.
Split	6 fl oz/170–180 ml bottle, generally used for coca cola, ginger beer etc.
Staff Feeding Allowance	An allowance given against the food stock result, for staff feeding during the period.
Statement	A monthly summary of all invoices and credit notes, stating the balance of any outstanding amount.
Stillage	A low structure on a cellar floor, generally made of wood or metal, designed to support casks.
Surcharge (Uplift)	1. An additional charge applied, on an extended stock report, to adjust results from more expensive bars, when the price structure of the cheapest bar is being used as the basis of calculation. (Not applied when a cellar control system (see entry) is in operation.)
	2. An additional charge applied when prices have increased during a stock period, so as to keep the final results correct.
Surplus (Overage)	The amount by which actual sales (or takings) exceed estimated or computed sales.
Tabular Ledger	A daily analysis of all business transacted on a specific date, often referred to as a Tab.
Takings	See *Income*.

Tariff	A list showing prices of items sold, displayed for both customers and staff to see.
Tenancy	Leasing by a tenant, at a regular rent, of licensed premises owned by a brewery. The licensee shares with the brewery the interest and income resulting from their joint activities; the brewer provides most of the capital, including the fabric of the building, and the tenant generally finances the stock and has responsibility for furniture and fittings.
Ullage	General term for all items considered unsaleable, e.g. bottles with necks broken when decapped, corked wines, drinks returned, and general wastage.
Uplift	See *Surcharge*.
Valuer	See *Broker*.
V.A.T.	Value Added Tax – a tax on commodities imposed by the Government and administered by H.M. Customs and Excise.
Vendor	The (outgoing) person selling the business.
Yield	The number of units a bottle or container will produce, when a specific measure is used.

APPENDIX 4
THE INCORPORATED SOCIETY
OF LICENSED TRADE
STOCKTAKERS

The Development of the Society

As far back as the late nineteenth century, many licensees were concerned that they were not producing the profits they anticipated; and realising that their trade was open to fraud, they looked for ways of monitoring the operation on a regular basis. It was then that small professional stocktaking companies began to emerge all over the country, set up by people who had either an accountancy background or a thorough knowledge of the licensed trade.

As the liquor industry expanded, taxation increased to a level which made liquor one of the highest-taxed of commodities; and thus the role of the Stocktaker became even more demanding. He was expected to provide not only accurate results, but also expertise and information relevant to every aspect of the trade, from advice on minor points of law to recommendations about how best to increase profitability.

As the demands on the profession became more exacting, a group of concerned Stocktakers formed an association with the aim of ensuring that all members reached the highest standards of efficiency and ethics. This was in 1953, and the association then formed was later to become the Incorporated Society of Licensed Trade Stocktakers.

In order to ensure that all members reached the high standards required by the Society, examinations were set up, a pass being essential to the granting of full membership. Training courses were also inaugurated, to help those wishing to learn the trade.

Membership

This is open to all Stocktakers and trainees; but before sitting the examination, they must have had either three years' experience, or two years' experience in addition to attendance at one of the Society's training courses.

The types of membership are:–

Student   Any Stocktaker or trainee who has applied for membership, but has not yet passed the examination, will qualify as a Student Member (subject to references).

Associate   Any member who has passed the examination becomes an Associate, and is able to use the letters A.I.L.S.

Fellow   Any member who has been an Associate for seven years, and whose application has been considered favourably by the Committee, will become a Fellow and be entitled to use the letters F.I.L.S.

All members benefit by informative newsletters, a readily-available Society Handbook, and free advertising in various trade journals. They are welcome to attend the A.G.M. and other social events, and receive discounts on training courses.

Examinations

Examinatons for Associate Membership are usually held twice a year, generally in the Midlands. The examination consists of two parts, and a candidate must achieve a pass mark in each if he is to become an Associate. If one section is failed, then that part only must be re-taken.

The Practical Paper requires examinees to complete a physical stocktake and bring their results to a conclusion. The time allowed is 4 hours and 45 minutes, and during this period each person will be asked to do a hydrometer test on a sample bottle of spirit.

The Theory Paper is combined with an oral session, for which an overall total of 2 hours is given. Questions relate to all aspects of the licensed trade, and also to food and ancillary stocktaking. An example of this paper, which is designed to test the student's knowledge of the profession, can be seen on page 306.

Training Courses

These are held twice a year, and usually extend over a four- to five-day period. They are devised to assist student members in preparing for the examination, and also to increase the knowledge of those associated with the trade. While they are primarily intended for people who envisage stocktaking as a career, they have always been popular with licensees, publicans and other people involved with the trade, such as brewery auditors and accountants.

They are extremely intensive; but the purpose of the Society is to ensure that members fully understand the background of licensed trade stocktaking, and the procedures adopted in producing a result. It is also important for them to be able to discuss these with clients and to advise them, and to have the knowledge necessary to inspire trust and confidence. It is interesting to examine the wide scope of the course, which necessarily reflects the breadth of knowledge required by Stocktakers today.

In this book, the Society has endeavoured to cover all pertinent aspects of the profession, and any trainee Stocktaker should find it of great value. (It is also hoped that all those connected with the licensed trade will find it genuinely useful, as it deals specifically with the control of stock and the methods for achieving maximum profitability.) It should not be assumed, however, that an intending Stocktaker need do no more than read this book. The profession is a highly skilled one, in which expertise is gained only through the years of training and experience.

Further Information

It is in the interests of both proprietors and staff to ensure that all stock results are produced by a person who is experienced and who has reached a high standard of proficiency, and they are therefore advised to engage the services of a qualified member of the Incorporated Society of Licensed Trade Stocktakers. For lists of qualified members; details of examinations, training courses and membership; or any other information about the Society, please contact:–

The Secretary,
The Incorporated Society of Licensed Trade Stocktakers,
15 Deanburn Walk,
Bo'ness,
West Lothian,
EH51 0NB.

*An Extract from the President's Speech at the First Annual General Meeting
of the Society on 27th November 1954 (E. Duncan Simonds, Esq.)*

The qualities required in a good Stocktaker are at least as exacting as
those required in most other professions, and the work is only for
those who are strong-minded and self-disciplined. Every Stocktaker
must, above all things, be possessed of absolute integrity, for it is on
the assumption of this integrity that the whole delicate structure of
control is built up. And do not forget that this integrity is a two-way
affair; not only does the employer rely on it to ensure the proper
control of his business, but managers and staff of licensed houses
rely on it equally, in order to protect their own position from false
claims and charges. Many a man's whole career may rest on the
absolute integrity of the gentleman who comes to take the stock.

The second important qualification is accuracy, and in this connection I would say no more than that accuracy, like justice, must
not only be done, but be seen to be done. Nothing creates more
confidence than to observe that the Stocktaker sets about his job with
obviously meticulous care and accuracy.

Many other qualities are required for your profession, and not
least of them a heightened power of observation and perception; a
Stocktaker should be a great chap for sensing straws in the wind,
and the direction in which they are blowing; he is a bit of a
policeman in that respect, and his employer greatly relies on his
confidential reports on the conduct of the establishments he visits. I
will, however, mention only one more quality, and one which tends
to be overlooked – I refer to humanity. With all this emphasis on
honesty and accuracy and objectivity, there is a risk that a Stocktaker
may come to regard himself as a machine, and, worse still, may
regard the managers and staffs of hotels as machines too. This is
definitely not so; we are all of us, whatever our jobs, first and
foremost human beings, subject to the weakness and weariness
which from time to time afflict the human mind and body. Never
forget this, and always make allowances for the difficulties of
whatever situation may prevail when you enter a house to take its
stock.

I would conclude by saying that the duties of a Stocktaker must
always be performed without fear or favour, bias or sentiment. You
should remain dignified, aloof, and ever watchful for the depreda-
tions to which our trade is so unfortunately subject.

APPENDIX 5

SAMPLE THEORY
EXAMINATION PAPER

INCORPORATED SOCIETY OF LICENSED TRADE STOCKTAKERS
THEORY EXAMINATION

Time Allowed: 1 Hour 45 Minutes

Questions 1–4 are compulsory. Two out of the remaining three must be answered if maximum marks are to be attained. You are advised to read the paper first and then answer the questions in any order you wish. Workings should be shown to all answers and a brief precise summary will be much more acceptable than a long protracted answer. As part of this examination there will be a short oral which will take place outside the allotted time and which will only be taken into account when candidates are within 5 marks of passing the theory paper. (*N.B. References to V.A.T. assume a rate of 15%.*)

Question 1 (Compulsory): 15 marks

Give ten examples of dishonesty or improper practice and state your recommendations for preventing each one. Also, state the advantages and disadvantages of computerised tills.

Question 2 (Compulsory): 15 marks

You are asked to do a changeover. You have never worked for either client before. Explain exactly what procedures you would adopt, what you would do if working for only one party, and with examples demonstrate how you would present your valuation. Beer is awaiting return in the cellar; some has been tagged and some not. Explain what action you would take.

Question 3 (Compulsory): 15 marks

(a)   At premises where you generally take food stocks, your client has expressed his dissatisfaction at the results and suggested that the poor profit margins may be due to errors in stocktaking. Explain exactly how you took the stocks and arrived at a gross profit. Explain to him what else could be wrong and how to cost his menus out to achieve a realistic gross profit.

(b)   He has a small shop and asks you to prepare a valuation. Explain the normal procedures to him and tell him how the valuation would be arrived at.

Question 4 (Compulsory): 15 marks

Using the following information, prepare a trading account:

Purchases		Income	
(excl. V.A.T.)	£120,010.00	(incl. V.A.T.)	£228,846.00
Closing stock	£10,467.00	Opening stock	£9,437.00

If you incorporate allowances at retail of £18,380 (incl. V.A.T.), how will this affect the result?

Because your closing valuation was up until close of business on 5th January 1988, the accountants have asked you to do an adjustment. Purchases for the five-day period are (V.A.T.-exclusive) £2,800 and income (V.A.T.-inclusive) £1,300. Prepare a new valuation figure and show how it will affect the trading account.

Question 5 (Optional): 20 marks

Explain briefly each of the following:–

(a)	Uplift	(f)	Obscuration
(b)	Corked	(g)	Fermentation
(c)	Sales mix	(h)	Tolerance
(d)	Gruyère	(i)	Corkage
(c)	Pin	(j)	Fitou

Question 6 (Optional): 20 marks

(a) Name 10 wines. State whether they are red or white, and their country of origin.

(b) Explain the difference between real ale and kegged beer.

(c) Give the yield ⅕ gill and ⅙ gill on each of the following:

(i)	Bacardi (magnum)	(iv)	Whisky (gallon)
(ii)	Brandy (bottle)	(v)	Drambuie (bottle)
(iii)	Glayva (50 cl)	(vi)	Gin (litre)

(d) Explain briefly with a diagram how a cellar ledger system works.

Question 7 (Optional): 20 marks

(a) A bottle of whisky costs £7.80 (incl. V.A.T.). Using ⅙ gill measures, what must it be sold for to achieve 60% gross profit?

(b) A client buys whisky at £7.80 (incl. V.A.T.). He sells it at 65p per ⅙ gill. What gross profit is he achieving?

(c) How many 2 oz measures would be produced from one litre of postmix (dilution 7.5 : 1)?

(d)   Consumption at cost   = £4,873.08
       Consumption at retail = £11,163.01 (incl. V.A.T.)
       Allowances   = £842.76 (incl. V.A.T.)
       Income   = £10,306.97 (incl. V.A.T.)
       Show the estimated and actual gross profits.
(e)   A meal costs £2.06 to produce. What price must it be sold for
       to achieve 60%?

ANSWERS TO SAMPLE EXAMINATION PAPER QUESTIONS

Question 1

Dishonesty or improper practices

(a)   *Theft of cash* – This would show up as a shortage when the actual income for any period was compared with the reading produced by the cash register.

Theft of cash can be minimised by good supervision of bar staff, efficient control of cash, and occasional unannounced spot checks, at which a reading is taken and any money in the drawer replaced by a spare float. This procedure will indicate whether staff are under-ringing, to build up cash for removal later. An accurate note of payouts must also be maintained.

(b)   *Theft of stock* – This would probably not show up on a daily basis, but might be noticed by the Stocktaker or by the proprietor/manager when too much of any one commodity was being issued to a bar. A computerised till is advantageous here: a discrepancy may be apparent between the reading and the Stocktaker's report.

All liquor must be properly controlled, where necessary by using a cellar ledger, and spare stock always kept properly secured. If necessary a par stock can be held, and replacement liquor only issued where an empty bottle is given in return.

(c)   *Delivery shortages* – These would show up as a deficit on the stock report.

Draymen should never be left in the cellar unaccompanied by a responsible member of staff. All goods received and deposits returned must be checked against the delivery note. New supplies should preferably be left apart from existing stock so that the latter are not inadvertently checked off as part of the delivery.

(d)   *Dilution of spirits* – This is generally done by staff to cover their own consumption or the theft of stock or cash. It would not show up on a stock report.

It will only be detected by regular hydrometer tests, or by reductions in the sale of certain commodities.

(e)   *Dispensing of 'Off-Sales' stock* – Where half-bottles are generally sold for around £5.00 they may, if put through the optic, retail at double that amount, thereby inflating the stock result.

'Off-Sales' stock should be kept apart, and where possible the income should be recorded separately. Any sudden increase in the sale of quarter- or half-bottles would justify immediate investigation.

(f)   *Drinks unpaid for* – The cash register reading would balance with the income, but the stock report would show a deficit.

Friends and family of staff should not be encouraged to use the bar. Other staff should not be permitted to drink alcohol on the premises.

(g)   *Cash register interference* – If staff have access to Z keys, they can clear the cash register after the first two or three days of a stock period and then re-commence it, pocketing the takings to date. It is not unknown for staff to produce their own till for certain periods. Both procedures would result in stock deficits.

The sequence of Z readings can be recorded, but staff should not have access to these keys. A reading should be taken on the day of the stocktake, which should roughly correspond with cash taken.

(h)   *Dilution of postmix syrups* – When the equipment is installed, the dilution ratio is set by the engineer. Any interference with this will reduce the strength of the solution, which will create inflated results and allow scope for dishonesty.

Checks should be made on the dilution ratio at regular intervals by the supplier (or by the Stocktaker, if he has access to Brix equipment or a refractometer).

(i)   *Stock introduced by staff for resale* – An employee may purchase a bottle of whisky for around £7.00. If he sells it over the counter, he may be able to charge double that amount – but the premises will not profit by the sale. Such activity will be detected neither by stocktaking nor by comparing income with cash register readings.

Regular checks on stock should be carried out. Surpluses should be investigated, and stock on display can be marked with an internal stamp or folio number.

(j)   *Wrong measures being used* – The customers do not receive the correct or full measure. This will create an inflated surplus, unless the benefit has been taken by the person concerned.

Measures, both hand-held and optic, should be checked regularly, and staff should be supervised to ensure that full units are being given.

Computerised tills

Advantages

(a)   Staff make fewer errors.
(b)   There is an instant price-change facility.
(c)   Comprehensive information is readily available.
(d)   There is a facility for comparing actual sales with cash register
       readings.
(e)   Staff are deterred from under-ringing.

Disadvantages

(a)   Staff are sometimes liable to register items of a similar price
       through one key – defeating the object (of accuracy).
(b)   Drinks, particularly in a large 'round', can be forgotten and
       consequently not charged for.
(c)   If one member of staff, while serving a customer, monopolises
       the machine, service can be slowed down considerably.
(d)   Management may assume that a computerised till is all that is
       required for complete stock control.

Question 2

The premises should, if possible, be visited prior to the stocktake.
The vendor should be informed that most types of draught beer
which are over six weeks old cannot be included in any valuation as
the brewers will only allow duty, if anything, when crediting the
return of such beer. Similarly, all bottles and cans displaying 'best
before' dates which have passed will be excluded, as will any very
close to the date in question. It should be explained to the vendor
that the purchaser might agree to buy these items at a reduced price,
but that he would be well advised to sell them himself, if at all
possible, prior to the changeover. He should also be made aware of
any overstocking, and advised to return any excess stock to the
suppliers.

Confirmation should be obtained as to what is to be valued, other
than liquor. It may be that food, cleaning materials, fuel oil, calor
gas and glassware will form part of the valuation, and the Stocktaker
should accordingly ensure that as many invoices as possible are
available for these items on or before the date of the changeover.

If the Stocktaker is working for only one party, he should agree
the count and the cost prices with the other Stocktaker when
calculating the valuation. It is essential for the Stocktaker to ensure
that his client is paying a fair price for good saleable stock, and that
agreement is reached between all parties prior to his departure.

Any beer awaiting return, whether tagged or not, should only be
included in the valuation if the purchaser agrees. If this consent is
not given, the vendor can arrange for its removal and for his own

receipt of any credit. The Certificate of Valuation would be presented as shown in the following example.

Society Hotel – Strange Street, Stafford

We certify that a fair valuation of stock on hand at the above
premises cost value excluding V.A.T. after close of business on
Saturday 3rd December 1988 would be Seven thousand seven
hundred and fifty eight pounds and ninety two pence made up as
follows

Draught beer	1488.29	
Bottled/canned beer	210.11	
Minerals	362.20	
Spirits	2444.90	
Vermouths/apéritifs	57.10	
Liqueurs	186.80	
Table wines	240.53	
Tobacco	96.80	
Nuts and crisps	30.10	
Deposits	222.36	
Sundries	72.00	
Liquor		5411.19
Food		1719.43
Cleaning materials		86.20
Heating oil		542.10
Total		£7,758.92

Stocktaker's signature . . . .

Question 3

(a)   The Stocktaker will have counted and listed all the food on the
       premises; preferably, a chef will have been present, to elimin-
       ate the possibility of any stock being missed. Once the listing
       had been prepared, the Stocktaker would apply cost prices (ex-
       cluding V.A.T.) before extending his sheets and preparing a
       valuation. Once this had been done, a trading account would be
       prepared, using further information as supplied by the client.

Opening stock		Closing stock	
1/10/88	£1,847.50	1/11/88	£2,203.76
Purchases (excl.		Income (excl.	
V.A.T.)	£5,480.73	V.A.T.)	£11,403.86
Gross Profit	£6,279.39		
	£13,607.62		£13,607.62
Gross Profit	55.06%		

If the client has given food allowances, e.g. 'Staff Meals of £183.36 at Retail Value excl. V.A.T.', then this figure would be added to the Gross Profit and divided by the income including the allowance figure:–

Gross Profit   6,279.39 + 183.36 = $\overline{6,462.75} \times 100 = 55.7\%$.

Income   11,403.86 + 183.36 = 11,587.22

This shows the client what percentage would have been achieved had there been no staff meals.

Poor profit margins on food sales can be improved by regulating the portions, negotiating better buying prices, controlling staff feeding, wastage and theft, and (not least) increasing selling prices.

Assuming that all the information given to the Stocktaker is correct and that all business has been correctly raised during the stock period, the Stocktaker should study the client's menus and advise him on costing procedures. The following is an example of what he must charge for a Sirloin steak platter if he wishes to make a gross profit of 60%.

8 oz Sirloin steak	Cost	£1.76
Vegetables	Cost	.70
Garnishes and sauces	Cost	.50
Total		£2.96
60% gross profit		
Total selling price		£7.40
Price on menu including V.A.T.		£8.51

It is not always possible to achieve the full profit margin on every item, and some may be below the projected figure while others are above it.

(b) Shop stocktaking often involves a considerable number of items, and because it is usually unnecessary to list them all, the Stocktaker will write down '5 at 20p' or '86 at 73p' etc., according to the quantity and the retail price. He will split his count into various categories, such as cards, stationery, tobacco, cigars, food excluding V.A.T., food including V.A.T. etc. He will then calculate a gross price for each section, deduct V.A.T. (where applicable), and thus produce the percentage gross profit for that particular range of products. This will enable him to calculate the cost price, on the basis of which he would then prepare a Certificate of Valuation.

Question 4

(a)   *Trading Account*

Opening
   stock 1/1/87
	£9,437.00	Closing
		   stock 5/1/88
			£10,467.00

Purchases		Income	
(excl. V.A.T.)	£120,010.00	(excl. V.A.T.)	£198,996.52
Gross Profit	£80,016.52		
	£209,463.52		£209,463.52

Gross Profit 40.2%

(b)   *Allowances*

Opening
   stock 1/1/87
	£9,437.00	Closing
		   stock 5/1/88
			£10,467.00

Purchases		Income	
(excl. V.A.T.)	£120,010.00	(excl. V.A.T.)	£198,996.52
Gross Profit	£95,999.13	Allowances	
		(excl. V.A.T.)	£15,982.61
	£225,446.13		£225,446.13

Gross Profit 44.6%

(c)   *Adjustment*

Purchases
   (5 days)
	£2,800.00	Income
		   (excl. V.A.T.)
			£1,130.43

		Less Gross Profit 40.2%	£454.43
Closing stock	£10,467.00	Cost of Sales	£676.00
Less Purchases	(£2,800.00)		
	£7,667.00		
Add Cost of Sales	£676.00		
Adjusted valuation 1/1/88	£8,343.00		

(d)   *Adjusted Trading Account*

Opening
   stock 1/1/87
	£9,437.00	Closing
		   stock 5/1/88
			£8,343.00

Purchases		Income	
(excl. V.A.T.)	£117,210.00	(excl. V.A.T.)	£197,866.09
Gross Profit	£79,562.09		
	£206,209.09		£206,209.09

Gross Profit 40.2%

Question 5

(a) *Uplift*
     This can refer to either (i) or (ii):–
(i) The surcharge applied to adjust the result where there are two
     or more bars with different price structures and where selling
     prices have been based on those of the cheapest bar.
(ii) Removal of goods for return to the supplier.

(b) *Corked*
     If air has penetrated the contents of a wine bottle and impaired
     the quality of the product, the wine is referred to as 'corked'.

(c) *Sales mix*
     Sales values of individual items or categories of products, shown
     as percentages of total sales.

(d) *Gruyère*
     A hard cheese from Switzerland.

(e) *Pin*
     A beer vessel with a capacity of 4.5 gallons.

(f) *Obscuration*
     The effect of sugar and colourings on the measured strength of
     items such as brandy and rum. When a hydrometer test is
     carried out, the reading may show a divergence from the legal
     volume percentage, and a specific tolerance must be taken into
     account.

(g) *Fermentation*
     The chemical change which turns sugar into alcohol.

(h) *Tolerance*
     An allowance for small amounts of error or wastage. If a bottle
     produces 48 measures at ⅙ gill, the client may ask the Stock-
     taker to charge only 47, to give the manager or steward a
     'tolerance' to cover losses from leaking optics etc.

(i) *Corkage*
     If wine or other drink is brought into premises by a client, the
     hotel will charge 'corkage' for opening and serving it.

(j) *Fitou*
     A dry red wine from France.

Question 6

(a)	Château Talbot	Red	France
	Monbazillac	White	France
	Château Rieussec	White	France

Hautes Côtes de Beaune	Red	France
Mainzer Domherr	White	Germany
Würzsburger Stein	White	Germany
Barolo	Red	Italy
Orvieto Classico	White	Italy
Vinho Verde	White	Portugal
Carta de Plata Rioja	Red	Spain

(b)   Real ale, normally known as traditional beer, goes through a fermentation in the cask and still contains yeast when delivered. The beer needs very careful handling, and must be allowed to settle for almost two days before being used. Finings may be rquired, to help clear it during the settling process.

Keg beer is conditioned at the brewery and packaged under pressure. This type of beer also requires pressure from CO_2 gas outside the keg to send it to the point of dispense.

			$1/5$ gill	$1/6$ gill
(c)	(i)	Bacardi (magnum)	52	63
	(ii)	Brandy (bottle)	24	29
	(iii)	Glayva (50 cl)	17	20
	(iv)	Whisky (gallon)	158	190
	(v)	Drambuie (bottle)	26	32
	(vi)	Gin (litre)	35	42

(d)   *Whisky 75 cl*

	Delivery	Public	Lounge	Cocktail	Balance
3/8/88	24				24
4/8/88				3	21
5/8/88		1			20
6/8/88			1		19
7/8/88		6			13
9/8/88	12				25
Stocktake	36	7	1	3	25

By the use of requisition books, transfers are recorded from the cellar to the bars. These figures are entered in the cellar ledger, as shown in the above example, the balance being entered each time to show what stock should remain in the cellar. The actual and theoretical figures should match. The system ensures strict security and, because purchases are allocated to each bar, enables separate stock reports to be produced for every outlet.

Question 7

(a)   Cost price = 7.80 (incl. V.A.T.)

$$\frac{7.80 \times 100}{100 - 60} = 19.50$$

19.50 ÷ 32 (measures) = 61p.

(b)   Cost price = 7.80 (incl. V.A.T.)
Selling price = .65 × 32 (measures) = 20.80 (incl. V.A.T.)

$$\frac{(\text{Selling price} - \text{cost price})}{\text{Selling price}} \times 100 = \text{Gross Profit}$$

$$\frac{(20.80 - 7.80)}{20.80} \times 100 = 62.5\%.$$

(c)   35.2 oz (1 lt) × 8.5 (yield) = 299.2 oz
= 149.6 × 2 oz measures.

(d)

Consumption at retail (excl. V.A.T.)	£9,706.97
Less allowances (excl. V.A.T.)	(£732.83)
	= £8,974.14
Less consumption at cost	£4,873.08
Estimated Gross Profit	= £4,101.06 = 45.7%
Actual income (excl. V.A.T.)	£8,962.58
Less consumption at cost	£4,873.08
Actual Gross Profit	= £4,089.50 = 45.6%

(e) $$\frac{2.06}{100 - 60} \times 100 = 5.15; \quad \frac{(5.15 - 2.06)}{5.15} \times 100 = 60\%;$$

Meal must be sold for £5.15 plus V.A.T. = £5.92.

INDEX

A.C. (definition)   221

accounts – *see* balance sheets;
  bookkeeping; profit and loss
  accounts; trading accounts

adjustments –
  for price changes etc.   4-6, 17-18, 39,
    84, 102, 132-9, 300, 315
  to year-end valuations   116, 124, 139-
    141, 314
  see also allowances; transfers, external
    (stock, borrowed or loaned);
    transfers, internal

alcoholic drinks, V.A.T. on   44, 175,
  177

alcoholic strength –
  legal definitions   61, 273-4
  beer   183, 185-6
  spirits   190, 192, 193, 274, 275
  wine   210-11, 220
  wines, fortified   195
  see also dilution – adulteration;
    hydrometer, use of

ale, real; ale, traditional – *see* beer,
  draught

allowances –
  correct recording of   viii, 3, 39, 42, 79
  in stock reports, extended   28, 49, 95,
    117-21, 126-31, 297
  in trading accounts   132, 159, 164-6,
    300, 313, 314
  see also adjustments; transfers, external
    (stock, borrowed or loaned);
    transfers, internal

alpha/numeric tills – *see* tills, pre-set
  (computerised)

Alsace, liquor products of   202, 204,
  220, 226, 227

amusement machines, in licensed
  premises   51, 71-5

'amusements with prizes' machines   51,
  71, 72, 74-5

annual licensing meeting – *see* licensing
  meeting, annual

antiques, valuation of   33, 144

apéritifs   93, 198, 207
  see also vermouth

appeals – *see* licensing decisions, appeals
  against

Armagnac   194

assets, valuation and depreciation
  of   33-6, 142-6

assortments and mixtures – *see* biscuits
  and biscuits, assorted; fruit and
  nut mixtures; petits fours

Auslese (definition)   221

Australia, liquor products of   197, 200,
  201, 203, 204, 211, 217, 218, 224,
  226, 231, 291

Austria, liquor products of   204, 205,
  222, 225, 291

baby (capacity)   297

'baby mixers'   99, 297

balance sheets   31, 33-6, 297

Balthazar (capacity)   281

banquets   80

bar –
  legal definitions   51, 53-4
  hygiene   76-8
  counting contents of   96-8, 178
  stock control in multi-bar outlets   21-
    29, 102, 136-7, 297, 300, 315
  see also price list (tariff); staff

bar, occasional – *see* licence, occasional

barley – *see* grain, malted

barrel (capacity)   87

barrelage   286, 297

Beaujolais, wines of   151, 211-12, 220,
  227, 230

beer, bottled and canned –
  production, types   185
  storage, 'shelf life'   29, 148, 311
  counting and valuing of   86, 87, 95,
    99, 105, 111, 148, 286, 297

beer, bright   185

beer, cask – *see* beer, draught

beer, draught –
  definitions (cask, natural or traditional
    beer, real or traditional ale; keg or
    pressurised beer)   185, 297, 299,
    316
  storage, 'shelf life'   29, 38, 148, 186,
    187-9, 311
  dispensing, measures   18, 21-5, 64, 79,
    88, 186-7, 298, 299, 316
  wastage, loss   viii, 38, 126-7

beer, draught (*contd.*)
  returns   4, 39, 42, 98, 138-9, 148, 311-
      312
  counting and valuing of   43, 87-8, 97,
      98, 105, 148, 286, 297
  profit margin   113
Beerenauslese (definition)   221
beerhouses, legal requirements *re*   70-1
beer, keg; beer, natural; beer, pressurised
      – *see* beer, draught
beers, foreign   99, 291-3
beer, traditional – *see* beer, draught
Belgium –
  liquor products   202, 291
  cheese   238
betting, in licensed premises   51-2
bin cards   29, 297
biscuits and biscuits, assorted, V.A.T.
      on   175, 176, 177
bitter lemon   99
bond   vii, 297
book debts   174
bookkeeping   xi, 3-14, 36-40, 43-9
  see also cellar control system; deliveries;
      income; purchases; sales
      (consumption), at cost and at
      retail; etc.
books – *see* newspapers, magazines and
      books
Bordeaux, wines of (including
      claret)   150-1, 213, 219, 222, 226-
      227, 229, 230, 281
borrowed stock – *see* transfers, external
      (stock, borrowed or loaned)
bottles (capacities) –
  apéritifs   93
  champagne   281
  liqueurs   92
  spirits   93
  wines   212, 281
  wines, fortified   93
bottles, cases and containers ('deposits'),
      counting and valuing of   42, 97-
      102, 116-18, 121, 124, 149, 153,
      173, 298, 309
bottles, part-, gauging contents of   28,
      84-6, 91, 148, 178
brandy –
  production, types (Armagnac, Cognac,
      grape brandy, marc)   193-4, 204
  alcoholic strength, age   193, 275, 315
  in liqueurs and wines, fortified   195,
      197, 198
  see also spirits

bread   164, 167
Brewers' Society   181
brewery companies – *see* licensed
      premises – tenancies, brewery
      companies and tied or managed
      houses
brewing –
  ingredients, processes   181-5
  conditioning   185, 189, 316
  racking   185, 316
  alcoholic strength of beer   183, 185-6
Britain – *see* U.K.
Brix meter – *see* refractometer (Brix
      meter)
broker (valuer) –
  role of, at changeovers, valuations
      etc.   33, 142-7, 297
  security procedures   143, 146
Budget, Chancellor's   30, 43
Bulgaria –
  wines   225
  cheese   238
Burgundy (including Beaujolais, Côte
      d'Or and Mâconnais, le), wines
      of   151, 211-12, 219-20, 222, 226,
      227, 228, 230, 316
  see also Chablis, wines of
Burtonisation   182
'business done' figure   3, 9, 10, 297
butt (capacity)   87

calculators, in stocktaking   270-3
California, wines of   211, 223, 226, 231
Canada, beers of   291
cans (tins), food (capacities)   160
caramel, in liquor production   185, 192,
      198
carbon dioxide – *see* gas (CO_2)
cards, greetings, counting and valuing
      of   171, 172-3, 175
cases – *see* bottles, cases and containers
      ('deposits')
cash balance, reconciliation   12-14
cash income, recording of – *see* floats,
      cash; income; tills, pre-set
      (computerised)
cash registers – *see* tills, pre-set
      (computerised)
cash, theft of   vii-ix, 19, 40-2, 309-10
casks (capacities)   87-8
Catalonia, wines of   222
cellar –
  management, hygiene, safety
      etc.   186, 187-9

counting contents of 97, 98
cellar control system –
    general 21-9, 102, 297, 316-17
    cellar ledger 25-9, 316
    cellar requisitions etc. 25, 30, 41-2,
        79, 178, 300, 316
Chablis, wines of 210, 220, 228, 229
Champagne, wines of (i.e.
        champagne) 152, 210, 211, 219,
        226, 230-1, 232, 281
changeover (change of tenancy or
        ownership), procedures and
        valuation for 29-30, 100-2, 121-4,
        142-58, 170-5, 311-12
cheap sales allowance 95, 128, 297
    see also 'off-sales' transactions
cheese –
    national varieties 235-8
    diagrams 258
    counting and valuing of 149, 160-1
children and young persons, legal
        requirements re 52-4, 66, 296
chocolates and chocolate goods – see
        confectionery (including chocolate
        and chocolate goods)
Christmas Day, hours permitted for 56,
        58, 60, 66
cider 54, 62, 64, 177, 286
cigarettes and cigars – see tobacco
claret (red wines of Bordeaux) 150-1,
        213, 219, 222, 226-7, 230
classico (definition) 223
cleaning materials, counting and valuing
        of 154, 311
'closing stock' figure 84, 105, 124-5
clubs, registered 12, 60, 72, 95-6
coca cola 90, 300
Cognac 193-4
cold room, counting contents of 160-1
Common Market – see E.E.C.
        regulations, rulings etc.
complimentary issues –
    drinks 15, 79, 130
    food 131, 164
    wrappings 174
composite figures 286, 297
computer programs (software), in
        stocktaking etc. 83, 269-70, 300
computers (hardware), in stocktaking
        etc. 6, 83, 113, 269-70, 299
    see also tills, pre-set (computerised)
conditioning, of beer 185, 189, 316
confectionery (including chocolates and
        chocolate goods) –

counting and valuing of 87, 95-6, 173
    profit margin 96
    V.A.T. on 164, 175, 176, 177
consumption, at cost and at retail – see
        sales (consumption), at cost and
        at retail
containers – see bottles, cases and
        containers ('deposits')
cordials, counting and valuing of 87,
        88, 98, 287
    see also liqueurs
corkage 40, 297, 315
corked (wine) 127, 297, 301, 315
Côte d'Or, wines of –
    Côte Chalonnaise 219
    Côte de Beaune 219, 230, 316
    Côte de Nuits 219, 230
credit sales 16, 21, 41, 79, 297
credits, credit notes –
    bottles, cases and containers
        ('deposits') 100-2, 117, 124
    purchases free of charge 134-5
    stock, borrowed or loaned 137-8
    stock, returned 4, 28, 39, 105, 124,
        138-9, 148, 298, 311-12
crème de . . . liqueurs 200-1
crisps etc. –
    counting and valuing of 87, 95-6, 98,
        100, 111
    profit margin 96
    V.A.T. on 96, 175, 176
cumulative figures 117
Customs and Excise, Department of vii-
        viii, 43, 49, 72, 74, 113, 138, 183,
        186, 301
Cyprus, liquor products of 197, 198,
        202, 291
Czechoslovakia –
    liquor products 200, 291
    cheese 238

dancing, licensing of – see licence –
        entertainment(s)
days stockholding 115-16, 270
debtors ledger 9, 12
deep freezes – see freezers and frozen food
deficit – see surplus (overage)/deficit
        (shortage)
deliveries –
    recording and monitoring of 28, 39-
        40, 97, 154, 167, 270, 309
    short vii, 39, 49, 100, 159, 309
    see also Goods Received Book

delivery notes   3, 25-8, 39, 84, 90, 91,
        96, 100, 105, 124, 159, 164, 298,
        309
Denmark – *see* Scandinavia
department keys, on tills   16-17
deposits –
    advance payments   10, 12, 298
    refundable items – *see* bottles, cases
        and containers ('deposits')
    sediment in liquor – *see* sediment
depreciation, of assets   33-5, 146
Deutscher Tafelwein (definition)   221
dilution –
    of fruit juices and minerals,
        postmix   88-91, 310
    adulteration   41, 274-5, 309, 310
    see also hydrometer, use of
dipstick, dip-rod, use of   93, 98, 99, 152-
        153, 298
discounts and special offers –
    on purchases   4, 86, 116, 124, 134-5,
        175
    on sales   95, 96; *see also* cheap sales
        allowance
    on sales, improper   40, 41, 310
    on excess or sub-standard stock in
        valuations   149, 154-5, 172, 311
dishonest practices – *see* deliveries –
        short; staff – dishonest practices
distilling   189-95
D.O.C. (definition)   223
D.O.C.G. (definition)   223
drawings   298
drinking-up time   54, 296
duty –
    rates of, for wines and wines,
        fortified   151, 152
    refund of, for beer, draught,
        returned   138, 311

Eau de Vie   198, 202
'edible products not classified as food',
        V.A.T. on   177
E.E.C. regulations, rulings etc.   43, 152,
        212, 219, 223, 274
Eiswein (definition)   222
'empty for full' system   41-2, 309
England –
    liquor products   181-2, 197, 203, 204,
        206, 224-5, 226, 292
    cheeses   237, 258
    English practices *re* licensed
        premises   60, 142, 147, 186

Environmental Health, Department
        of   78
examinations, stocktaking   303, 306-17
extended hours, extended hours order,
        extension of permitted hours   56-
        59, 65
extended reports – *see* stock reports,
        extended

fermentation (conversion of sugar to
        alcohol)   181, 183-4, 185, 189-90,
        193-7, 210-12, 276, 315
finings –
    in beer   185, 316
    in wine   212
Finland – *see* Scandinavia
firkin (capacity)   87
fish, fresh –
    seasonal availability   234-5
    diagrams   254-6
    counting and valuing of   160
floats, cash   10-12, 42, 155, 298, 309
food –
    lists and diagrams   233-62
    hygiene   76, 77-8, 161
    purchases, deliveries, storage,
        preparation   167
    V.A.T. on   43-4, 96, 164, 175-7
    see also menu planning and costing;
        portion control
food, canned – *see* cans (tins), food
        (capacities)
food, 'carry out', V.A.T. on   43
food, frozen – *see* freezers and frozen food
food stocktaking –
    counting and valuing of stock   149-50,
        159-64, 311, 312
    trading account and allowances   159,
        164-6, 300, 312-13
    see also transfers, internal
food store, counting contents of   160
France –
    wines   150-1, 213-14, 219-21, 226-32,
        315-16
    other liquor products   193-4, 197-8,
        199-206, 292, 293
    cheeses   235-6, 258
free drinks etc. – *see* complimentary
        issues
free houses – *see* licensed premises – free
        houses
free stock – *see* credits, credit notes;
        promotions, promotional stock

freezers and frozen food, counting and
    valuing of   149-50, 160
fruit –
    seasonal availability   260-2
    counting and valuing of   161
fruit and nut mixtures, V.A.T. on   176
fruit juices –
    dispensing, dilution, postmixes   90-1
    counting and valuing of   90-1, 99, 297
fruit machines – see 'amusements with
        prizes' machines
fuel, quantifying and valuing of   152-4,
        311
furnishings, fixtures and fittings,
        valuation and depreciation of   35,
        142, 144-6

gallonage   287
game –
    seasonal availability   233
    diagrams   252
gaming, in licensed premises, Gaming
        Act, Gaming Board   51, 52, 66,
        73
    see also amusement machines
garages, stock in – see stock, wholesale
gas (CO$_2$) –
    in dispensing of beer, keg   185, 187,
        189, 316
    counting and valuing of cylinders   98,
        116
gas (fuel), quantifying and valuing
        of   152-4, 311
general order of exemption   58-9, 65
general stocktaking   152-5, 311
Germany –
    wines   151, 216, 221-2, 226, 228, 229,
        230, 316
    other liquor products   199, 200, 202,
        203, 205, 206, 292, 293
    cheeses   236
gin –
    production, types (Genever, London,
        Plymouth)   194
    alcoholic strength   274, 275
    legal measures   64, 65, 296
    see also spirits
ginger ale, beer   99, 300
ginger wine   93
glassware –
    in bars   76-7, 298
    diagrams   294-5
    beer glasses (brim/line)   79, 88, 187
    wine glasses (sizes)   93-4, 232

counting and valuing of   143, 155, 311
    see also measures
Good Friday, hours permitted for   56,
        60, 66
Goods Received Book   3-4, 10-12, 25,
        84, 105, 121, 164, 298
grain, malted –
    in brewing   181-3
    in distilling   190-2, 194
grape brandy   194
gravity, original – see alcoholic strength
Great Britain – see U.K.
Greece –
    liquor products   201, 204, 205, 225
    cheeses   238
grocery goods, counting and valuing
        of   173-4
GTZ or Z2 key, on tills   16

'happy hour' prices and allowances   17,
        23, 24, 128
hardware –
    computers – see computers (hardware)
    non-consumable items   299
Havana cigars – see tobacco
'head', on beer   77, 187
hock – see Rhine wines (hocks)
hogshead (capacity)   87
Holland –
    liquor products   194, 199-206, 292
    cheeses   238, 258
hops, in beer   181-3, 186
Hotel Proprietors Act   60, 61, 65
hours permitted for consumption of
        liquor   54-5, 56-60, 65, 296
Hungary –
    liquor products   197, 199, 206, 225,
        229
    cheese   238
hydrometer, use of   41, 42, 148, 274-6,
        290, 299, 303, 309, 315
hygiene –
    bar, food, staff, stocktakers   76-8, 161
    cellar   187-9

ice-cream, V.A.T. on   164, 175, 176
Imperiale (capacity)   281
imprest book and system – see petty cash
income –
    definition   299
    recording and monitoring of   viii, 3-21,
        31-3, 36-42, 79, 270, 297, 309-10
    see also stock reports, extended; trading
        accounts

Incorporated Society of Licensed Trade
    Stocktakers (development,
    membership, examinations,
    training courses)   iii, vii, 80, 302-
    305, 306-17
    see also stocktakers
ingoer (purchaser or tenant,
    ingoing)   29-30, 102, 142-55, 170-
    175, 300, 311
Inland Revenue   vii-viii
innkeeper (legal definition, legal
    liability)   60-1, 65-6
input tax – *see* V.A.T. – input tax/output
    tax
International Organisation of Legal
    Metrology (O.I.M.L.)   274
inventories   142-6
invoices –
    definition   299
    re cellar ledger   25-8
    re discounts   4, 134
    re stock reports, extended   3-4, 39, 84,
        86, 100, 105
    re trading accounts   118, 124, 159, 164
    re valuations   141, 150, 153, 154, 172,
        311
Ireland, liquor products of   190, 203,
    292
Israel, liquor products of   200, 205, 292
Italy –
    wines   221, 222-3, 226, 228, 229, 230,
        316
    other liquor products   197, 198, 199,
        200, 202-6, 292
    cheeses   236, 238

jackpot machines   72, 74
    see also amusement machines
Japan, liquor products of   200, 204, 205,
    292
Jeroboam (capacities)   281
juke boxes   71-3, 74
    see also amusement machines
justices' certificate – *see* supper hour
    certificate (justices' certificate)
justices' licence – *see* licence – on-/off-
    (justices' licence)

Kabinett (definition)   221
kilderkin (capacity)   87
kitchen, counting contents of   159-61
kitchen drinks   127
kitchen transfers – *see* transfers, internal

lager – *see* beer, bottled and canned;
    beer, draught
Landlord and Tenant Act   63
Landwein (definition)   221
Lebanon, wine of   225
ledger – *see* cellar control system – cellar
    ledger; debtors ledger; tabular
    ledger (Tab.)
'ledger balance brought forward'   9-10
lemonade, counting and valuing of   88-
    89, 98
liabilities, financial   35
licence –
amusement machine   51, 72, 74,
    75
    betting office   51
    entertainment(s)   55-6, 57-8
    for sale of beer   62-3, 64, 71
    for sale of cider   54, 62-3
    for sale of wine   62-3, 64, 71
    justices' – *see* licence – on-/off-
        (justices' licence)
    occasional   66-7, 79
    on-/off- (justices' licence)   50, 60, 62-
        63, 65, 66, 68, 71
    provisional   50, 62-3
    residential   68-9
    restaurant   68-9
    removal of   50, 62, 63, 65, 67
    renewal of   50, 63, 68
    transfer of   50, 62, 63, 67, 69-70, 142-
        143
licensed premises –
    legal requirements etc.   50-78
    tenancies, brewery companies and tied
        or managed houses   12, 51, 71-5,
        142-4, 149, 299, 301
    free houses   71, 146, 147, 149, 298
    see also changeover (change of tenancy
        or ownership); management
Licensing Act   53-4, 56-7, 60, 65, 66, 70,
    71, 296
licensing decisions, appeals against   50-
    51, 55, 56, 69
licensing meeting, annual   50, 59, 63
licensing sessions   50, 62-3, 63-4, 70
    see also transfer sessions
liqueurs –
    production, types ('creme de . . .', Eau
        de Vie, fruit liqueurs, herbal
        liqueurs, marc)   194, 198-206,
        275
    counting and valuing of   84, 87, 91-2,
        105, 116, 282-3

liquors, intoxicating, legal definitions of –
    see alcoholic strength – legal
    definitions
liquor stocktaking –
    counting and valuing of stock:
        yield   87-96, 282-3, 301
        physical count   84-6, 96-102, 147-9,
        178, 286-9
    stock report, extended:
        basic calculations   83-6, 103-21
        adjustments   4-6, 17-18, 39, 84,
        102, 132-9, 300, 315
        allowances   28, 49, 95, 117-21, 126-
        131, 297
    trading account:
        basic calculations   118, 124-5, 314
        allowances   131-2, 314
    valuation:
        basic calculations   121-4, 147-9,
        150-2
        adjustment (year-end) 116, 124, 139-
        141, 314
loaned stock – *see* transfers, external
    (stock, borrowed or loaned)
Loire, wines of   151, 212, 220, 226, 227,
    229, 230
lollies, V.A.T. on   176
lotteries, in licensed premises   52

Mâconnais, le, wines of   219-20, 227
madeira   152, 196-7
    see also wines, fortified (madeira, port,
    sherry etc.)
magazines – *see* newspapers, magazines
    and books
magnum (capacity)   281
malpractice – *see* deliveries – short; staff
    – dishonest practices
malt – *see* grain, malted
managed houses – *see* licensed premises –
    tenancies, brewery companies and
    tied or managed houses
management –
    responsibilities, security procedures,
    supervision of staff   vii-ix, x-xi,
    18, 19, 36, 41-2, 79-80, 159, 309-
    310, 311, 313
    consumption of food and liquor   54,
    128, 130, 164
marc   194, 204
mark-up – *see* profit, gross
mead   197
meals, consumption of liquor with   53,
    54, 56-8, 68-9

measured pulls   299
    see also beer, draught – dispensing,
    measures
measures –
    Imperial/metric   91-4, 232, 274, 283-5
    legal, for different drinks   64, 65, 296
    beer glasses (types, legal)   187
    wine glasses (sizes, approved)   93-4,
    232
    monitoring use of   viii, 38, 40, 79,
    178, 310
    in assessment of yield   91-4, 282-3,
    301
meat –
    diagrams   239-51
    purchasing and costing of   167-9
    counting and valuing of   149, 160,
    161
mechanical equipment, valuation and
    depreciation of   35, 143
menu planning and costing   168-9
    see also portion control
meters, in dispensing of liquor – *see* beer,
    draught – dispensing, measures;
    minerals, postmix – dispensing,
    dilution; minerals, premix –
    dispensing
'méthode champenoise'   219, 220
Methuselah (capacity)   281
Mexico, liquor products of   199, 200,
    203, 204, 206, 291, 292
Midi, wines of   220-1
milk   90, 164, 167
minerals –
    storage, 'shelf life'   29, 148, 311
    counting and valuing of   86, 87, 95,
    99, 105, 111, 148, 287; *see also*
    'baby mixers'
minerals, postmix –
    dispensing, dilution   18, 21, 88-90,
    310
    counting and valuing of   18, 87, 88-
    90, 99, 288-9
minerals, premix –
    dispensing   18, 21, 88
    counting and valuing of   18, 88-90, 99
'mis-en-place'   161
mixers – *see* 'baby mixers'
mixtures and assortments – *see* biscuits
    and biscuits, assorted; fruit and
    nut mixtures; petits fours
Mosel wines   221, 226, 228, 229
music, licensing of – *see* licence –
    entertainment(s)

Nebuchadnezzar (capacity)   281
newspapers, magazines and books,
        counting and valuing of etc.   43,
        171, 174
New Zealand, liquor products of   224,
        231, 292
Norway – *see* Scandinavia
'no sale' rings, on tills   19, 41
notices in licensed premises   57, 58, 61,
        64-5, 72, 296
    see also price list (tariff)
numeric tills – *see* tills, pre-set
        (computerised)
nuts, etc. –
    counting and valuing of   87, 95-6, 98,
        100
    V.A.T. on   96, 175, 176

'obligations to serve the public'   65-6,
        67-8
obscuration   275, 299, 315
'off-sales' transactions   ix, 28, 42, 128,
        309-10
    see also cheap sales allowance
oil, quantifying and valuing of   152-3,
        311
O.I.M.L. (International Organisation of
        Legal Metrology)   274
'opening stock' figure   83, 103, 124-5,
        159
original gravity – *see* alcoholic strength
outgoer (vendor or tenant,
        outgoing)   29-30, 142-55, 170-5,
        301, 311-12
output tax – *see* V.A.T. – input tax/
        output tax
overage – *see* surplus (overage)/deficit
        (shortage)
overheads   ix, 33, 298, 299
overstocking   viii, 30, 84, 116, 149, 172,
        270, 299, 311
ownership, change of – *see* changeover
        (change of tenancy or ownership)

par stocks   30, 41-2, 299, 309
payouts   10, 309
Performing Rights Society (P.R.S.)   72-3
permissions, occasional – *see* licence –
        occasional
perry   53, 54
petits fours, V.A.T. on   176, 177
petrol, quantifying and valuing of   152-3
petty cash   3, 4, 9, 10-12, 40, 49, 299

Phonograph Performance Ltd
        (P.P.L.)   72-3
'physical count' (of stock) – *see* food
        stocktaking – counting and
        valuing of stock; liquor
        stocktaking – counting and
        valuing of stock: physical count
Piemonte, wines of   222, 316
pilferage – *see* cash, theft of; stock, theft
        of
pin (capacity)   87, 315
pin tables   72, 74
    see also amusement machines
pipe cleaning   15, 21-5, 126-7
P.L.U. keys and numbers, on tills   16-
        17, 24
Poland –
    liquor products   194-5, 203, 206, 292
    cheese   238
pool tables   72, 73
port –
    production, types   30, 195, 198, 207
    counting and valuing of   87, 91-3
    duty on   152
    see also port, vintage
portion control   159, 299, 313
    see also menu planning and costing
Portugal –
    liquor products of   199, 202, 207-9,
        225, 230, 292, 316
    cheese   238
port, vintage   30, 92, 207-9
poultry, diagrams of   253
price differences (between bars),
        adjustments for   102, 136-7, 300,
        315
price list (tariff)   38, 65, 79, 85, 141,
        231-2, 301
prices, cost –
    definition   297
    in stock reports, extended   84-6, 103,
        111, 270-1, 272
    in trading accounts and
        valuations   121, 150, 152-5, 159-
        161, 170-2, 175, 311, 312, 313
    changes, monitoring of and
        adjustments for   xi, 86, 132-3,
        270
    see also profit, gross; purchases; sales
        (consumption), at cost and at
        retail
prices, retail (selling) –
    definition   300
    establishing of   x, xi, 231-2

ensuring correct charging of 18, 38, 178, 311
in stock reports, extended 84-9, 94-6, 103, 111, 159, 270, 271, 272
in valuations 170-3, 175, 313
changes, monitoring of and adjustments for ix, 17-18, 79, 84, 102, 133-4, 270, 300, 311
V.A.T. element 43-4, 49, 65, 86, 103, 170-1, 231, 278-80
see also profit, gross; sales (consumption), at cost and at retail
printer, computer 269
profit and loss accounts 31-3, 36-8
profit, gross –
definitions (gross/net; actual/estimated; on sales/on cost, or mark-up) viii, 33, 38, 115, 166, 298, 299
in stock reports, extended viii, 80, 111-15, 117-21, 270, 317
in trading accounts and valuations viii, 83, 118, 124-5, 131, 141, 164-7, 170-2, 175, 312, 314
effects of allowances and adjustments on 3, 97, 118-21, 127, 129-32, 134-5, 164-6, 313, 314
ways of improving xi, 112-13, 168-9, 277-9, 313
see also profit, gross, percentage; profit margins, variability of; surplus (overage)/deficit (shortage)
profit, gross, percentage –
in stock reports, extended 92, 111, 112-13, 115, 270, 317
in trading accounts and valuations 124-5, 132, 166-7, 312-13
see also profit, gross – ways of improving
profit margins, variability of 96, 113, 170-2, 175, 232
see also profit, gross
profit, net 31-3, 299
programs – see computer programs (software)
promotions, promotional stock 4, 17, 128, 130, 135-6, 300
proof (definitions) 273-4
see also alcoholic strength
property, valuation and depreciation of 35

proportion of alcohol – see alcoholic strength
protection order 67, 142-3
Provence, wines of 220-1
puncheon (capacity) 87
purchaser – see ingoer (purchaser or tenant, ingoing)
purchases –
recording and monitoring of 3-4, 10-12, 25-9, 40, 42, 79, 164, 299
in stock reports, extended 84, 100-2, 105, 117
in trading accounts 118, 124-5, 159, 164
discounts on 4, 86, 124, 134-5, 175
input tax (V.A.T.) recoverable on 43-9, 299
see also deliveries; prices, cost
purchasing, advice on xi, 167, 313

Q.b.A. (definition) 221
Q.m.P. (definition) 221

Race Relations Act 67-8
racking, of beer 185, 316
refractometer (Brix meter), use of 90, 310
refrigerators, counting contents of 100, 161
Rehoboam (capacity) 281
reports, extended – see stock reports, extended
requisitions, cellar – see cellar control system – cellar requisitions etc.
residents on licensed premises, consumption of liquor by 54
restriction order 50, 65
retail outlets – see stock, retail
revenue – see income
Rhine wines (hocks) 151, 216, 221, 226, 228, 229, 230, 316
Rhône, liquor products of 197, 203, 210, 214, 220, 226, 227
Rioja, wines of 215, 222, 230, 316
rum –
production, types (Barbados, dark, light) 30, 195
alcoholic strength 274, 275, 299, 315
legal measures 64, 65, 296
see also spirits
Russia, liquor products of 194-5, 203, 205, 206, 292

sales (consumption), at cost and at
    retail –
    recording and monitoring of   15-21,
        38-42, 79, 159, 309-10
    in stock reports, extended   84, 94-5,
        105, 111, 113-18, 270-3
    output tax (V.A.T.) payable on   43-9,
        299
    see also adjustments; allowances; prices,
        cost; prices, retail (selling); sales
        (mix) ratios; surplus (overage)/
        deficit (shortage)
sales (mix) ratios   49, 97, 113, 115, 232,
    270, 271-2, 315
Salmanazar (capacity)   281
Scandinavia –
    liquor products   199, 201, 204, 205,
        206, 291, 292, 293
    cheeses   238
Scotland –
    liquor products   190-2, 200, 202, 203,
        292
    cheeses   237
    Scottish practices re licensed
        premises   142, 147, 186-7
security procedures – see broker (valuer)
        – security procedures;
        management – responsibilities,
        security procedures, supervision of
        staff; stocktakers – security and
        checking procedures
sediment –
    definition ('deposit')   298
    in beer   98, 185, 186, 189
    in port, vintage   92, 207
    in wine   151, 211-12
'sell by' date – see stock, 'shelf life' of
shandy   88
shellfish –
    seasonal availability   234
    diagrams   257
sherry –
    production, types   195-6, 197
    counting and valuing of   84, 87, 91-3,
        105
    duty on   152
sherry, cask   87, 93
shift key level, on tills   17
shops – see stock, retail
shortage – see surplus (overage)/deficit
        (shortage)
Sicily, liquor products of   197, 222
Sikes hydrometer and scale   273-5
    see also hydrometer, use of

smokers' sundries – see tobacco
soda water   87
soft drinks, V.A.T. on   175, 177
software – see computer programs
        (software)
South Africa, liquor products of   197,
        206, 224, 293
South America, liquor products of   199,
        200, 205, 224, 291
Spain –
    wines   211, 215, 222, 224, 226, 230,
        316
    other liquor products   195-6, 197, 199,
        200, 201, 203, 204, 205, 293
    cheeses   238
spare parts, counting and valuing
        of   175
Spätlese (definition)   221
special hours certificate   50, 57-8, 65
special offers – see discounts and special
        offers
special order of exemption   54, 59
spirits –
    production, types   189-206
    alcoholic strength   190, 192, 193, 274,
        275
    adulteration   41, 274-5, 309
    legal measures   64, 65, 296
    counting and valuing of   42-3, 87,
        100, 105, 111, 148, 282-3
    profit margin   113
    discounts on purchases   135
    see also hydrometer, use of
split (capacity)   300
staff –
    hygiene   76-8
    supervision of   41-2, 79-80, 309-10,
        311, 313
    dishonest practices   vii-ix, xi, 18, 19,
        30, 40-2, 49, 84, 134, 159, 275,
        309-10, 311, 313
    consumption of food, staff feeding
        allowance   164, 300, 313
    consumption of liquor   54-5, 127, 310

standard rating – see V.A.T. – standard
        rating/zero rating
Statement of Settlement   156-8
statements (of account, suppliers')   3,
        300
stationery, counting and valuing of   154-
        155
stillages, stillions (gantries), cellar   98,
        186, 189, 300

stills, in distilling –
  patent   190, 192, 194
  pot   189-91, 193, 194
stock, borrowed or loaned – *see* transfers,
    external (stock, borrowed or
    loaned)
stock, brought in   17, 41-2, 310
stock reports, extended   viii, 3, 49, 83-7,
    103-21, 159, 269-73
  see also liquor stocktaking
stock, retail –
  counting and valuing of   170-5
  V.A.T. on categories of   43, 170-1,
    175-7
stock, returned –
  general   4, 84, 100, 105, 124, 164
  beer, draught   4, 39, 42, 98, 138-9,
    148, 311-12
stock rotation   29-30, 147, 167
stock sheets –
  prepared   83, 103, 155, 160, 270
  recording of information on   3-4, 25-8,
    103-13
  checking of information on   98, 99
stock, 'shelf life' of   29-30, 147-9, 170,
    172-3, 311
stock, storage of –
  general   29-30, 79
  beer   29, 186, 187-9
  food   167
  minerals   29
  port, vintage   208
  tobacco   265-6
  wine   150, 297, 315
  'other locations'   39, 98, 100, 161, 178
stock, theft of   vii-ix, 18, 30, 40-1, 49,
    159, 309-10, 313
stock, wholesale, counting and valuing
    of   175
stocktakers –
  professional qualities and conduct   ix-
    xi, 84, 146-9, 161, 170-2, 175, 178,
    302-5
  client and staff relationships,
    confidentiality   ix-xi, 34, 97, 144-
    145, 146-9, 170-2, 178, 275, 303,
    305
  security and checking procedures   ix,
    39, 42-3, 96-100, 147-9, 161, 178
  see also Incorporated Society of
    Licensed Trade Stocktakers
stocktaking, principles and benefits
    of   vii-ix, 31, 36, 38, 49, 80, 159,
    302

sugar –
  (added) in liquor production   185,
    198, 200, 211, 221
  in liquor, *re* hydrometer testing   275-
    276, 299, 315
  see also fermentation (conversion of
    sugar to alcohol)
Sundays, hours permitted for   56, 60
supper hour certificate (justices'
    certificate)   56-7, 65
surcharge (uplift) –
  for price changes   118, 133-4, 300
  for price differences between
    bars   102, 118, 136-7, 300, 315
surplus (overage)/deficit (shortage) –
  definitions   298, 300
  contributory factors   ix, xi, 38-42, 128,
    135, 272-3, 309-10
  in stock reports, extended   viii-ix, 49,
    115, 117-21, 132, 170, 270, 272-3
'sweat pint'   127
Sweden – *see* Scandinavia
sweets – *see* confectionery (including
    chocolates and chocolate goods)
Switzerland –
  liquor products   200, 203, 293
  cheeses   238, 315

tabular ledger (Tab.)   6-10, 39, 300
Tafelwein (definition)   221
takings – *see* income
tank, measuring capacity of –
  cylindrical   154
  rectangular   153
tannin, in wine   211, 212
tax – *see* Customs and Excise,
    Department of; duty; Inland
    Revenue; V.A.T.
taxable take   74-5
temperature control –
  beer, 186, 188-9
  tobacco   265
tenancies – *see* changeover (change of
    tenancy or ownership); licensed
    premises – tenancies, brewery
    companies and tied or managed
    houses
tenant, ingoing – *see* ingoer (purchaser or
    tenant, ingoing)
tenant, outgoing – *see* outgoer (vendor or
    tenant, outgoing)
thermometer, use of –
  in beer cellar   188-9
  in hydrometer testing   274

tied houses – *see* licensed premises –
  tenancies, brewery companies and
  tied or managed houses
tills, pre-set (computerised) –
  use of information from   3, 15-24, 41-
    42, 128, 133, 311
  monitoring use of   41-2, 79, 309-10
tobacco –
  Havana cigars:
    production, types   262-4
    storage, 'shelf life'   265-6
  cigarettes, cigars and smokers'
    sundries:
    counting and valuing of   87, 94-6,
      98, 100, 111, 171-2, 265-6
    profit margin   96, 171
tolerance –
  for error or wastage   92, 315
  for obscuration in hydrometer
    testing   275, 315
tonic water   65, 99
trading accounts –
  bottles, cases and containers
    ('deposits')   102
  food   159, 164-6, 312
  liquor   viii, 83, 118, 124-5, 314
  with/without allowances   132, 159,
    164-6, 300, 313, 314
training courses, stocktaking   302, 303,
    304
transfer sessions   63, 69, 143
transfers, external (stock, borrowed or
    loaned)   38-9, 40, 79, 137-8
transfers, internal   28-9, 79, 118-21, 127,
    129-32, 164
triple magnum (capacity)   281
Trockenbeerenauslese (definition)   221-2
Turkey, liquor products of   204, 205,
    293
turnover, *re* V.A.T.   43, 44, 49
Tuscany, wines of   222, 230

U.K. –
  liquor products   181-2, 190-2, 197,
    200, 202, 203, 204, 206, 224-5,
    226, 292
  cheeses   237, 258
  see also England; Scotland; Wales
ullage – *see* wastage (ullage)
Umbria, wines of   222, 316
under-ringing, on tills   ix, 40, 42, 309,
    311
unlicensed premises, consumption of
    liquor on   55

uplift –
  removal of goods   315
  surcharge – *see* surcharge (uplift)
U.S.A. –
  liquor products   199, 200, 201, 203,
    205, 206, 211, 223, 226, 231, 291
  cheeses   237

valuation –
  of assets   33-6, 142-6
  of stock – types:
    stock at valuation, stock on hand (as
      at changeovers)   29-30, 100-2,
      116, 121-4, 146-56, 170-5, 273,
      311-12
    year-end   100-2, 116, 153, 155, 170
    insurance   146, 150
    bankrupt stock, dissolution of
      partnership, probate   146
  of wine – types:
    current replacement value   150
    open market   150
    transfer of stock   150-2
Valuation, Certificate of   111, 121, 122-
    123, 148, 149, 155-6, 173-4, 312,
    313
'valuation' figure (in stock reports,
    extended)   84, 111
valuer – *see* broker (valuer)
V.A.T. –
  standard rating/zero rating   43, 74,
    96, 164, 170-1, 173, 174, 175-7
  input tax/output tax   43-9, 74-5, 270,
    278-80, 299, 301
V.D.Q.S. (definition)   221
vegetables –
  seasonal availability   259-60
  counting and valuing of   161
vehicles, valuation and depreciation
    of   33, 35
vendor – *see* outgoer (vendor or tenant,
    outgoing)
Veneto, wines of   222, 229
vermouth –
  production, types (French,
    Italian)   197-8
  counting and valuing of   84, 87, 91-3,
    148
video games   72, 74
  see also amusement machines
Vin de Pays (definition)   221
Vino Tipico (definition)   223
vintage years – *see* port, vintage
V.O. (definition)   193

vodka –
    production, types (Polish,
        Russian)   194-5
    alcoholic strength   274, 275
    legal measures   64, 65, 296
    see also spirits
V.Q.P.R.D. (definition)   223
V.S.O. (definition)   193
V.S.O.P. (definition)   193
V.V.S.P.P. (definition)   193

wages   33, 298, 299
Wales –
    liquor products   200, 225
    cheese   237
    licensing hours   60
warehouses, stock in – see stock,
        wholesale
wastage (ullage) –
    food   159, 164, 167, 313
    liquor   38, 79, 91, 92, 127, 148, 301,
        315
water –
    in beer   182, 185-6
    in brandy   193
    in fruit juices and minerals,
        postmix   89-91
    in whisky   192
weekdays, hours permitted for   56, 58,
        59-60
Weights and Measures Act   40, 64, 65,
        232, 296
    see also measures
West Indies –
    liquor products   195, 199, 204, 205,
        206
    tobacco   262-5
whiskey (Irish)   190, 199
whisky –
    production, types (blended, malt,
        vatted malts)   190-2
    alcoholic strength   192, 274
    legal measures   64, 65, 296
    see also spirits
whisky (Scotch)   190-2, 199
wine bars, legal requirements re   70-1

wine lists   17, 100, 225-32
wines –
    production, types   210-25
    alcoholic strength, age   210-12, 220
    storage, 'shelf life'   150-1, 212, 297,
        315
    purchasing; duty on   30, 116, 135,
        150-1, 152
    sale by glass, by bottle; measures,
        bottle sizes   64, 93-4, 152, 212,
        232, 281
    counting and valuing of   87, 93-4,
        100, 150-2, 282-3
wines, dessert   195-7
wines, fine   30, 150-1
wines, fortified (madeira, port, sherry
        etc.)   30, 84, 87, 91-3, 105, 152,
        195-8, 207-9
wines, 'house'   152, 220-1, 228, 231
wines, red   151, 152, 211-12, 219-28,
        230, 231, 315-16
wines, rosé   211, 220, 225, 230, 231
wines, sparkling   152, 211, 219, 220,
        222, 226, 230-1
wines, white   151, 152, 210-11, 219-30,
        231, 315-16

X key, on tills   15
X.O. (definition)   193

year-end valuations and
        adjustments   100-2, 116, 124,
        139-41, 153, 155, 170, 314
yeast, in liquor   181-6, 190, 210, 212,
        316
yield, of liquor   87-96, 282-3, 301
young persons – see children and young
        persons, legal requirements re
Yugoslavia, liquor products of   197, 204,
        205, 225, 226, 293

Z key, on tills   15, 16, 41, 310
Z2 key, on tills – see GTZ or Z2 key, on
        tills
zero rating – see V.A.T. – standard
        rating/zero rating